W9-AFJ-715

Crisis in the Courts

Crisis in the Courts

by HOWARD JAMES

This book is based on a series of articles that appeared weekly in *The Christian Science Monitor,* April to July, 1967.

DAVID McKAY COMPANY, INC.
New York

CRISIS IN THE COURTS

Second Printing, April 1968

Library of Congress Catalog Card Number: 68-18723

MANUFACTURED IN THE UNITED STATES OF AMERICA

VAN REES PRESS • NEW YORK

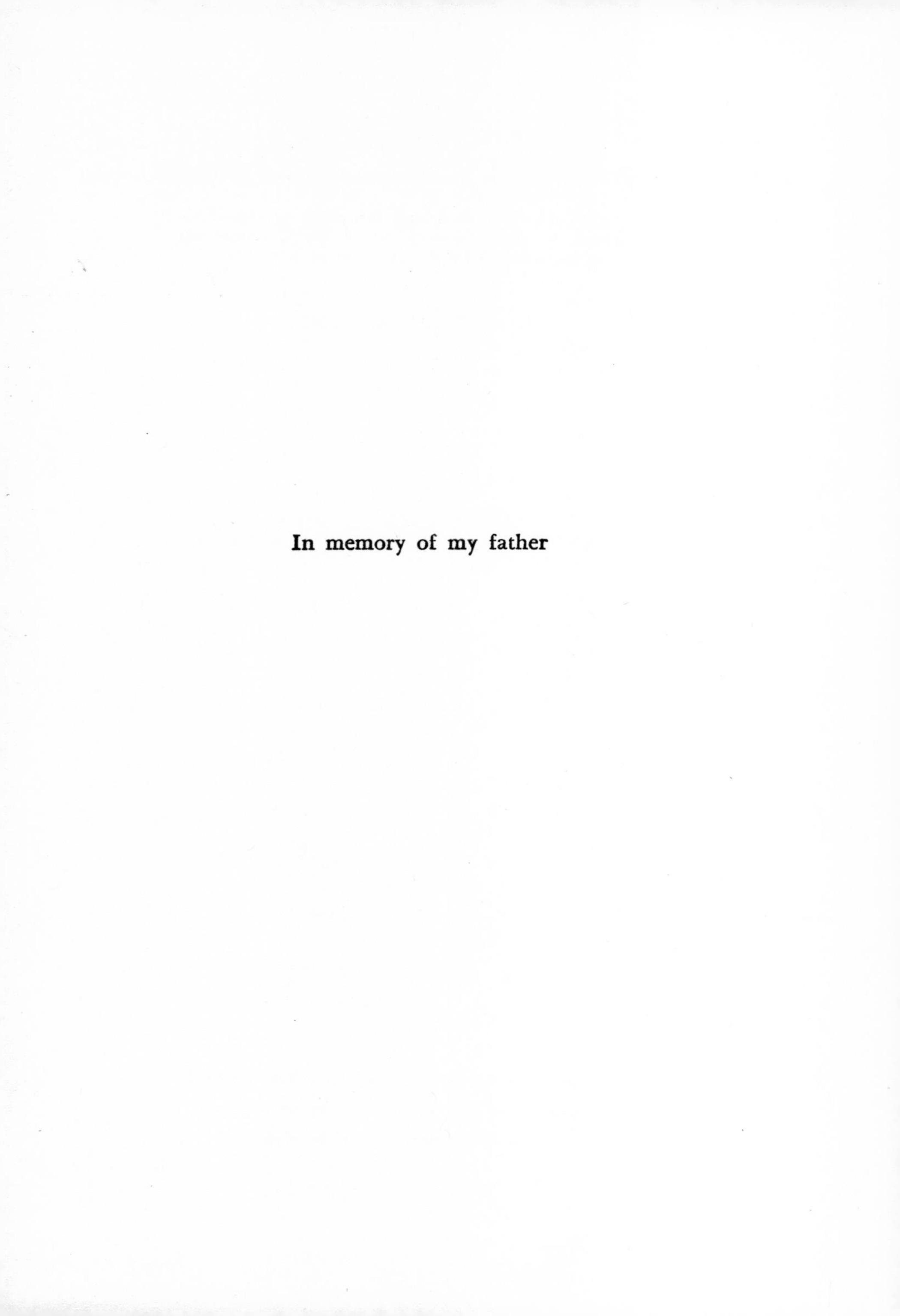

In memory of my father

Foreword

We are living in an era of marked tension and rapid social and technological change, characterized in increasing measure by confusion and uncertainty.

Because of this, our system of justice carries an ever increasing burden. It is obvious that it must be strong, efficient, and just if our way of life is to survive. This book shows, however, that there are serious flaws—some of which may come as a surprise even to the professionals.

A book on this subject cannot be taken lightly. It must be read and pondered. This is because it serves both as a warning signal, describing the challenges we face, and as a beacon of hope, pointing to possible solutions.

Surely no one can doubt that crime is the most pressing domestic problem facing our nation. Riots, with their attendant looting, arson, and murder, have shaken our cities, and we are confronted by the continued pervasiveness of organized crime, a steadily increasing crime rate, and the constant rise in juvenile delinquency.

The report of the President's Commission on Law Enforcement and Administration of Justice tells us: "The criminal court is the central, crucial institution in the criminal justice system." This means that all efforts to conquer crime will go for naught if the courts—"the institution around which the rest of the system has developed and to which the rest of the system is in large measure responsible"—do not administer justice efficiently and effectively.

In 1906, Roscoe Pound, then a young Nebraska lawyer, but later to be recognized as one of the outstanding legal scholars of our time, shocked the legal profession with a speech at an American Bar Association meeting on "the causes of popular dissatisfaction with the administration of justice." In this talk, Pound discussed the faults and deficiencies of American courts. The profession was shaken because never before had anyone publicly, and so articulately, pointed out the weaknesses of the judicial system. But despite the astonishment at Pound's verbal thunderbolts, his speech can be considered as the beginning of the judicial reorganization movement in America. What Pound said sixty-two years ago was valid; and his words continue to have a ring of verity today.

For some in the legal profession, as well as for laymen, portions of this book may seem equally shocking. Yet we dare not ignore the book, because the problems are real and they must be resolved.

In 1906, the population of our country was small and largely rural. The automobile was just coming into limited use. America's problems were comparatively simple ones.

Since that time, our population has ballooned; millions of cars travel our streets and highways; crime and juvenile delinquency have grown to unprecedented proportions; enormous corporations have developed; labor unions have attained great power; our society is a complex, and sometimes disturbing, amalgam. All of this has meant a tremendous increase in the business of our courts. Yet many of the procedures of judicial administration suited to the "horse and buggy days" remain with us, and many of the concomitant problems still exist.

Too many courts have not yet learned that a key to effective justice is the operation of the courts in a businesslike manner. Justice William Brennan of the United States Supreme Court has written:

"There is actually no difference between the business of judicial administration and the business of running an industrial or commercial enterprise in the sense that the efficient and businesslike conduct of both means better service for the public. And inefficient and wasteful judicial administration can and does result in a denial of justice, however earnestly an honest and upright judge may strive to prevent that lamentable result."

But instituting businesslike methods, thus decreasing delay, is only part of the answer as we strive to insure equitable treatment for all who come in contact with the judicial process—criminal and civil.

This book deals with a wide array of problems.

It is important to recognize that if we are to resolve these problems, all citizens, not just lawyers and judges, must work together. And we must also remember that the struggle is for neither the faint-hearted nor the short-winded.

EARL F. MORRIS, *President*
The American Bar Association

Prologue

> Justice is the great concern of man on earth. It is the ligament which holds civilized beings and civilized nations together. Wherever her temple stands, and so long as it is duly honored, there is a foundation for social security, general happiness and improvement and progress of our race. And whoever labors on this edifice with usefulness and distinction, whoever clears its foundations, strengthens its pillars, adorns its entablatures, or contributes to raise its lofty dome still higher in the skies, connects himself in name and fame and character with that which is and must be as durable as the frame of human society.
>
> —Daniel Webster

It is in the spirit of the words of Daniel Webster, uttered nearly a century and a half ago, that this book has emerged.

It was conceived in the fall of 1966 when the editors of *The Christian Science Monitor* pondered the weakened foundations and crumbling pillars of American Justice.

For 1966 was a year when more and more citizens expressed alarm over soaring crime statistics—apparent evidence of a crime explosion in the United States.

It was a year that brought verbal attacks on the police, even as they battled minority groups in the streets over the effects of social and economic injustice of centuries.

The Supreme Court of the United States remained under fire from those who believed it had gone too far in forcing desegregation, in eliminating prayers from schools, in the reapportionment of state legislatures, and in protecting the rights of men and women accused of criminal acts.

Others berated the High Court for moving too slowly.

The logjam in our civil courts made it almost impossible to bring about speedy and fair justice.

New scandals were uncovered in the nation's lower courts. Philadelphia's magistrates' courts were so bad that it was being proposed that they be abolished. The justice-of-the-peace system had already been replaced in Maine and Illinois, and other states were thinking of similar changes.

There was a great deal of talk about the "generation gap"—the breach between adults and children—in 1966. There were more divorces, and the family lost more ground, while state and institutional responsibility increased.

While the things some youngsters did were worse than before, other things that were "childish pranks" before World War II, when this writer was growing up, had become "juvenile delinquency" by 1966 as our society grew more mobile, citified, and impersonal and less tolerant.

In 1966 television was still growing up, and sometimes the more bizarre aspects of our society were brought into our living rooms so often that they began to seem like the norm.

As in years past, the number of traffic accidents climbed. Safety experts told us this was the result of speeding, drinking, and a youthful love for the daring and reckless (sometimes involving immature adults) combined with flaws in automobiles. More and more Americans were—whatever the reason—hailed into court.

The headlong, sometimes violent rush to urban areas continued to be a concern. Yet Wilfred Owen, an authority on urban affairs, predicted that this nation *could* become "urbanized and civilized, as well as motorized and mechanized."

It caused Governor Daniel J. Evans of the State of Washington to comment at a Citizens' Conference called to improve his state's courts:

> Too few people, I am convinced, understand the vital role—the key role—which the courts must play, and which the administration of justice must play, in an urbanized society. The sweep of history that lies behind us—whether of the nation or of this state—has been largely constructed on the law.

Government derives its power from the laws established by the people; people derive their freedom from the laws, and limit it according to the majority consent of those who are governed.

The courts are bound by the law, and laws in turn are both adjudicated by the courts and administered by them.

Laws govern the formation of cities, the conduct of commerce and industry, the control of traffic, and the relationship of every citizen to every other citizen.

And it is therefore the law and the courts of law which in large measure will determine whether or not we can succeed as a civilized people in a complex, integrated, and urbanized society.

Our concept of law is often governed by our relationship to it and our experience with it.

Not long ago I walked across the plaza on the south side of Chicago's new Civic Center, where the civil courts are housed. Two ragged little boys were scrambling after pennies tossed into the fountain just west of the city's new tourist attraction and symbol of culture—the rusting iron Picasso goddess.

No one was paying much attention to the boys, although the plaza was crowded. No one, that is, except two men in blue uniforms, who came waving and pushing and shouting their way across the plaza.

I was not quite close enough to hear, but I am certain one boy shouted to the other, "Run, it's the law!"

The concept of the "law" for these boys is an angry, red-faced man in blue, shouting and pushing and waving his arms. The rules say you must escape from "the law."

The impression could have hardly been worse—unless the men had been shooting, which happens more often than many of us suspect in the poor neighborhoods of our cities.

In the spring of 1967 a New England state supreme court chief justice—Frank R. Kenison, of New Hampshire—had his secretary type out something for me from a book. He handed it to me with a smile, and said that "I think you will find a place for this."

What the paper said was:

In a book by G. K. Chesterton is a chapter entitled, "The Twelve Men," in which he described a jury trial through the eyes of a layman: "And the horrible thing about all legal officials, even the best, about all judges, magistrates, barristers, detectives, and policemen, is not that they are wicked (some of them are good), not that they are stupid (some of them are quite intelligent); it is simply that they have gotten used to it.

"Strictly they do not see the prisoner in the dock; all they see is the usual man in the usual place. They do not see the awful court of judgement; they see only their own workshop."

Not all judges and lawyers and policemen fit this mold, but too many do. One who does not is Judge Sam P. McKenzie, of Atlanta, Ga. Not long ago he said: "I wish I could tell you that once the courthouse doors are closed a trial judge can free his mind of the cases that have come before him and go home without worry. This is just not possible if a man has done his job properly. The consternation and bewilderment of the people who have appeared before him burn deeply into his memory and rise before him in the waking hours of the night."

I have met many strong, sensitive men and women working to upgrade our system of justice in our cities and states. Among these are Glenn Winters, director of the American Judicature Society; Robert C. Finley, Chief Justice of the Supreme Court of the State of Washington; Alfred T. Sulmonetti, of the Circuit Court of Portland, Ore., and the 1967-68 president of the National Conference of State Trial Judges; George B. Richter, district judge in Waukon, Iowa; Eugene A. Wright, who retired from the bench in Seattle in 1967; Maurice Rosenberg and Harry W. Jones, law professors at Columbia University; Geoffrey C. Hazard Jr., University of Chicago law professor and administrator of the American Bar Foundation; Stanley Schrotel, former chief of police in Cincinnati; Laurance M. Hyde Jr., former circuit judge in St. Louis; James P. Economos, who heads the American Bar Association's Traffic Court Program and the other dedicated ABA staff members who gave me so much assistance; and officers and staff of the American Trial Lawyers Association.

A special word of gratitude to attorney Peter T. Kennedy and Stanley Hall of the *Monitor* editorial staff, who provided much-needed criticism and counsel.

There are dozens of others who deserve mention. Most are specialists, and thus "experts."

Yet specialization has become such a fad, and perhaps a necessity, in our era, that it seems essential to take the big overview. This, too, prompted the series in *The Christian Science Monitor*, and thus this book.

For we have much to learn from the puzzle-makers who cut pictures into fragments. They always expect the pictures to be assembled again, and they know if the pieces remain scrambled and unassembled there is little hope of understanding what the picture is about.

At the urging of my editors I have attempted to take the widely scattered pieces of a complex puzzle called Justice in America and assemble them for all to see.

In keeping with a long-standing tradition of *The Christian Science Monitor*—a newspaper that searches for solutions—I tried to do more than assemble a picture. As I talked to judges and lawyers around the nation and as I sat in courtrooms for hours, I looked for ways to improve justice in America.

This, too, helps explain the thrust of the series I wrote for the *Monitor*, and the direction this book takes.

I believe no other news-gathering organization has yet attempted such a sweeping study. The cost in both dollars and man-hours has been high, and much credit must go to DeWitt John, the editor of *The Christian Science Monitor*, and his associates. Without their support and guidance this book would never have come into being.

It is limited in scope to state courts, and from the level of our courts of general jurisdiction down. This is simply to keep the study under control, and yet see as complete a picture as possible.

It is also because these are the courts that most Americans face, and the courts they can do most about. They are within reach.

A higher concept of justice is needed in the United States. Perhaps this book will help move more citizens to action.

It should be pointed out that these people are in no way responsible for what appears in this book. Rather, I mentioned them out of appreciation for the time they gave and the ideas they generated.

Contents

Crisis in the Courts

CHAPTER I

Judging the Judges

It is 11:43 A.M. on a Wednesday in late February. Spring is edging into Louisville, Ky., and on the street people have shed their coats and are nodding and smiling.

But in the courtroom of Circuit Judge R—— there are no smiles. A middle-aged barber, accused of wounding a man, is worried. His freedom and future are at stake.

On the witness stand his daughter, an attractive woman, tells the jury how the victim provoked the shooting by taunting her father and by getting youngsters to block the barbershop driveway with their bicycles to keep customers away.

As she testifies, an aging newsboy enters the courtroom and hawks papers.

With considerable rustling, Judge R—— opens his newspaper to the comic page. After reading for several minutes he pulls the section out, folds it into a smaller square, and counts quietly to himself, apparently working the crossword puzzle.

The young woman seems nervous. She speaks rapidly.

Judge R—— looks up from his paper and tells her to slow down. There is a note of irritation in his voice when, a few minutes later, he again orders her to speak more slowly, so the court stenographer can keep up.

The stenographer, who already has put down her pen and is checking her fingernails, says, "Oh, I gave up a long time ago."

When the defendant's daughter finishes, two other witnesses take the stand briefly. Judge R—— denies the prosecution request to let a woman use the chalkboard to clarify her testimony.

At 12:38 P.M., the judge adjourns court for lunch until 2 P.M.

A visitor, after buying license plates in another office, has stopped by to watch. With adjournment he rises to leave before the jury has departed. Judge R—— orders him stopped by a bailiff, brings him before the bench, and gives him a lecture on courtroom decorum.

What happened on this day in Louisville is unusual. But it is far from unique in the nation's state courts.

In criminal court in Manhattan a judge read his newspaper-sized law bulletin while holding hearings. Lowering a corner to listen now and then, he kept the paper in front of his face as defendants appeared before him. To those involved each case was an important matter—worthy of his full attention.

In Cincinnati a new common-pleas magistrate, Judge K——, was reading, ironically enough, copies of the *Journal of the American Judicature Society* during a narcotics trial. (It is the Judicature Society that has pioneered in improving the administration of justice.)

Behind a bench in Manhattan, Judge S—— became furious with a defendant when the man's lawyer did not show up in court. The defendant said his attorney was in a higher court in another city. The judge refused to listen and raised the man's bail—putting him behind bars "until your attorney shows up." He also ordered the man to phone the lawyer, James Horan. The defendant button-holed another attorney, Irving Unger, and asked Mr. Unger to help. When Mr. Unger, who confirmed the fact Mr. Horan was in court, tried, the judge shouted him down and stormed off the bench.

One recalls that Harry W. Jones, Cardozo professor of jurisprudence at Columbia University, once said, "Every multijudge trial court of general jurisdiction has at least one tyrant in residence."

Later that day, perhaps after thinking it over and learning that a newspaper reporter had been watching, the judge reversed himself.

In San Francisco Municipal Court, Judge F—— was hearing traffic cases. He argued with the defendants, seemed to have trouble reading police accident reports without help from aides, and made sarcastic remarks.

When a woman with a Spanish accent, who was trailed by several children, said she couldn't pay an $18 traffic fine, he asked her if her husband worked. Upon her explanation that he had left her, Judge F—— demanded: "Why don't you throw him in jail?"

Later he did show some compassion by giving her a 30-day suspended sentence—but not before he had embarrassed her before her children and a courtroom full of spectators.

When I asked others in the courthouse about Judge F——, I was told he was "a brilliant criminal lawyer who thinks he is above hearing traffic cases" but must, under the system, take a turn at it.

At present there are more than 3,700 state trial-court judges in the United States. The number climbs slowly year by year as more state legislatures face up to a mushrooming population, an ever-higher highway accident rate, and an increase in crime and violence.

Below these trial courts (called courts of general jurisdiction) are other, lower, levels of courts. It is here the bulk of our citizens have their first, and perhaps only, court experience as they stand accused of traffic violations, charges of drunkenness, shoplifting, indecent exposure and other immoral acts, failure to pay small bills, city-ordinance violations like burning of rubbish in the street, and a host of other minor crimes known as misdemeanors in legal jargon.

Fantastic as it seems in this age of the electronic computer and punch card, no one knows how many lower-court judges there are in the United States. This provides a clear clue to the low level of interest in our courts in general and helps explain why so many problems exist.

Compiling my own figures and comparing them with estimates made by one of the most knowledgeable authorities on minor courts in the nation, James P. Economos, director of the American Bar Association's Traffic Court Program, I discovered there are far more judges than you might suspect. For my figures show there are more than 15,000 men and women presiding over lower courts and at least 10,000 are nonlawyers.

If my sampling is a fair indication (I simply sat down in courtrooms selected at random around the country and listened), perhaps half of the trial judges are, for one reason or another, unfit to sit on the bench.

Because so little attention is paid to minor-court judges, and because so many are housewives, gas-station attendants, farmers, retired workers, and businessmen rather than qualified lawyers, incompetence on the lower-court bench is far more widespread than in the trial courts. Probably not more than one in 10 lower-court magistrates is, in most states, really qualified to dispense justice today. Exceptions would be found in Maine, Illinois, and in other states where laymen judges have been eliminated or are on the way out.

After talking with hundreds of lawyers, prosecutors, policemen, and judges, I can add that most agree the level of incompetence is high, although many would not say so publicly because they fear retaliation.

But others, from New York to California, have the courage to speak out, commenting as does Joseph Harrison, a well-known Newark, N.J., lawyer, who told me, "About half are good judges. The others have various kinds of shortcomings."

Still others, in states like Pennsylvania, New York, Kentucky, Texas, Oklahoma, and Indiana, where court problems are especially acute, complain that my estimate of the percentage of incompetent judges is far too low.

Generalizations upset many judges. They prefer to have adverse publicity swept under the rug, for it might harm their image or professional pride.

Many with high standards find it hard to believe that other judges can falter and fall. Even today some Oklahoma judges refuse to believe that members of their State Supreme Court took bribes, even though one has confessed and another is in prison.

Some judges fear that a public airing of dirty judicial laundry will further reduce respect for law and order.

Others, like Robert C. Finley, Chief Justice of the Supreme

Court of the State of Washington, take a balanced view, arguing that while courts must be criticized and improved they are not beyond hope: "Otherwise our society would have broken apart long ago."

Certainly few lawyers or laymen have followed a path as far-reaching as that taken by this writer. Judges are in a poor position to evaluate the magnitude of the problem because they seldom visit other judges' courtrooms. They tend to overlook faults that they themselves have. Beyond this, there is a fraternal relationship between judges that can blot out objectivity.

In a conversation in his office in the Supreme Court Building, former Associate Justice Tom C. Clark told me that he knew most trial judges in America and believed them to be "pretty good."

Yet Mr. Justice Clark, a leading exponent of court reform and instrumental in establishing the promising National College of State Trial Judges, knew these men from seminars and friendly discussions. I am convinced he would change his mind if he saw them as I did—as I sat on hard courtroom benches across the country.

Lawyers have a limited view of the courts because so few spend time in court, and that is normally in a single city or section of the country.

I can best describe my own reaction to what I saw as shock and disbelief—at least for the first few weeks of court-watching.

But as I traveled and talked to judges, lawyers, and ordinary citizens, I began to realize that I was dealing with what must be the most important, and at the same time most ignored, segment of state and local government. And because of public and official apathy, problems have grown like weeds in an untended garden.

Perhaps most curious of all, I discovered that judges across the nation operate without supervision (there are a few states where this is not true, New Jersey for one) and without guidance or standards to live up to.

In fact, I found that few people agree on what makes a good judge, or what he should do or be.

"What qualifications should a judge have?" I asked as I toured the nation. I found opinions vary widely.

In fact Columbia University Professor Harry W. Jones points out that "no person or organization has been rash enough to offer an authoritative definition of . . . 'qualified.' "

Vincent A. Carroll, who is chief judge in Philadelphia's Common Pleas Court, suggests that "a man doesn't have to be a genius. He does need a substantial background in the community and a good legal education."

Most judges feel experience as a trial lawyer is essential. Many contend top-flight, small-town lawyers make the best judges because they have broad experience in trying both civil and criminal cases.

The American Bar Association's canons of judicial ethics state that a judge should be, among other things, "conscientious, studious, thorough, courteous, patient, punctual, just, impartial, fearless of public clamor, regardless of public praise, and indifferent to private, political, or partisan influences. . . ."

Professor Jones suggests that "only a man of first-rate [intellectual] capacity can make sound, split-second decisions on questions of criminal law and procedure, exercise sentencing responsibilities thoughtfully and wisely under exhausting pressure of time, and improve procedures to make assembly-line law enforcement seem less cut and dried."

Incompetent judges can be classified into one or more of the following 11 categories, all too frequently observed in action by this writer since January.

1. **The hacks:** These men are given judgeships as a reward for long and faithful service to a political party, or to some political leader. While many make excellent judges, dozens of others do not belong on the bench.

"The most important thing, if you want to become a judge, is to have good political contacts," says one bitter New York trial lawyer. "You don't get to be a judge by practicing law. You've got to sit in the clubhouse and build your contacts."

"Almost all state judges are picked because of their experience in public life—in politics," says Geoffrey C. Hazard Jr., executive director of the American Bar Foundation.

2. **The retirees:** One of the largest groups, these men seek the bench as semiretirement from the trying life of practicing law. They arrive at work late (if at all), take frequent recesses, spend two hours at lunch, and go home early. Some play golf or go fishing while men languish in jail and civil cases pile up.

3. **The failures:** These men were incompetent lawyers who sought judgeships because they had trouble earning a living as lawyers. They can be found in every section of the nation, but are most prevalent in states where judicial pay is low and prestige is little higher.

4. **The inattentive:** These men have heard it all before, find judging a bore, or simply couldn't care less. They lean back with their eyes closed, read, doodle on a legal pad, or stare out of the window. I have watched some chat on the telephone or hold whispered conversations with aides who want papers signed while witnesses testify. And this has happened in non-jury cases.

In Miami, Fla., Judge T—— leaned back in his chair with his eyes closed, his arms up behind his head, as he tried two men for running a bookie joint. A few minutes later he admitted in open court that he "wasn't paying attention" to some of the evidence.

Both men were sentenced to a year in jail.

"It isn't just a question of a judge sitting there in a robe," says Delmar Karlen, director of the Institute of Judicial Administration in New York. "He must be putting his mind to it."

5. **The misfits:** Another large group, these are competent lawyers with personality quirks that keep them from living up to the canons of judicial ethics. Many are abrasive and short-tempered. Others come to court with their minds made up, refusing to acknowledge that each case is different. In each state a few men simply cannot make decisions. And some, who were

skilled trial lawyers, are irritated by the unskilled men who argue cases before them.

A top Pittsburgh trial lawyer, Gilbert Helwig, sums it up this way:

"A good judge has a judicial temperament. He must give up a certain amount of vanity and be willing to listen. He cannot decide the case before he hears it. Then there is the question of discipline. Nobody tells a judge how much work he should do. And in criminal court there is a need for compassion."

6. The informal: In some cities "open court" is a misnomer. Most business takes place in the judge's chambers, with little dignity or decorum. It is an experience not unlike having to appear in the office of a political boss for favors or to be reprimanded.

7. The incapacitated: A judge, complaining of old age or ill health and unable to serve, can continue to draw full pay while preventing an active replacement from taking over. Last year only 22 of 30 common-pleas judges (the court of general jurisdiction) in Philadelphia were available for regular assignments. One has been disabled for several years, but is serving a 10-year term and cannot be removed.

8. The inexperienced: Judging is not a career in the United States, as it is in some countries. The subject is not taught at law schools. Further, "a man can have a distinguished career in the law today and yet he may have almost never appeared in court," says Professor Jones.

In terms of formal training, then, every judge who takes the bench is inexperienced. Fortunately, most begin to measure up within a few months or years. Unfortunately, too many lawyers fail to recognize the drastic differences between practicing law and sitting on the bench as an impartial judge.

9. The lazy: Dozens of judges never look up the law. They "wing it," trusting memory or the lawyers who appear before them, and usually rationalizing that they are "too busy." This group also sees little need to challenge the prosecutor or others who appear in court to see that justice really wins out.

An excellent example of how a good judge can protect justice:

Tom Daniel Grammer, a 19-year-old in Portland, Ore., with little education pleaded guilty to first-degree arson before Judge Alfred T. Sulmonetti with the support of the district attorney and his court-appointed lawyer.

Before accepting the plea, Judge Sulmonetti questioned the boy. He learned that the boy had been working for his brother-in-law helping to demolish a condemned building. His pay: $1.25 an hour plus "all the copper wire" found. To remove the insulation from the wire he set fire to it in the basement of the building being demolished.

Leaving the fire for two or three minutes, he returned to find it out of control. He quickly called the fire department. For this the district attorney charged him with arson.

Judge Sulmonetti turned down the guilty plea, and a trial was held. Instead of going to prison the youth returned to a state home for the mentally retarded.

10. The weak: It takes a strong man to rule against a close friend or a political sponsor, knowing that an adverse decision may end the friendship or end the support. For these and other reasons—especially fear of reversal—dozens of judges are pushed around by lawyers or let outsiders influence justice. One of the greatest offenders: the press.

Adds Mr. Karlen: "I hear constantly of judges who are afraid to try cases. Afraid they may make fools of themselves. And some judges let others—bail bondsmen, the clerk, a district attorney, or defense attorney—run their courtrooms."

11. The prejudiced: When a lawyer becomes a judge, he does not simply shed his old opinions and wiggle into a robe of objectivity. Instead he brings with him a viewpoint developed by his experiences. These include such influences as his economic, religious, and ethnic background.

A wealthy corporate lawyer, educated in the best private

schools, may have little understanding of the problems of an uneducated laborer who says he cannot hold a job long enough to pay his ex-wife back alimony. A clean-cut Midwestern judge may give little justice to a dirty, long-haired teen-ager, thus making the inscription "equal justice under law" meaningless.

And there is old-fashioned prejudice. When I asked a Miami, Fla., judge why he gave a surprisingly severe sentence to a Spanish-speaking youth, he explained that the boy was from a migrant family.

In the series that ran in *The Christian Science Monitor* and served as the basis of this book, these 11 categories, coupled with my estimate that half the trial judges are not fit for office, created the greatest stir.

While some judges reacted negatively, dozens of others called these 11 points the most useful list of dos and don'ts they had seen.

One California judge wrote that he was 64 years old, had been a lawyer more than 30 years, has now served as a judge for two years, and believed that if any judge could give defendants a fair trial he was that judge.

That was before he read the list just cited. Afterward he said he realized he was violating several of the 11 points, was grateful to have this list to use as a set of standards, and was determined to try to live up to these standards.

Now additional research by this writer adds a 12th problem area: alcoholism. Many state court officials agree that it is one of the most serious problems of the bench—although the "number of alcoholics is about the same as in the general population."

But the problem is more acute in the courts simply because of the nature of the judge's job. It is clear that judges, if our system of government is to work, must be a cut above the rest of the population. In fact, most Americans believe that they are—an unfortunate assumption that leads to public apathy.

State trial courts have incompetent judges for many reasons. Often it is because of politics or because the system of selection is so poor. In many communities there is little or no screening of candidates. Frequently the voters pay no attention to the screening committee, or no qualified lawyer wants the job.

One capable judge, Maurice A. David, of Columbus, Ind., is very candid on this point. He retired from the Marine Corps in 1964 and opened a law office. His experience had been in military law. Five months later a group of local lawyers came to his office and asked him to run for judge.

"I put this question to them," he says. " 'If you have such a burning desire to find a new judge, why don't you run yourselves?' Any one of them would have been qualified.

"Their answer: 'We can't afford to run. The pay is too low. Judge ——— is an honest enough person, but he is irascible and unpleasant to deal with."

With this urging, plus a military pension of $6,000 a year, and a judicial salary of $18,500 in the offing, Mr. David agreed to run as a Democrat in a county that often elects Republicans.

"I was elected by the Johnson landslide in '64," he says. "And I can easily lose in the next election."

About 70 miles west, in Spencer, Ind., Circuit Judge Austin B. Childress had not—when I visited him—filed court records with the county clerk for over four years. At my request the clerk showed me the books. The first entry was made in February, 1819, the last Sept. 29, 1962.

Judge Childress says he is unable to bring the records up to date because he is overly concerned with commas and periods and the perfect use of words.

"I am too meticulous," he told me. "I have made it a practice to hire inexperienced girls from business schools and train them, and I have had two operations. Each kept me away for six weeks."

Yet only recently did the six lawyers in Spencer ask the State Supreme Court to step in. And none apparently wants the job of judge. Experienced lawyers in Spencer net $25,000 a year or more, one said. The judgeship pays only $12,500.

Many judges are deeply embedded in politics, or owe allegiance to a political boss who may be able to influence decisions.

The chief judge of the Circuit Court in Cook County, Ill.,

John S. Boyle, has the reputation for being a tough, demanding administrator as well as a close friend of the Mayor of Chicago. The day I visited him, campaigning for the spring election was under way. On his desk was a sign: "Daley for Mayor." Court personnel, including deputy state's attorneys, wore Daley buttons.

As I traveled from state to state I told judges and lawyers what I saw—without naming Judge Boyle, Chicago, or Mayor Daley. To a man they condemned any judge who would so blatantly violate the judicial canons of ethics which prohibit "the public endorsement of candidates for political office."

A highly respected New Jersey jurist added that not even wives can mix in politics in his state. One judge, whose wife did, complained he could not control her. The problem was quickly resolved when the judge was told to tell her she had a choice: get out of politics or see her husband resign his judgeship.

Why this concern over mixing politics and justice?

"The need to find funds to finance a political campaign and the low pay of judges are leading reasons why we have corrupt judges," says Elvin J. Brown, a highly respected district judge from Norman, Okla.

One of the great problems facing the courts: Few states have anyone to keep watch over judges. As Bernard G. Segal, a top Philadelphia lawyer, points out, "A judge is just a lawyer elevated to the bench. He may be a poor administrator, or poor at research, or have other shortcomings."

As I have pointed out, sometimes he is not even a lawyer. This is often the case in small-town traffic courts and in other courts that handle large numbers of "minor" cases that are very important to those involved.

Some of these men with limited legal skill push their way up into higher courts.

In Ardmore, Okla., Judge Joe Thompson, who sits in five counties as a district judge, was on the bench, his robe open, his collar loose, his tie askew, and his shirt front gaping. He was not wearing an undershirt.

Although he attended law school in Oklahoma City, he admitted to me he knows little about the law. He got on the bench more than 12 years ago when his home county (he lives in Marietta) needed a county judge—a secondary post that includes presiding over county governmental meetings and probate matters. With no one else willing to serve, the two district judges asked the State Supreme Court to give him a special permit until he passed the bar exam.

A cloud hangs over his passing the exam. He failed it several times. Some say three. Others say four. Judge Thompson says he has forgotten the details, but that he passed with ease on the final try, whatever the number.

He denies reports that he cannot read and write, explaining he is left-handed and "can't read my own scribbling." His clerk reads his instructions to juries, he says, because "I've got sore eyes."

After serving eight years as county judge he ran against W. J. Monroe (one of his benefactors who helped him get the initial appointment) and won the seat as district judge in the court of general jurisdiction. He is now in his second term.

"He's not the smartest man on the bench, but his heart is as big as a washtub," says former District Judge John Caldwell, who served as Judge Thompson's court reporter during his first four-year term in District Court, often backstopping the judge by giving him points of law.

Commenting on complaints that some of his practices raise big questions, Mr. Caldwell says, "Judge Joe lets some lawyers take advantage of him. And when he doesn't like you he lets you know it. So some people get the wrong impression."

The judge also has a reputation for helping out home county folk who get in trouble with the law. But not always.

A man accused of arson made a deal with the assistant district attorney in Judge Thompson's home town of Marietta. The two agreed that a guilty plea probably would net him "only" 25 years.

But Judge Thompson, before sentencing the man, recessed court to find Willis Choate, the young business manager of the local paper.

"He asked me what kind of sentence he should give, and I told him the people are pretty hot, and I'd sentence him to 50 years," Mr. Choate says.

Judge Thompson did. It was later reduced by the Court of Criminal Appeals.

Public indifference must be blamed for most court problems.

Much has been said and written about the nation's probate courts in recent years. Thousands of families have found funds they both needed and counted on slip into the pockets of lawyers—too often a crony of the probate judge. Yet little has been done to stop this practice.

In some states judges of trial and appellate courts remain as directors of corporations, own businesses, oil wells, or have other business interests while serving on the bench. During the summer of 1967 it was announced on the business pages of the Chicago papers that a newly elected Illinois Supreme Court justice was being named a director of a financial institution.

Many judges disqualify themselves in cases where there is a clear conflict of interest in a case. But others won't or don't. And I found few states have conflict-of-interest laws covering the judiciary. In fact, many state officials told me they have never thought about such legislation.

While the criminal courts, because of the nature of their work, have the worst reputation, I found divorce courts can be in a class by themselves.

Take the case of a young salesman living in the suburbs northwest of Chicago. He admits he was having difficulties with his wife and that she talked of divorce. But he swears he didn't know she filed suit against him.

On July 24, 1967, he says she told him she was going shopping. But court records show she went to the Cook County courtroom of Circuit Judge Alfonse F. Wells.

Without the husband present, Judge Wells ruled the divorce uncontested and gave the wife, mother of two small children, the family home and the bulk of the husband's income.

To Judge Wells's credit, in September, after hearing the husband's side of the story, he tossed out the divorce.

Little wonder a group called the Divorce Reform League has

been formed to change divorce laws and to combat divorce-court practices.

I found that in many cities judges handle these all-important family matters in their spare time, often before hearing the regular court docket. Yet even in Chicago and other cities where judges preside full time over divorce courts, problems that have a serious impact on our society exist.

Perjury, the three-syllable word for lying in court, is as common in divorce cases as turning back the speedometer in used-car lots. Perhaps more common. The judges know it. The lawyers know it. Open, wholesale lying—with the court apparently helpless to do anything about it—must have a serious impact on attitudes toward law and courts.

Yet often it is the attitude of judges that creates disrespect for our courts and our system of laws.

In Sioux City, Iowa, Judge George Paradise made news not long ago when he became bothered by noise outside his home one evening. He went out on the street and told several young men to leave, that he was a judge, and that it was a court order. The youths reportedly became rough. The next morning he cited them for contempt. The case was appealed to the Iowa Supreme Court, where the judge was upheld, though the punishment was reduced.

In Savannah, Ga., a woman judge was challenged in 1967 by the grand jury. Stella Akin, who has served since 1957, is said to have "repeated and protracted absences" from the bench, throwing the burden on an associate municipal judge.

From time to time charges more serious than incompetence are brought against judges. But corruption is hard to prove. A judge who takes bribes obviously does it in secret. And neither party involved will shout it from the housetops.

"There are many ways for a judge to be corrupt," adds Prof. Hazard. "It doesn't always mean he's going to take a satchel of money."

In the spring of 1967 a Suffolk County, N.Y., judge, Floyd Sarisohn, appeared before a five-man panel of the New York State Supreme Court's Appellate Division on charges of helping a prostitute stay in business, fixing a speeding ticket for a friend, jailing an innocent woman, setting bail at $1.5 million on a burglary suspect, and freeing three men in a case before another judge. The judge was removed from office.

While problems are numerous across the country, I saw many excellent judges in action. Municipal Judge Murray Goodman of Miami Beach was fair and friendly. When five men corrected violations to city building ordinances he praised them for their cooperation, reopened the cases, and set aside findings of guilty so that they would not have court records. Emphasis is on getting cooperation and compliance. Yet he does not allow people in court in beach attire, nor can they smoke, chew gum, or read in court.

One young woman in Los Angeles, Bonnie Lee Martin, a municipal court commissioner, selected by the judges themselves, was without a doubt one of the finest judges I observed. She handled tough morals cases and difficult points of law with dignity and skill.

While Los Angeles judges were all among the best in the nation, I found the younger municipal judges there more alert and pleasant while on the bench than a few older men sitting in Superior Court.

Oklahoma, despite many judicial problems, also produces men of high caliber—like Elvin J. Brown, district judge in Norman.

How can the quality of judges in the United States be improved?

- Many say raising salaries would help.

Eugene A. Wright, one of the nation's outstanding trial judges, retired from the Superior Court of Seattle, Wash., in the fall of 1966 to become vice-president of a bank.

In Pittsburgh, Common Pleas Judge Ruggero J. Aldisert, an excellent judge, had a six-figure income as a successful trial lawyer.

"My wife and I have, after five years, adjusted to our new budget," he says.

He makes $30,000 as a judge, but his take-home is far lower after taxes, pension pay-out, life insurance, and other expenses.

And as a judge he is unable to write off business expenses on his income tax.

But some say pay is only part of the answer. A burning desire to see justice done and the prestige of office help.

• The majority of states need a better system of selecting judges. Though it has its detractors, most court critics point to the merit-selection plan proposed in 1913 by Elbert M. Kales, a Northwestern University law professor, and backed since that year by the American Judicature Society.

Under the plan, an impartial committee of lawyers and laymen receives nominations and then draws up a list of qualified candidates, usually three for each vacancy. The governor then appoints new judges from this list. At regular intervals each judge's name is submitted to voters, without party designation, on a ballot that reads: "Shall Judge———, of the ——— Court, be retained in office? Yes——— No———."

First adopted in St. Louis and Kansas City in 1940, it is often called the Missouri plan. Alaska included it in its constitution when admitted as a state in 1948. In 1962 Iowa and Nebraska joined. During this same era other states began to use it in selected cities or for certain courts. Interest is slowly beginning to grow 54 years after the plan was first proposed.

Seven states, Connecticut, Delaware, Massachusetts, New Hampshire, New Jersey, Rhode Island, and South Carolina, have appointed judges since colonial times, while several other states have returned to the appointive system after finding popular election unsatisfactory.

Yet some 36 states continue to follow the tradition attributed to the Jacksonian era of democracy some 125 years ago under which, in order to win office, judges must raise funds and give speeches to people who often couldn't care less.

• Tenure, the length of appointment or elected term, is a key factor. Massachusetts judges serve for life, as in the federal system. New Jersey judges serve seven years, and then for life. Pennsylvania judges are elected for 10 years. In many states judges serve four years. These include Arizona, Arkansas, Idaho,

Oklahoma, South Carolina, South Dakota, Washington, and several others.

Vermont judges for years were elected to two-year terms by the Legislature. Terms were recently lengthened to six years.

Few top lawyers are willing to give up a successful practice for a short term on the bench. And it takes time and experience to become a good judge. Thus long terms are generally supported.

Six years is common. In five states judges serve for 8 years. In Delaware they serve 12, and in Maryland 15 years.

• Coupled with tenure is the need for a good removal system. California's system is cited as an excellent solution, for it does not put judges at the mercy of politicians, but does keep a check on judges.

Los Angeles Judge William B. Neeley, former chairman of the California Commission on Judicial Qualifications, says anyone—lawyer, defendant, or citizen—is able to file a complaint against a judge. There are no forms to fill out. Only a letter to the commission is required.

To protect judges from cranks and political enemies, the complaints are kept confidential. So are the names of the complainers, to protect them from reprisals.

In California it has been found there is little need for formal action against a judge. Usually a letter asking him to respond to complaints results in reform, although the commission "sometimes gets flimsy excuses."

One judge was accused of "becoming very arbitrary and often sharp with witnesses." The judge wrote back that the "complaint is well-founded. I have had many health and family problems, and I can see how this has affected my actions in court." Although the complaining group was never notified of steps being taken, they soon told the commission that "the judge is doing much better."

A few states have adopted the California system, or are considering it.

In New Jersey the Chief Justice of the Supreme Court oversees judges, sets working hours, and generally controls the bench. A judge "can't even take a day off without reporting in," says one official. Yet a proposed system of removing unfit judges has been held up by the New Jersey Legislature for years.

Most states require impeachment proceedings, which usually means it is almost impossible to remove an incompetent or corrupt judge.

Most judges have their own "kingdoms," with no one having power to make them work, keep them from becoming abusive or arbitrary, or correct other human failings. Appeals courts only rule on errors of law. Lawyers across the country say they are afraid to challenge judges because it will harm their practice and their clients. And in most cities the public doesn't know what is going on, nor does it care.

Yet many judges and lawyers point out that reform will not come from within. It will be up to laymen to make changes.

CHAPTER II

Delay Defeats Justice

If you are arrested on a hot summer day in Cleveland on a serious charge and can't make bail, you may still be in jail awaiting your day in court when Christmas rolls around. Even if you are innocent.

Or take the case of a New York housewife. Driving her auto down a Bronx street she is hit by another car. Doctors say she is seriously injured and expenses pile up.

If the other driver's insurance company haggles over a settlement, it could be 1973 before she collects a dime. It often takes that long to get a civil case before a jury.

Nor are Cleveland and New York exceptions. Most state courts, especially those in large cities, are bogged down with business. They are struggling with what members of the bench and bar call "backlog."

Justice is delayed for many reasons. More civil cases are filed —mostly auto accidents—than the courts can handle. The crime rate keeps climbing. Criminal trials take longer than in the past because of recent Supreme Court rulings. There aren't enough judges in most jurisdictions. And both judges and lawyers throw up roadblocks, too often for selfish reasons.

"The backlog of civil trials continues to mount until our courts are rapidly approaching the point where the maxim 'Justice delayed is justice denied' may apply to all civil litigants," asserts Judge J. Gilbert Prendergast of Baltimore, where delay from filing to trial now totals more than two years.

"Saying 'I'll see you in court' has become the great national pastime," asserts Maurice Rosenberg, Columbia University law professor.

Common Pleas Judge Herbert Levin of Philadelphia warns:

> A terrible thing has happened to justice in America, and the tragedy is that while it was occurring, there were so few who, recognizing it, warned us of its consequences.
>
> I'm talking about the House of Justice in the big city. The termites of slums, industry, unemployment, two world wars, highway accidents, labor-management disputes, and myriad other problems never known before bored their way into the walls, floors, and beams of a once-commodious structure. . . .

Yet in my visits with judges, lawyers, prosecutors, policemen, and everyday citizens I find:

• Widespread public apathy despite these warnings.

• A tendency toward putting paper patches on the state systems of justice, rather than reinforcing foundations or building an entirely new structure.

• A chronic lack of communication among courts, both within a state and nationwide. This, coupled with a trial-and-error approach to problem-solving, means a judge in Massachusetts can't profit from the success or failures of courts in Oregon, Texas, or Florida. Communications even break down among judges sitting in one city.

• Rigid opposition to change on the part of many lawyers and judges. This is partly because they are overly concerned with tradition and partly because of self-interest.

"Members of the bar engaged in trying civil matters could well be financially distressed if personal-injury litigation goes out the window," says Geoffrey C. Hazard Jr. of the American Bar Foundation in Chicago.

Taking auto accidents out of the courts is being suggested as one possibility to end backlog. Lawyers are worried.

"Unless lawyers do something about court backlog, laymen will take over," warns James A. Dooley, one of the busiest trial lawyers in Chicago. "Within our framework we must do away with existing ills and bring about a streamlining of trials to protect the judge-and-jury system."

The problem of court delay is exceedingly complex. Each court in each state is different, and most face a wide variety of troubles.

At least on paper, Cook County, Ill., has the worst civil backlog in the nation. But John S. Boyle, the circuit court's chief judge, accuses other courts around the country of juggling statistics.

"We're the only court in the nation that keeps accurate backlog figures," he said in an interview. "New York has several million cases unaccounted for. Using bookkeeping gimmicks Los Angeles wiped out its backlog [on paper] overnight. Besides, Chicago has become the personal-injury-litigation center of the world."

In Judge Boyle's court system it now takes five or six years from the date of filing to get a case before a jury. Latest figures compiled by the Institute of Judicial Administration in New York City show:

A backlog of up to 5 years in civil courts around New York City; 38 months in the Boston area; 34 months in Cleveland (the chief justice of the Common Pleas Court there told this writer it is nearer 40 to 48 months now); 32.7 months in Detroit; and 30.1 months in San Francisco.

While most concern centers on civil litigation—largely auto-accident suits—this reporter found an alarming growth in criminal-court business. Soon criminal-court delay may be making national headlines.

In Los Angeles, for example, the home of one of the best court systems in the nation, criminal-court volume has hit crisis proportions and is still climbing.

Arrests are up 30 percent in five years there. Of greater concern, the number of defendants demanding jury trials has increased 300 percent in the same period. This, officials say, is largely due to recent Supreme Court rulings restating the rights of the accused and cracking down on police practices.

Similar reports are heard in other cities coast to coast.

"Ten years ago we had two criminal-court judges, and they weren't overly busy," says Judge Prendergast in Baltimore. "Now we have five judges there, plus a full-time juvenile judge, hearing criminal cases."

The number of criminal cases filed in Hennepin County (Minneapolis), Minn., increased by 50 percent in 1966 over 1965. The statewide average for new criminal filings in 1966 in Minnesota was up 46 percent.

As noted, Cleveland has one of the worst big-city criminal backlogs in the nation. Donald F. Lybarger, chief justice of the Common Pleas Court, reported 1,409 criminal cases pending as of March 27, 1967. Those in jail sometimes wait 8 to 10 months to go to trial, he adds. Defendants out on bail may wait longer.

Criminal backlog hurts both society and the accused. Prosecutors complain they lose too many cases as witnesses disappear and memories dim.

The accused, when arrested, may lose his job. His family faces great hardship. Reputations are tarnished. Often this adds to already fat welfare rolls, for the defendant's family must eat. Those who cannot make bail may sit in jail longer than a judge would sentence them for the crime. This is the city picture in some states.

Delays also occur in rural areas where judges are not sitting full time and courts operate on the old "term" system. This is as true in Massachusetts or Kansas as in South Carolina or Georgia.

Since most state courts use the same judge to try criminal and civil cases, reasons for delay in both divisions can be combined as follows.

1. Acute shortage of judges

While populations mushroom in urban areas, many courts operate with about the same number of men on the bench as they did two or three decades ago.

In Cuyahoga County (Cleveland), Ohio, "We have 24 judges for 1.8 million people. We ought to have 32," Judge Lybarger said in early 1967.

Minneapolis, in a county with a population of 900,000 and with 16 full-time judges, needed 20 in 1967, officials report. The same officials asked for several retired judges to work part-time to clean up the backlog. Neighboring St. Paul, in a slightly less-populated county, required three judges to boost the total of full-time judges to 13 in order to stay even.

Boston is operating with fewer judges than a generation ago because many of them are transferred out of the city to meet the huge growth of court business in other Massachusetts counties, says G. Joseph Tauro, chief justice of the Superior Court. Yet crime in Suffolk County has increased more than 50 percent in the past 10 years, the civil load is up, and the need for more judges is acute.

2. Too few courtrooms

"We need more judges, but even if we get them we don't have any place to put them," says Judge Prendergast of Baltimore. "Our courthouse is jammed, we have no way to expand, and so the only answer is a new building."

"We are reduced to using what resembles City Hall's converted closet space—both clothes and water," asserts Philadelphia's Judge Levin. "And while a few decent rooms are on the planning board, these will only meet present and long-overdue needs, not tomorrow's."

The report of the Citizens' Conference on the Administration of Justice in Hawaii states: "Physical facilities throughout the [court] system are woefully inadequate."

I found similar complaints in more than 30 other states.

3. Lazy judges

While many judges work in their chambers before taking the bench in the morning, during the noon hour, or in the afternoon, hundreds of judges average a 25- or 30-hour work week. This in spite of the backlog.

Tradition is one excuse. Judges keep short hours because

"that's the way it's always been done." Others assert that a judge's job is so demanding that it would be unfair to expect them to work longer (to which still others reply: "Hogwash").

In Chicago, the city with the biggest civil backlog, this reporter has checked all 114 courtrooms in the new Civic Center several times.

On a typical day he found judges on the bench in only 11 of the 114 courtrooms between 9:30 and 10 A.M.; 58 of the 114 benches filled between 10 A.M. and 10:30 A.M.; 45 judges sitting between 10:30 and 11 A.M.; and the same number between 11 and 11:30 A.M. Between 2:30 and 3 P.M. there were only 34 of the 114 benches with judges sitting.

And while almost every other chief judge in the nation helps reduce backlog by hearing cases or handling the court calendar, Chief Judge Boyle functions as a full-time administrator.

A veteran Chicago court observer, who says, "Cook County courts are 100 times better than they were," asserts Judge Boyle has his hands full "knocking heads, taking care of political matters, and acting as a buffer between the politicians and the prima donnas on the bench."

Some Chicago judges should be praised. One this reporter always found hard at work is Judge Harold G. Ward, who heads the law division.

"He works from 8:30 to 5:30. You can find him anytime," agrees Mr. Dooley, a lawyer with plenty of business in Judge Ward's court.

Among the nation's conscientious pace setters:

Judges in Los Angeles arrive between 8 and 8:30 A.M., reach the bench promptly at 9, take a 10-minute recess in the morning, lunch from 12 to 1 or 1:30, and quit between 4:15 and 4:30.

New Jersey judges start at 9:30, lunch from 1 to 2, and adjourn at 4, with 10-minute recesses in the morning and afternoon. Hours are stringently regulated by the New Jersey Supreme Court. Assignment (administrative) judges are the busiest. They start by 8:30 and seldom leave before 5.

In most districts judges pick their own working hours, and there is no one to keep tabs on them. New Jersey is one exception. There are others. In some cities judges work out a gentleman's agreement on hours. Some rural judges, often for lack of business, work only four or five days a month, while in the cities judges fight backlogs.

Howard Kline, senior judge in Wichita, Kan., says his court has a backlog ranging from four months to 2½ years. Until the State Supreme Court stepped in recently, each judge was given the same number of cases, kept his own docket, and proceeded at his own speed—without outside supervision. Pressed for a reason for the wide variation there, he says, "Some judges know how to operate their docket and others don't. And I guess if you get right down to it, there may be some lazy judges."

In every state visited this reporter saw a few judges working long hours to keep dockets current. Sometimes they were doing it just to keep other judges afloat.

Most judges still take long vacations. During the summer months many courts shut down.

Cleveland closes down in August. Pittsburgh judges take two months off during the summer. So do Memphis judges, says Judge John W. Wilson, but "somebody is always around for emergencies."

Long vacations date to the day when courthouses weren't air-conditioned. Many still aren't. Judges who take most of the summer off argue that witnesses, jurors, and lawyers are often hard to find.

Yet times are changing.

In Massachusetts Superior Court the recess during the last week of March was eliminated last year by Chief Justice G. Joseph Tauro. He says judges will sit all summer to expedite criminal matters.

Rhode Island's Superior Court Presiding Justice, John E. Mullen, asked the Legislature to pass an amendment that would provide a summer docket so that criminal trials can be held during the traditional layoff. This, he says, would eliminate excessive delay for those held in jail.

Judge Joseph G. Jeppson of Salt Lake City says his judges only get "two weeks for sure, and three weeks maximum," depending on court business. Their civil backlog is less than a year.

4. Dilatory lawyers

Much of the court delay can be blamed on lawyers. This is true in both criminal and civil courts.

"Lawyers as a whole are procrastinators," says Mr. Dooley, one of Chicago's busiest negligence lawyers. "Some think getting continuances is a good day's work. But continuing cases doesn't bring money into a law firm. Cases should be prepared, settled, or tried."

While civil-practice lawyers have much more going for them, only a handful enter courtrooms in most cities. (And for that reason, like most citizens, they often have little idea of what really is going on.)

Out of thousands of Chicago lawyers, 36 handle the bulk of auto-accident cases. Each firm has from 300 to 1,000 cases pending today, according to court officials.

"In Cleveland 55 lawyers try 82.3 percent of all cases," says Judge Lybarger. "And we have a bar of about 3,000."

The story is the same across the nation. Lawyers who take trial work find it extremely lucrative. Many grab every case that walks in the door. Some even solicit business. But they simply do not have enough days in the week to go to court. Sometimes they forget they have cases pending. They frequently ask for continuances or delay justice by being tied up in another courtroom, perhaps in federal court, when their case is called.

"When a trial lawyer has too many cases he tells the judge, 'I'm too busy to come to court,' " says Henry Ellenbogen, senior judge in the Pittsburgh Common Pleas Court. "So the lawyer on the other side twiddles his thumbs."

The system of justice is, in itself, a cause of delay.

Lawyers battle it out in court, and as one judge succinctly puts it: "Neither wants to see justice done. Each wants to win." In civil cases they are urged to settle out of court. So lawyers waste time trying to outbluff each other. The attorney for the plaintiff holds out for every cent he can get. The insurance company lawyer tries to bring the plaintiff's price down.

Both judges and lawyers have, in interviews and in print, compared what goes on behind the scenes in an auto-accident (negligence) case with back-room poker. Yet this wheeling and dealing goes on in cities across the nation week in and week out.

I have watched the process and found it fascinating. In one Western state the insurance-company lawyer kept calling his home office long distance, checking on offers. With each proposal the other lawyer, representing the plaintiff, or injured party, would go out to the courtroom and talk to his client.

The jury, which had spent hours listening to testimony, waited and wondered over the delay. The plaintiff, an elderly woman who had been injured while riding in a friend's car, was extremely uncomfortable.

The insurance company knew she should have something. It was a matter of how much. The logic seemed to be: This is an old woman. She will not live many more years. Why give her money that only will go to her children and to the state?

Finally the old woman settled out of court for $6,800, although in the suit she had asked for more than $30,000.

Her lawyer collected a fat fee—a third of the settlement, or $2,040. The defense lawyer was well paid. The insurance company did not have to risk thousands of dollars, should the jury have felt sorry for the woman and awarded her a larger sum. At the same time, she did not have to take the chance that the jury might award her less than $6,800. And so she went home with $4,760.

The 12 jurors went home too—each paid $5 by the taxpayers of the state for his trouble.

I left that courtroom feeling a little unclean and uncomfortable, wondering if there is not a better way of resolving these questions.

In some crowded areas lawyers even use the court backlog as a lever. But insurance companies are not always winners.

"A few say, 'Settle for what we offer, or wait six years'," says Chicago attorney Dooley. "It's a lousy choice. Someday they'll learn that those who can wait it out will get two or three times what they would if they settled without the delay."

In Cook County 95 percent of the cases are settled out of court before a jury reaches a verdict, says Judge Boyle. Plaintiffs' lawyers use the jury as a big stick to get insurance companies to pay off; thus the lawyers function largely as collection agents, using the courts as a tool.

Criminal lawyers across the country admit that they try to delay justice if they have a tough case, hoping that witnesses will forget or change their minds. They believe they have nothing to lose and everything to gain, since their client will probably go to jail anyway.

One problem is a critical shortage of competent attorneys, especially those who will take criminal cases. The report of the President's Commission on Law Enforcement and the Administration of Justice, puts it this way:

> The shortage of criminal lawyers, which is already severe, is likely to become more acute in the immediate future. . . . Criminal defendants can pay only a small fee. . . . Counsel for the defense must expect to lose more cases than he wins. . . . All but the most eminent criminal lawyers are bound to spend much of their working lives in overcrowded, physically unpleasant courts, dealing with people who have committed questionable acts. . . . In nearly every large city a private defense bar of low legal and dubious ethical quality can be found. . . . The public image of the criminal lawyer is a serious obstacle to the attraction of young, able lawyers and reputable and seasoned practitioners. . . .

As could be expected, I found reasons for delay complex. To many court officials the problems are frustrating.

But strong judges can at least resolve the civil backlog.

"If the judge really wants to do it he can clear the dockets," says Warren Burnett, of Odessa, Tex., one of the busiest lawyers in the Southwest. "All he has to do is make a courtroom available and tell the lawyer to be there. Then he runs that lawyer's cases through like boxcars, and you settle or go to trial as fast as they roll by."

Mr. Burnett knows, for as head of a small firm with some 2,000 cases pending, it has happened to him.

Judge Boyle asserts some Chicago lawyers slow down the pace in November and December because they have made so much money by then the fees "all go to the government." (Civil lawyers usually take a 25 to 50 percent cut of the settlement.)

In the few states where judges have firm control of their courts—and Illinois is not one of them—judges interviewed see the Cook County complaint as just another example of judicial weakness.

It may well point up another flaw: the unwillingness of local bar associations to discipline their members. I was sorry to find that in most states there is a "you protect me, I'll protect you" approach to bar discipline. And it also extends to the bench.

Mr. Burnett, when told of the charge that lawyers slow down court business for tax reasons, said flatly, "Those lawyers ought to be disbarred."

5. "Expert witnesses"

The use of "expert witnesses" like doctors and psychiatrists leads to problems of delay. Each lawyer, in trying to knock down the opposition's case, produces his own experts, who testify at length.

These experts are often hard to get to court because they are busy professionally. So lawyers ask for delays to accommodate them.

Their testimony is usually long-winded and highly technical, and it is too often used to confuse jurors rather than to help them make knowledgeable decisions. It has been proposed that a "neutral" expert take part in trials to help sort facts and translate terms.

This might speed up trials if the third expert is able to cut through the obfuscation created by the other two—or it could cause further delays.

6. Lax legislatures

State legislatures too often refuse to face the problems of the courts. Often they do not provide enough judges or funds.

In Illinois, where a new judicial article was recently passed, there is still a law that requires court docket books to be written and bound by hand, even though Cook County has rented a computer that could produce the information in minutes.

Los Angeles, while generally ahead of the nation in court administration, is blocked by archaic laws and the state constitution from making additional improvements, says Andrew L. Schultz, executive assistant court administrator.

Most states lack laws governing the forward progress of civil cases.

Michigan judges can throw a civil case out if it isn't making headway.

In New York City and Philadelphia, criminal defendants are brought in for hearings 24 hours a day. Pittsburgh operates one courtroom till after midnight. Several states have laws limiting the time a man can be held without starting him through the trial process.

7. Inefficient methods

Nearly every state requires criminal cases to proceed through the system at a "reasonable" speed. But each judge and prosecutor may have his own theory on what "reasonable" means.

The courts themselves often refuse to try modern business techniques.

Each year a few more hire court administrators so judges can be free of paperwork and other mundane activities. Richard E. Klein has been working as court administrator in St. Paul, Minn., since January, while Minneapolis has had an administrator for a year.

Judge Jeppson, in Salt Lake City, says the State Legislature has just provided for an administrator. The new law went into effect June 1, 1967.

I found Seattle's administrator, Robert C. Wetherholt, deep in paperwork. Until February he wore a second hat, handling noncontested matters too. In April he was still trying to clean up the backlog.

8. "Cats and dogs" cases

Wholesale filing of what some judges call "cats and dogs" cases.

These end up with a verdict of only a few hundred dollars, or at most a few thousand, and cost courts a great deal of time and money. Pittsburgh's Judge Ruggero J. Aldisert has studied the problem, and in his county "72 percent of all settlements and verdicts are under $5,000."

Nationally, thousands of plaintiffs ask for sizable sums and settle for a fraction—sometimes less than $1,000.

Not only are settlements small. Often the area of disagreement between the plaintiff and defendant is relatively narrow, Judge Aldisert adds.

"If a trial lasts four days, then, depending upon what formula you use, it costs the taxpayers between $1,800 and $2,400 for a jury trial," he asserts. "If the parties are only $500 or $1,000 apart in a $5,000 or $10,000 case why should the taxpayers pay $1,800 to settle this difference?"

Criminal-court judges also complain about the filing of "cheap" cases, while those involving serious crimes and with good evidence against the defendant are held up. In too many instances the prosecutor is too busy to screen cases, or wants the judge to take the blame for throwing them out.

There are, of course, other reasons for delay. And while the list of problems is fairly universal, it does not apply in every court in every state.

Without a doubt the problem could be resolved quickly if more judges and lawyers and the general public really cared. But justice is a sometime thing for most of us. We never expect to go to court. Even when we find ourselves there, we have no way of knowing if our experience—good or bad—is typical.

Almost no one is watching the courts, not even that curious collection of retired and bored men who once kept courtroom benches polished with their well-worn trouser seats. Television, retirement money for travel or a home in a warm climate, the availability of automobiles, and other inventions of our era have changed that.

Many judges fight change. This is often laid to the conservatism of the profession. Others credit it to the fact judges often take the bench when they are beyond the midpoint of their careers, or are approaching retirement. By then many are rather rigid in their ways.

I have found humility is not the best-known trait of lawyers. Many are not interested in suggestions—especially from outsiders like business-management consultants. Members of the bench and bar have a beautiful way of putting laymen down with four words: "Are you a lawyer?"

Many believe the law and the courts are the private domain of their profession, not the possession of the people of America. Too many judges are not there to serve. Rather they consider a judgeship a special honor and expect to *be* served, cajoled, and catered to.

Even with this to contend with, in almost every state I found a few citizens and the more thoughtful members of the bench and bar working to bring about changes that will eliminate delay and other court problems.

Many solutions are being offered—beyond providing more judges and courtrooms and demanding more work from those who earn their keep in the courts. Included are:

• A strong chief judge who can make assignments, set working hours and make them stick, and keep judicial business flowing. He should have a good business-oriented court administrator.

• Team spirit in the courts. "We have perfect cooperation of judges," says Judge John W. Wilson, of Memphis, where the backlog is one of the lowest in the country. "Say I have three suits on my docket when I open court at 10 A.M. and they all announce settled. I don't leave the courthouse, although I could. I go to the other judges to see if they have any cases I can take."

• The use of certificates of readiness. Before a trial date is set, lawyers must sign a statement that they are ready for court.

• Computers and other electronic equipment for recordkeeping and other judicial administration requirements.

• Liberal transfer or assignment policy. In some states a judge is sent where he is needed. A rural judge may well spend part of his time in the city.

• Arbitration. In Pittsburgh three-lawyer arbitration panels hear minor civil cases with excellent results, often handling six cases per panel per day.

• The six-man jury and split verdicts in civil cases. Some lawyers feel a smaller jury works as well as the large one and that a 9-3 or even 7-5 jury verdict in civil cases is better than the normal 12-0 vote.

• Much has been said about pretrial, and nearly every court in the nation is using some form of it or has tried it to clarify issues, find areas of agreement, and settle civil cases. In San Francisco Judge Charles S. Peery, with the help of an appointed commissioner, pretries 40 to 50 cases a week—two every half-hour. Yet some judges call it a waste of time.

• In auto-accident cases there are several suggestions. Judge Alexander P. Waugh of Morristown, N.J., notes these: (a) a system similar to workmen's compensation; (b) recovery on your own insurance policy; (c) abolition of the jury trial; (d) court costs being paid by one or both of the parties in the suit, rather than by the taxpayers.

While judges, lawyers, and concerned laymen are divided on solutions and will even argue over which court problems are most pressing, few deny that a crisis exists.

It is easy to file a civil suit. Thousands of people go to court for the first time every month—either as plaintiff or defendant. But for many, justice grinds slowly—sometimes to no avail because it grinds too late.

Many in the legal profession agree that laymen will indeed "take over" unless the profession acts to speed up the wheels of justice.

But whether reform comes from within or from outside the

ranks of the legal profession is perhaps of less importance to concerned citizens than that it come. And there is hope that it will.

Says Maurice Rosenberg, professor of law at Columbia University, "The problem of delay may be old, but it is by no means obsolescent; it is complex but not insoluble; it is stubborn but not hopeless."

CHAPTER III

Courts for the Common Man

She was a pretty girl from Wisconsin. Attractively dressed, she sat with the more scraggly prisoners on the platform and stared at her hands. Only once did she let her eyes meet those of her fiancé in the crowd below.

Coming to Philadelphia a few months before to be near him, she was working while he finished college—saving what she could for their marriage.

Now she was in Philadelphia's night court, charged with shoplifting.

When her name was finally called, she walked weakly down the steps and stood, white-faced, before the bench. A department-store clerk said the girl had tried to steal a sweater.

In less than five minutes the magistrate found her guilty. Given the choice of paying a $25 fine and $2.50 costs or spending 10 days in jail, she let her fiancé pay the fine. Her conviction was entered in the record book.

A few minutes later a dirty old man with bagging pants and a three-day beard stood before the magistrate, charged with stealing 14 pairs of ladies' hose. The magistrate grinned, recognizing him as a resident of a flophouse in his district.

"Didn't all 148 of you [residents of the flophouse] vote against me?" the magistrate asked, half joking.

"No, no, no, Your Honor, we all voted for you," the old man whined. "I'm begging you to give me a break. I'm begging you."

The magistrate grinned again and let the man go.

On the two nights I visited this court, the magistrate, his clerk, a deputy district attorney, a stenographer, a deputy public defender, and two police officers smoked. This despite large signs tacked to the bench reading: "No Smoking."

One man, waiting for hours for a case to be called, asked if he, too, could smoke. The cheroot-puffing assistant district attorney told him no—only court personnel could "ignore the law."

As this reporter traveled across the nation looking at the state courts, these events in Philadelphia became symbolic of flaws most clearly seen in the minor courts and sometimes present in the higher trial courts as well.

Through friendship, political station, and sometimes bribery (although this point was not an issue on this night in Philadelphia), Americans have established a curiously privileged class of citizens—a group of people who stand above or beyond the law, almost as once was the case with the rich and the royal.

The President's Commission on Law Enforcement and Administration of Justice expressed concern in its recent report over the widespread inequities it found in the American system of justice and stated the over-all problem clearly:

> The commission has been shocked by what it has seen in some lower courts. It has seen cramped and noisy courtrooms, undignified and perfunctory procedures, and badly trained personnel. It has seen dedicated people who are frustrated by huge case loads, by the lack of opportunity to examine cases carefully, and by the impossibility of devising constructive solutions to the problems of offenders. It has seen assembly-line justice.

And this is what I saw in Philadelphia and in too many other cities across the nation.

The Philadelphia magistrate I watched in action is not a lawyer. Like thousands of other minor-court magistrates, he became a judge of his fellow men by running for office and winning it. Day after day he dispenses justice like an Army mess sergeant dishing out boiled potatoes and meat loaf.

Only 30 states keep court statistics, and most do not include minor courts.

Though there is little accurate information available, it is estimated that every year some 35 million Americans come in contact with these so-called minor courts. Some, of course, are repeaters. Most—between 20 and 30 million—are charged with traffic offenses.

The President's commission found that in 1965 more than 2 million Americans entered prison, juvenile training schools, or were placed on probation. How many others were fined (like the Philadelphia girl), jailed briefly, or "given a break" is nearly beyond comprehension.

The majority get their first taste of American justice from more than 10,000 judges who are laymen or who work part time. The rest appear before the roughly 5,000 better-qualified lawyer-judges who preside over slightly higher-level minor courts.

Minor courts vary widely in name. The largest number are still known as justice-of-the-peace courts, a carryover from early England. Other titles include magistrate, municipal judge, city judge, police-court judge, district judge (in some New England states), common-pleas judge (which may also be the name of the highest trial court, depending upon the state), and county judge.

Their duties are equally diverse.

Conditions are not what you expect in the revered American system of justice.

Take Judge C——, an Oklahoma City justice of the peace, for example. Some months before I met him, his fellow JPs had asked him to speak for them before the Legislature to try to block a move to abolish the courts.

I found his courtroom in the back of an old store-front building that housed several related offices, including a bail bondsman.

The room, about 20 by 20, was in need of dusting and fresh paint. A story-and-a-half high, the upper portion was a dirty white, the lower an off blue-green.

An American flag was thumbtacked to the wall. Metal-framed, chicken-wire-glass windows needed washing. Four bare bulbs dangled on their electric cords. Pictures of Indians were spotted around the walls.

Those awaiting the 9 A.M. session sat on a battered, unmatched collection of chairs and old pews. The judge's bench was a desk on a wooden platform. The witness stand was in one corner, also on a platform, in front of shelves filled with large red and gold docket books. In another corner was a sink and a tattered folding screen.

Men and women, as well as policemen in uniform, file in and fill up the seats. Others mill around in the hall.

From my old wooden pew (I arrived early) I spot Judge C—— in his gritty, glass-enclosed, turn-of-the-century-style office. People press in and out, chatting with him.

Roughly the time court is scheduled to begin Judge C—— ambles from his office to the desk in the courtroom, sits down, and lights a cigarette. Then he tells those who are interested enough to listen that he will call four cases first—apparently the result of the conversations I had watched in his office.

People still stand around the bench, block the doorways, talk to each other, mill noisily in the hall.

Judge C—— calls the four cases and does not seem surprised when the parties are not present. He tells the witnesses to go home, explaining they will be told when to return again.

He calls another case. The defendant, out on bail, is not present. Someone says the defendant's lawyer "called and said he broke one of his plates, so he can't make it." Everyone laughs because the lawyer with the broken false teeth is well known in Oklahoma City. I had had lunch with him the day before.

Three young men handcuffed together and wearing jail garb —blue mechanic's coveralls—file in. They sit under guard with the rest of the audience.

Another case is called. Nobody is present. Some witnesses ask about their case. They are told it has been rescheduled for 1:30 P.M. and so they go home.

It is 9:15 A.M. and the noise in the hall continues. Two cases "hanging fire since last September" (this was February) will be tried together, the judge announces. Several policemen are sworn together.

The defendant asks for a continuance of two weeks so that he can finish paying off the bad checks, which are "90 percent paid." The policemen leave with the other witnesses. More people come in from the hall and fill up the seats.

It is now 9:26 and still no hearings have been held. Another case is continued for a week. Another defendant is not present. His name is shouted around and up and down the hall.

A Negro prisoner is called. He stands. The arresting officers' names are called. There is no answer. They call the policemen again. No response.

"Sit down, son," Judge C—— tells the prisoner, who asks why his lawyer is not there.

The next case is called, including a long list of witnesses. One policeman is present, along with the defendant. Judge C—— says that since the witnesses are not present (the case is not described) it will be dismissed—if the defendant agrees to pay court costs.

It is 9:35, and Judge C—— lights up another cigarette. Others are smoking and the room is nearly blue.

Another prisoner stands when his name is called. Several police officers are not present. The judge asks the youth if he has a lawyer. The boy replies "No," and so Judge C—— turns to a man standing at his elbow and says: "Here, you take it."

Finally at 9:41 the first witness, a white factory worker, is sworn. He testifies that he was awakened by police "about 6 A.M." one day and was told they had recovered his pink and white '55 Cadillac with a fender smashed.

He is asked if he knows who took it and he points at one of the youngsters and says, "That one." But according to the police, he was not present when the youth was picked up.

The judge calls for the arresting officers to testify. Somebody says, "They called in and said they're on their way." Judge C—— announces he will "hold the case in abeyance" until they arrive.

The next case is called. He has a whispered conference with the district attorney, who makes a motion to dismiss if the defendant pays costs.

Then a woman from a bank takes the stand in another case. Another waiting lawyer is appointed for a defendant.

The woman testifies that she closes FHA and VA loans for

the bank. The defendant had signed an affidavit that he had no liens outstanding, but "it turned out that he had several mechanics liens filed against the property."

The judge asks for more details. The district attorney objects, but the judge brushes it aside, explaining, "Overruled. I'm learnin' something here and I want to hear these answers."

While the judge and witness discuss how the system operates, someone brings the judge coffee. He sips it. The assistant DA objects to the questions again, but the judge says, "No, I want to know about this. I want to hear these answers."

Finally the judge binds the case over to district court (the trial court) and tells the defendant to visit the bonding company across the hall.

In the next case the defense attorney tells Judge C—— his client has been in court "each time the case was called since October," but so far the police officers have not been in court. The judge orders subpoenas issued again, and the case is rescheduled.

Then one of the white youths who arrived in handcuffs is told his case was "set by error" for this day, and that it is being reset for the following Tuesday. The boy is returned to jail.

After a brief pause another lawyer standing near the judge is assigned a case, and the attorney and his "client" move to a corner to whisper.

The next case is called and a policeman takes the stand. The case is postponed because the complaining witness has not been subpoenaed.

And so the morning goes: a man charged with using somebody else's credit card; more missing policemen, witnesses, and defendants; the two defense lawyers getting more assignments.

In the afternoon Judge C—— hears a child-manslaughter case. The father of the infant, born out of wedlock, is accused. Charges are dismissed because no one saw the man strike the baby, and a doctor testifies that the child might have fallen. Before the judge agrees to dismiss he makes sure he gets $42.50 court costs.

Much of his time is spent handling grocery bills and other credit matters. In a case where a man's wages are garnisheed for nonpayment of a bill Judge C—— collects $5, but $3 goes to his constable to serve papers.

The story is much the same in many sections of the country.

In Anderson, S.C., Magistrate Bruce Davis points out that "there are obvious defects in the system in light of the fact that few magistrates have legal training, and some, because of their small volume of business, have little opportunity to become familiar with legal procedure."

Yet Judge Davis, who has his office in the basement of the Anderson County courthouse, is an exception: a former schoolteacher, he is a college graduate. But he has no training in the law.

Much of his time is spent working on "domestic problems—trying to keep families together." Yet, he adds, "I have no jurisdiction in this."

In most states minor courts have jurisdiction over misdemeanors—the legal term for minor offenses like public drunkenness, vagrancy, shoplifting, and violations of local ordinances. The National Council on Crime and Delinquency reports nine-tenths of all American crime falls into the misdemeanor category.

Fines vary from state to state and sometimes from court to court. Most are limited to $200 or $300—at the top $1,000. Most minor courts can sentence from 30 to 60 days in jail—some up to one year. In those where the minor courts heve been upgraded into district courts with lawyer-judges, fines and sentences can be considerably higher.

County courts in Wisconsin, for example, have had their jurisdiction enlarged so that they can hear the cases traditionally handled by the circuit courts—except for treason. The Milwaukee area is an exception. Here only crimes punishable by a year or less in prison or by fines under $1,000 can be heard.

Again, depending upon the state, minor courts also may hear minor civil matters. Sometimes, as in South Carolina, the top limit is a few hundred dollars. In Kansas minor courts have civil jurisdiction in cases up to $1,000, and occasionally as high as $2,500—depending upon the county. The variation in Missouri is from $1,000 to $2,000. The cutoff in South Dakota municipal courts is $500, with $1,000 tops in county courts there.

Minor-court judges also hear most or all traffic cases, and sometimes probate, juvenile, divorce, and other family matters.

In addition to this they perform marriages, issue criminal warrants, and often set bail for all crimes, including murder.

Most can cite citizens for contempt of court. In Kansas a justice of the peace can send you to jail for 10 days for contempt. In Louisiana the limit is $10 or 24 hours. Montana and Nevada limit contempt penalties to $100 or one day. The same is true of Utah, South Dakota, and Idaho. Some states, like Alabama, limit the penalty to $6 or 6 hours or similar short periods.

At last count, 32 states let their minor-court justices and judges earn all or part of their keep by collecting fees in criminal cases. This is a horrible system that can lead to finding nearly everyone guilty and heaping on costs to make a profit; for the magistrate's cut is often tied to the size of the fee.

More progressive states have replaced the fee system with a salary. And some states pay justices a fee when cases are dismissed.

The President's commission found that in at least three states justices of the peace are paid only if they convict and collect a fee from the defendant—a practice held unconstitutional by the Supreme Court 40 years ago.

Thousands of minor-court judges work only part time. In New Hampshire only one among 73 district and municipal judges works full time. Of the 73, 34 are laymen, according to Frank R. Kenison, Chief Justice of the New Hampshire Supreme Court.

In Pendleton, S.C., Justice J. W. Holliday is a retired schoolteacher who sits on the bench a few hours each day handling "fines and forfeits."

"I never run out of family troubles," he said, as we sat on his front porch one evening, chatting.

Now and again he is called on to hold a jury trial. When he does, he usually finds himself serving as prosecutor as well as judge. And he gives the six-man jury a chance to "ask a few questions too, so they get enough facts" to make a decision.

Minor-court record-keeping checked by this reporter in a national tour would make most business executives shed bitter tears. In Pennsylvania, where every hamlet and crossroads has its own JP, there are between 4,000 and 5,000 minor-court judges. William W. Litke, former president of the Pennsylvania Bar Association, has said:

"Only the accounts showing fines transmitted to local and state governments and costs for handling criminal cases which are reimbursed by the county are audited. This leaves a large volume of criminal, as well as noncriminal, transactions unaudited.

"Moreover, responsibility for auditing is divided among state, county, and local officials. Often the auditing is performed by elected or appointed personnel who lack professional training and who are not aloof from political considerations."

Two years ago, when Illinois court reform abolished the lowest level of courts, revenue collected by some courts soared. Cook County suburbs are taking in so much now that they are building new courthouses, says one state official. He wonders aloud about where the money was going before.

Interestingly enough, in some downstate areas in Illinois the amount collected by the new courts is lower than in the past.

This undoubtedly is in keeping with the tired old saw that JP stands not for justice of the peace, but instead for "justice for the plaintiff." Thus less money is being collected because there are fewer convictions than in the past.

As I traveled the nation, I found in almost every state a few JPs won the bulk of police business. This is partly attributed to the availability of the justice. In fee states it can be partly blamed on kickbacks. But more often JPs are busy simply because they are willing to convict.

"Policemen don't bring 'em in unless they're guilty," explained one veteran Texas magistrate. His words were echoed, although often more subtly, in every corner of the country.

At least 40 states still permit badly flawed minor-court systems to operate. And this system of justice is supported—if only through permissive silence—by the American people.

Actually, few know what goes on in the minor courts. Few

lawyers practice there. The average citizen may appear once or twice in a lifetime to face speeding charges or some other minor offense. His stay is brief—perhaps a few hours in city courts or five minutes or less in rural areas where the workload is low. And he has little or no way of evaluating what happens, except that he may be rather angry about his personal experience.

Lawyers who do practice in the lower courts are often struggling to keep meat on the table. In several cities I saw them waiting for cases like hungry alley cats—this because tidbits are thrown to them. In some cities appointed lawyers, though supposed to work without fee or to be paid by the county, push a client to fork over a wrist watch, television set, auto title, or even a deed to a home before the lawyer will appear on behalf of the defendant. In many cities higher-court judges will grant a continuance without a word when a lawyer mentions a code phrase that indicates his client has not yet paid his fee.

Many lower-court judges in the United States get first crack at serious (felony) offenses. They hold preliminary hearings to see if police have enough evidence to establish probable cause to bind over a case to a higher court or the grand jury.

By law, minor courts must take on these preliminary hearings. Yet better screening practices by prosecutors could be more effective.

Thousands of minor-court judges are not qualified to make decisions on the merits of the case. So many times they simply move them along to a higher court, making such hearings a farce. Only the public is fooled—believing that somehow justice is being "done."

Thus a preliminary hearing can often be a waste of time and tax money. Many defendants waive these hearings in states where this is permitted. Lawyers sometimes use them to discover what kind of evidence the police have against a client.

The lack of screening results in overloading higher courts with petty cases.

"To clog up criminal courts with 20,000 cases, 12,000 of which could be thrown out or handled by a [competent] magistrate, is ridiculous," says Adrian Bonnelly, president judge in Philadelphia's intermediate County Court.

Most of the nation's minor courts have little or no supervision from outside—certainly less than the 3,700 judges sitting in the highest state trial courts.

In a letter in response to a question by this reporter, William D. Radcliff, administrative assistant to the Ohio Supreme Court, stated that in Ohio "there is no supervisory authority vested in the Supreme Court to control or regulate the intermediate appellate court or the trial court. There is a great deal of autonomy and discretionary power vested in each judge and each court."

Checking further, I found that while Ohio has a Judicial Conference (used in more enlightened states to upgrade courts by training judges and magistrates), minor-court judges—who need the most help—are not permitted to belong.

Ohio is not alone.

Iowa's minor-court hodgepodge can only be described as awful.

To its credit, Iowa officials have counted their magistrates, thanks to Clarence A. Kading, Judicial Department statistician. Yet nobody supervises the courts.

The Iowa Legislature has provided for some 3,320 JP courts, but in 1964 only 552 JPs took office.

As in most states, the only qualification is that the justice be a resident of the township in which he runs. He has civil jurisdiction up to $100, and may hear cases up to $300 if both parties agree.

The JP acts as a committing magistrate for both felonies and misdemeanors. That means he can clap people in jail to await trial by a higher court or in his court, depending upon the magnitude of the crime. And he can sentence alleged offenders to 30 days in jail (certainly long enough to lose a job) or levy fines up to $100.

Then there are the mayors' courts. These are authorized for all cities and towns under 15,000 population. Exactly 901 were reported to be functioning or eligible to function in 1965.

Next in the line-up of Iowa courts is the police court. Criminal jurisdiction is the same as in the JP and mayors' courts, but unlike the other two, it has no civil jurisdiction. As in the other two, judges do not need to have legal training. Police courts are required in all communities of 15,000 or more people, and can be established by local ordinance in smaller cities. In 1965 a total of 29 were operating.

Next in line is the municipal court, which may be established by election in any city with more than 5,000 residents. Only 13 existed in 1965 in Iowa. It may be more than coincidental that municipal judges must be licensed lawyers.

This is also true of the fourth category—the superior court. Only Keokuk has established a superior court, although any community with a population of 4,000 or more can open such a court.

Both municipal and superior courts have larger jurisdictions than the other minor courts. In fact, superior courts have the same jurisdiction as the district courts—the courts of general jurisdiction in Iowa.

Lower-court hodgepodge is nationwide.

Utah has both city and justice-of-the-peace courts, and both hold preliminary hearings in felonies. City-court judges must be members of the bar, but JPs need only to be residents. And the justices operate on the fee system.

When I asked Leland Cummings, clerk of the Utah Supreme Court, how many JPs operate in his state, he assured me "nobody knows . . . no list is kept anywhere in the state."

And as in most states, nobody controls or supervises these minor courts.

Kentucky has some of the worst minor courts in the nation. There, too, information is available largely because of one man, James T. Fleming, director of the Legislative Research Commission.

In Kentucky each county is divided into districts, and each is entitled to a JP. Fortunately, the Court of Appeals "took the JPs off the fee system," he says. And some counties "won't pay them a salary." Those who are paid "don't do much work" because without the fee "there's little point in working."

In addition, there are about 350 police courts and 120 county courts, plus city judges. To run for office, would-be judges must be 24 years old and residents of Kentucky.

As pointed out earlier, perhaps fewer than half of the higher trial courts have judges that can be classified as "good." On this basis, since roughly two-thirds of the nation's 15,000 or more minor-court judges are not lawyers, and since pay for lawyer-judges in the minor courts is usually low, with many working only part time, perhaps only one in 10—if that many—could be considered "competent."

There are exceptions. In some states, including Maine, Colorado, North Carolina, and Illinois, nonlawyer courts have been abolished recently. In these states lawyers can sometimes work up through the system like college instructors moving up to associate and then full professorships.

Even this can cause shortcomings, says Milton G. Rector, director of the National Council on Crime and Delinquency in New York.

"Once a minor-court judge shows that he is capable, he is appointed to a higher court," Mr. Rector says. "This means we siphon off the best judges in courts that handle 90 percent of the people. The answer is to upgrade these lower courts."

Reform is already in the sprinkle stage, and there is hope it will soon grow into a downpour on what has been a thirsty desert.

How many cases are "fixed" by minor-court judges?

No one in the United States has any idea. But most states have a fixing scandal every few years—usually in areas where there is an aggressive newspaper to keep watch.

Chicago's traffic court has been rocked by scandal constantly. One recent shake-up came in early 1967. Four magistrates were fired and 13 others transferred. This despite the fact the Illinois court system was reorganized three years ago and the traffic courts have been under the supervision of the chief judge of the circuit court since then.

Maine prides itself on having a first-rate judiciary. In 1961 it began replacing part-time trial and municipal justices with district judges. When Paul A. MacDonald, a former secretary of state, took the bench he found one magistrate in his district had 116 cases "pending." Since they were beyond the legal time limit, all had to be dismissed.

"The fellow was a lawyer, and I suppose he put these away as a favor to fellow lawyers," Judge MacDonald says. "The old system wasn't much different than in states where judges run for office and have to collect campaign funds from attorneys and friends. It was all political."

Now Judge MacDonald, who is appointed, can do his job without caring "whether I hurt somebody's feelings or not."

Many minor-court judges are pushed around by prosecutors and police. This is partly because of their lack of knowledge of the law and partly because prosecutors and police will take their cases elsewhere if, in their eyes, a magistrate is "soft" toward defendants.

In Seminole, Tex., a small town not far from the New Mexico border, Judge Jim Vining, a retired oil field driller and newsstand operator, collects $360 a month to dispense justice.

Often, he says, when "a drunk says he is not guilty" he is thrown in jail "for two or three days" until he changes his mind, pleads guilty, and pays his fine. Sometimes sheriffs' deputies put on stronger pressure.

The day I visited Seminole, a man had been released from jail when his employer paid his $50 fine and costs.

He was arrested by the Texas State Highway Patrol. Officers had found a car stopped along a barren stretch of highway. The man was standing alongside, relieving himself. He was arrested and jailed, then brought before Judge Vining by a deputy sheriff who had no connection with the arrest.

"They told the man he better plead guilty to drunk and vagrancy or they'd get him for indecent exposure," Judge Vining told me. Later the sheriff admitted this was a fairly common practice.

Drunks fill minor-court dockets. In nearly every large city justice is performed in rapid-fire fashion.

San Francisco Municipal Judge Joseph Kennedy, a lawyer who expressed as much compassion and dignity as time would allow, had them file into his courtroom two dozen at a time on the Monday morning I was there.

Even before he reached the bench, you could hear the cell doors clanging and the jailers shouting names so the men could line up.

Each group of 24 filed out behind a large steel-pipe barrier. There Judge Kennedy advised them of the charge against them and of their rights. One after another they pleaded guilty. Each had roughly 30 seconds before the judge, and most were given 30-day suspended sentences. Some were encouraged to leave town.

One frequent visitor was told he was being sentenced to 15 days to "break the cycle." A few younger men were allowed to go to the "AA school so you can learn the evils of this problem." Several told Judge Kennedy they had been out "only an hour" before they were picked up again, to which Judge Kennedy replied: "That isn't our fault, is it?"

In 53 minutes he processed more than 140 men.

In Indianapolis the scene was the same—as it is in most large cities. Judge Harry F. Zaklan often recognized defendants.

"Ernie, you back again?" he would ask. Or, "Joe, you've been picked up 150 times. It's still cold out. For your own good I'm going to send you up until it gets warmer outside."

In rural areas I found judges tougher—socking drunks with $25 or $50 fines and long jail stretches.

At best, minor courts are unpleasant places. At worst they are bad beyond belief.

The county criminal court in Louisville, Ky., was packed and noisy. Although I sat near the front I found it difficult to hear court business—until a young woman who was picked up in a bar charged a young man with attempted rape. Suddenly everybody was listening.

The Louisville criminal-court judge was sarcastic with nearly everyone who appeared before him. He embarrassed a long-haired youth from a home for boys who was brought in by the prosecutor to testify for the state in a case.

"Whatta they do for you out there [at the home]?" the judge asked, "just let you sit around all day and talk and let your hair grow?"

Many minor-court judges are retired men who take the low-paying jobs to pad out Social Security checks. But others find these jobs extremely profitable.

Justice Jack Treadway is a lawyer in Houston. I asked him how he could afford to take such a low-paying job.

"I perform 2,000 marriages a year," he explained. "My minimum fee is $10, and it goes up to $35 or $50."

Yet down the hall the office of another justice was empty. He continues to draw his $12,000 salary as a justice of the peace, although court officials say he has been "bedridden for two years."

Judge Treadway says that nonlawyers are not qualified for justice-of-the-peace posts in Harris County and that only two out of nine JPs are lawyers.

Justice Treadway also notes the importance of screening cases.

"I dismiss at least 25 percent of all cases that come before me for lack of evidence," he says. (Yet by conservative estimate, the national average must be closer to 2.5 percent thrown out of minor courts.)

As in the higher courts, seldom is there communication between justices.

In Mr. Vining's court in Seminole he fines offenders $18.50 for running a stop sign; $20 for a red light. A habitual drunk pays $200 and usually serves a long jail sentence instead—"so we get rid of him."

A block down the street Mrs. Lorine Basham, a housewife and grandmother, presides over the city court from 9 A.M. to 12, and from 3 to 5 P.M.—all for a $250 a month salary, compared with Mr. Vining's $360.

"I handle everything the city police bring in—mostly drunks and disturbances and traffic cases," she says.

Her fine for running a stop sign: $5. Red lights cost violators $10. And drunks pay $25 for the first offense, $50 for the second, and $100 for the third.

It is in the traffic court that most of us learn how the American system of justice works. What we experience there influences our attitudes toward all courts and our system of justice as a whole.

When talking to groups about courts I have asked audiences for a show of hands indicating those who have received at least one traffic ticket. The room is always filled with raised hands.

James P. Economos, head of the ABA Traffic Court Program, estimates that 30 million traffic tickets are issued each year. Of these, some 10 million Americans appear before a judge or magistrate. The rest plead guilty without a court appearance.

In Los Angeles one Thursday evening I watched 754 people processed in less than three hours by three judges. Less than 8 percent plead not guilty, says Judge Thomas C. Murphy, who sits at the hub of this three-courtroom setup and dispenses justice with a light touch that keeps people from getting angry. He includes a "20-minute talk" every hour so defendants will understand their rights and how the court operates. Most plead guilty "with an explanation."

He even invites parents to let their children sit with him on the bench—if they promise to "take them when they go home." And adds: "You can even burn your driver's license in protest on the front steps."

Hundreds of communities, large and small, use traffic tickets to raise funds—ignoring what experts say is the primary reason for traffic court: to promote driving safety.

In Indianapolis I was surprised to hear Judge John C. Christ handing down fines of $1 or $1.25 and costs. That is, until I learned costs vary from $7.25 to $17.25, with the money going to the city general fund, to the state, and to state and county prosecutors.

Much of the $2.5 million yearly revenue (including parking revenue) produced by a one-judge court in Seattle (recently enlarged) goes into the general fund, says Judge Vernon W. Towne. "Our practices here are no different from any other city, and it bothers me when we are merely considered a revenue-producing court."

Most traffic courts tend to encourage defendants to plead

guilty—although in several of the states they may request jury trials.

The 8 percent pleading not guilty in Los Angeles must come back another day—perhaps missing work and losing more money than the cost of the ticket. Anyone who has spent time around traffic courts has heard citizens complain that they are not guilty but will pay the fine anyway to save time and money.

And there is little possibility of keeping track of money that is never turned in to the state or county by the minor courts—especially in rural areas. Millions may be lost this way each year.

In 1966 Philadelphia's traffic court reportedly lost $30,000.

In Pittsburgh, Chief Magistrate Ernest C. Jones has been using IBM equipment for "eight or nine years," along with professional accounting procedures.

When he took over, tickets were "stacked around in boxes and bushel baskets." He cleaned up a 200,000-ticket backlog and has a Better Traffic Committee working with citizen groups. To make sure all are properly treated and that no money disappears, other safeguards are used. The cash is balanced every day and deposited in a bank. The city is paid by check, and he can listen in on people dealing with the public by punching a button in his office.

Part of the problem with traffic offenses: Everybody who drives a car commits one or more violations almost every time he takes it out of the garage. So he hardly classifies the offense with other "crimes," although the law in most states does. Only a minute fraction of all violations are ticketed.

In a paper delivered at the traffic sessions of the 1966 National Safety Congress, Donald A. McIntyre Jr., research supervisor for the American Bar Foundation, said:

> I believe the image motorists have of traffic laws and traffic enforcement is most unwholesome. Judging from the considerable literature in this field, the fault stems in part from the fact that traffic laws are so numerous, so comprehensive, so restrictive, and so in need of precision that there is no sound basis for an appreciation and desire to obey the law.

He quoted the Oklahoma Supreme Court:

> There are one-way streets, no parking zones restricted to parking of particular kinds of vehicles, zones restricted to pedestrian traffic, no left turn corners, some left turn after stop, some, after arm signals. In some places a tail light signal is sufficient to indicate a turn or stop, other places require an arm signal; there are various lanes in some metropolitan areas, some restricted exclusively to various classifications of traffic, and requiring a genius to get out of after once getting in, without violating the law.

It seems worth noting that the Oklahoma high court comments were made in 1953—before many of our expressway spaghetti-bowls were built; before radar units were strapped to every village and hamlet police car; and in a time when most two-car families were at least in the middle class, for the flight from the cities and newly arrived Negroes was really only beginning.

Yet I found some improvement in traffic courts as I moved about the country looking at our system of justice. In a handful of areas the courts operate with the same honesty, professionalism, and dignity that one can find in the better trial courts.

If traffic courts are better today than a decade or two ago, one man, the ABA's Mr. Economos, must have most of the credit.

A large, friendly bear of a man, he has devoted much of his life to upgrading these courts. It has been an uphill battle.

In the spring of 1967 I attended one of his three-day meetings in Concord, N.H. It was the first time in 18 years that he had been able to get these New England minor-court judges to agree to meet and discuss their duties. This came about largely because of pressure that was being put on the courts by women's clubs.

Many magistrates grumbled about the session—apparently convinced that they didn't need anyone to tell them how to run *their* courts. In states where the chief justice of the supreme court had no control, many judges simply did not bother to come.

I left convinced that while several were inspired by the meeting, the majority of magistrates were about as impressed as the teen-agers who appear before these magistrates for speeding and reckless driving offenses. An interesting parallel since so many of these judges simply "cannot understand the attitude" of the youngsters.

I have often wondered what impact the attitude of the judge has on the decline in respect for law and order in America.

As a newspaper reporter for a dozen years I have visited jails and prisons, talked with rebellious teens, interviewed both whites and minority groups in both the North and South, lived in Northern slums, covered riots and other acts of violence, and watched our system of justice in operation.

And I have seen a wide gap between what we say is true about justice in the United States and what is really true.

If I am entitled to an opinion, it is that what I found in the minor courts has a major impact on the problems our society faces today.

If I may qualify that opinion, it should also be said that perhaps the problems of the minor courts also reflect the problems of our society.

In either case, changes are needed.

It is not enough that justice is "done," to use the revealing word so common in reference to our courts. Those who have justice "done to them" must recognize it as justice. Sometimes the smallest things can make a difference.

While many justices run honest courts, a judicial setting is lacking. In Loving, N.M., Justice L. C. Burkham runs a gas station. Sometimes when police bring in a speeder or other offender, he wipes the grease off his hands and holds court right there.

Others still hold court in their homes. Some motorists tell of a farmer who dispenses justice from a tractor, or from the back of the barn, where he is doing chores.

In this discussion of the lower courts I have paid most attention to the criminal side of the docket. More should be said about the civil actions that are heard before these magistrates.

As pointed out earlier, JP also stands for "justice for the

plaintiff." That means the merchant and bill collector. And rightly so in this era of easy credit, high mobility, and deadbeat philosophy.

Yet many who enter these courts do not have lawyers. Who sticks up for the little guy?

In Los Angeles it is Judge M. Peter Katsufrakis, once a lawyer for a large movie company. He operates in a huge cavern of a court—the most impressive in the Los Angeles court system. You are immediately aware of and awed by the magnitude and majesty of the law.

I watched on "store day." During the rest of the week a wide variety of cases—all under $200—are heard.

Judge Katsufrakis is not awed by the bill collectors. I watched him order them to tell him exactly how much interest they were charging, to explain hidden costs, and why they had delayed filing suits.

In one case a loan company sued for $162. The defendant was a man who had cosigned for his daughter. The actual bill was for $142.

In a voice strong enough to wilt the thorns on a desert cactus he asked the loan-company representative, "What do you people do, just pluck figures out of the air?"

Then after further questioning he asked the defendant if he "ever, ever, ever had been contacted" about paying the debt.

"No, Your Honor," the man said.

"Why do you have to bring him into court?" Judge Katsufrakis boomed. "I will not let you continue accumulating interest without trying to collect the bill."

In another discussion he commented: "The friendly loan companies are not so friendly in this court." Then asking if there was "still fat in this claim," he added: "Do we still have to check you as closely as we have in the past since your boss was up here?"

The loan-company official said meekly, "No, Your Honor."

Few if any other judges in America look so hard for truth—regardless of the level of court.

As I have tried to point out, the minor courts are seriously misnamed. In many ways they are far more important than state supreme courts. For in the lower courts the people of America actually come in contact with our system of justice. It is here they form concepts about law and order.

This writer's study of the courts suggests a need for the following changes:

• Training in the law—and preferably a law degree—for traffic-court judges.

• Pay adequate to attract high-caliber judges.

• Abolition of the fee system.

• Strong lawyer-judges for small-claims courts—as is the case in Los Angeles—to help resolve money disputes.

• An arbitration system—as found in Pittsburgh, where three-lawyer panels resolve disputes over minor money matters.

• Diversion of divorce, juvenile, and other family matters to higher courts, where specially trained judges are backstopped with proper facilities and staff to resolve these problems.

• The most drastic solution offered is to follow the lead of those states that have simply done away with minor courts.

"Study commissions have pointed out the scandal of the lower criminal courts for over a century," the President's commission explains. "More than 30 years ago the Wickersham Commission concluded that the best solution to the problem would be the abolition of these courts. The commission agrees."

CHAPTER IV

Children in Trouble

A petite 16-year-old with brownish-blond hair and blue eyes, very bright and alert, she was also decidedly pregnant. And very much alone.

Police had picked her up after she tried to kill herself.

Now, as she looked hopefully around the courtroom, Judge Joseph Sprankle had to explain that her mother had phoned to say she was "too busy" to come down to the Los Angeles Juvenile Court for the hearing.

The girl's case was not decided that day. I will never know what happened to her. Nor will the public ever find out. For in most states juvenile hearings—for better or worse—are not open to the public. With special permission, newspaper reporters sometimes can sit in, but few do.

In fact, until the spring of 1967 when the United States Supreme Court handed down another precedent-shattering decision (*Gault* v. *Arizona*), children's-court judges across the land were debating whether lawyers should be allowed in the courtroom.

Now, not even the most rigid judges can question that right. For the high court ruled that not only can the child have a lawyer in court, but added that the judge must provide an attorney if the child's family cannot afford to hire one and if the youngster may be committed to an institution as the result of a hearing.

In the Gault case, 15-year-old Gerald Gault, who earlier had been before the juvenile court, was alleged to have made an obscene telephone call to a Mrs. Cook. The juvenile court disposed of the case without telling Gerald or his parents of charges against him, without advising of his right to remain silent, without the presence of a lawyer, without granting him the right to confront witnesses against him, without having a transcript made of the hearing, and without apprising him of his right to appeal.

Basically what was being asked was: Do children have constitutional rights?

The High Court, in an 8-to-1 decision, affirmed that they do. And it scuttled the long-standing theory that the juvenile judge is a substitute parent (*parens patriae*) when the natural parent fails as a parent in the eyes of the court.

Yet the Supreme Court did not oppose juvenile courts that are separate from adult courts and closed to the public.

It did rule that children, like adults, must not be forced to incriminate themselves. Without a valid confession the court cannot find the child delinquent without hearing witnesses who give sworn testimony—a hearing where the child's lawyer can cross-examine the witnesses in an effort to uncover truth and expose falsehoods and errors.

The Court did not rule on two other questions: Must juvenile courts provide transcripts of hearings? And does the child or his parents have the right to appeal the judge's decision?

It also declined to outline the exact form of the hearing. It did make it clear that juvenile courts are not to become junior-sized criminal courts.

Emphasis, according to the Supreme Court, is to remain on rehabilitation rather than on retribution—as it too often is in the case of adult courts.

The Supreme Court has taken a significant step in resolving serious problems in our juvenile courts, but, to paraphrase Robert Frost, "we have miles to go before we sleep."

What I found out about the way we handle juveniles can only be described as shocking.

To begin with, we hear alarmed cries about juvenile crime,

yet we really know little about the problem. As the President's Commission on Law Enforcement and Administration of Justice points out:

> To prevent and control delinquency, we must first know something about the nature of delinquency and the dimensions of the problem. . . .
>
> But we are severely limited in what we can learn today. The only juvenile statistics regularly gathered over the years on a national scale are the FBI's Uniform Crime Reports, based on arrest statistics, and the juvenile court statistics of the Children's Bureau of the U.S. Department of Health, Education, and Welfare, based on referrals of juveniles from a variety of agencies to a sample of juvenile courts. These reports can tell us nothing about the vast number of unsolved offenses, or about the many cases in which delinquents are dealt with informally instead of being arrested or referred to court.

From my study I am convinced half or more of all youngsters who come in contact with "the law" are dealt with informally. The percentage may be considerably higher.

And I found that police departments, juvenile-court judges, and juvenile correctional institutions are too often simply guessing at how to handle youngsters—and are running in two dozen different directions.

From the statistics that have been gathered, as inaccurate as they may be, there is little question that the juvenile problem is huge—and growing.

In 1965, the Children's Bureau estimates, more than a million youngsters under 17 moved through the nation's courts.

While hard figures are not available, HEW estimates that of these million there were: 697,000 juvenile-delinquency cases; 460,000 youngsters charged with traffic offenses; and 157,000 children neglected, battered, abandoned, or orphaned.

The President's commission reports: "Almost all youths commit acts for which they could be arrested and taken to court. But it is a much smaller group that ends up being defined officially as delinquent."

Self-report studies, according to the commission, reveal that "perhaps 90 percent of all young people have committed at least one act for which they could have been brought to juvenile court. Many of these offenses are relatively trivial—fighting, truancy, running away from home. Statutes often define juvenile delinquency so broadly as to make virtually all youngsters delinquent."

The Children's Bureau studies show that 1 in 9 youngsters—1 in every 6 male youths—will be referred to juvenile court in connection with a delinquent act before his 18th birthday. And that does not include traffic offenses.

These figures show part of the picture.

But it was the young girl crying in the courtroom in Los Angeles who helped me understand why more thoughtful judges told me that the problems which come before the nation's courts—juvenile and adult—are bigger than the courts.

No legislative or Supreme Court formula can resolve the deep-seated problems of this girl. No robed judge has all the answers in his lawbooks.

Yet it is within this inadequate judicial framework that the United States tries to handle problems of those who refuse to conform or fail to fit into the "norm" of society. This is a major reason why the conflict is so huge in the juvenile field.

As I toured the nation I found:

• Police departments, juvenile-court judges, and correctional institutions are, as stated above, simply guessing at how to handle juveniles.

Most attempts are failures, for young people too often graduate from minor offenses to full-blown crime while under the supervision of these agencies.

• Animosity is far more common than cooperation among the agencies dealing with youngsters. Schools should be included on this list, along with the police, the courts, and the institutions.

• Thousands of policemen, most from our rough-and-tumble lower and lower-middle class, the majority with only a high-school diploma or less, are daily asked to cope with the most difficult problems of our society.

They are picked because they have the "right temperament." As one experienced juvenile officer in a Midwest suburb explained to me, that means "we pick the officer who has enough experience and maturity to handle kids without losing control and blowing up."

It does not mean he is otherwise qualified. He simply has more self-control than his fellow officers.

• Few juvenile-court judges are really qualified to handle juvenile cases. At best, most are simply lawyers. This says they can look up the law, but may have little understanding of complex sociological problems.

Yet a recent study of juvenile-court judges shows half had no undergraduate degree. A fifth had no college education at all. A fifth were not lawyers. And nearly three-quarters of them spent less than a fourth of their time handling juvenile and family matters. Most I talked to admitted they really didn't know if they were doing a "good" job.

"We get a lot more credit than we deserve," says Walter P. Dahl, one of Chicago's better judges and head of the juvenile courts there. "I don't know how many kids we help. We just pray we don't hurt any."

In many juvenile courts, judges handle only a small percentage of the cases. Many children appear only before a social worker or court-appointed referee.

Even the better-qualified judges face criticism for "coddling kids" if they follow the dictates of their training and experience.

• Too often the system of justice for young people is subject to a judge's whim.

While Los Angeles's Judge Sprankle agrees that every judge looks at each case in the light of his own background, he argues that "we don't sentence youngsters in juvenile court. Everything we do is—in theory, at least—considered rehabilitation."

Yet in the Gault case the youth lost his liberty "for duration of his minority or until released." This could have been six years (it wasn't) for an offense that would net an adult two months in jail at most.

• Some juvenile-court critics complain that it is far too easy in most states for employees of the juvenile courts to take a child from his parents. This may be simply on the say-so of neighbors or others who complain.

Judges lack facts in juvenile cases often because of the volume of business and the time available for hearings. One Milwaukee lawyer points out that at best a judge has perhaps one-eighth of the facts, "yet we expect him to rule with the wisdom of a Solomon."

• There is also a growing debate over whether young traffic offenders profit most from adult courts or by having their cases channeled into juvenile court.

• Court after court processes children for acts that never would have brought them into court a generation ago. The parents would have settled such cases.

In Chicago one youngster had simply been with another boy who smashed a neighbor's window in anger. Under Illinois law he was "aiding and abetting" because he neither ran away when he saw what was going to happen nor did he turn the other boy in.

While the judge made the youngster's mother pay for the window, he also commented that the case should never have come into court.

The other boy and his parents, defying the court, never showed up. A bench warrant was issued. I never heard the outcome.

• In several cities school officials could reasonably be described as vindictive in truancy cases.

One bright 14-year-old (who had been allowed to skip the fourth grade earlier) was in Chicago's Juvenile Court because he had just run away from a school for troublesome pupils. He had been "sentenced" to that institution because he sometimes sulked and sometimes "exploded" in the classroom. During the hearing, the judge learned that the boy's problems stemmed from a father who constantly beat and cursed the youth. Now the boy wanted to return to his mother and his old school because the father was no longer in the home and a divorce was pending.

The school official seemed little interested in what was best for the boy. Instead he testified that the boy "ran away," and if "he gets away with it others will try it." The judge ignored this argument and ordered an investigation by a social worker, noting the child's future was at stake.

• Police and judges find themselves in conflict, usually with the police wanting to get tough with youngsters.

In Anderson, S.C., Sheriff James H. Williams threw a 7-year-old and 10-year-old in the county jail overnight without notifying juvenile authorities. The children were charged with "desecrating a church." They had used the floor of the church as a toilet.

The day I was in Denver, court officials were complaining about how police had picked up several youngsters for "riding in a stolen motor vehicle." A boy had stolen a motorcycle and had given rides to several unwitting youngsters. Court officials saw the pickup of these youngsters as harassment that could undermine respect for the police and perhaps push youngsters into crime instead of preventing it.

"We found in 21 states police hold kids without any kind of petition or judicial review," says Milton G. Rector, executive director of the National Council on Crime and Delinquency. "In one city six kids had been held three weeks. They were arrested for fighting."

To iron out police and court differences in Massachusetts a special series of workshops—the first of their kind—was held last year by the National Council of Juvenile Courts.

• With the exception of Hawaii, where a new system is in operation, too new to be evaluated, there seems to be very little coordination between juvenile, family, civil, and criminal courts. Thus a youngster may be in juvenile court as a result of strife at home, while in another corner of town his parents are getting a divorce, with little thought of the needs or problems of the children.

"One of the great scandals of our country is the easy divorce," says Eugene Wright, retired Seattle judge. "That, and the lack of judicial understanding of the effect of divorce on juvenile crime."

• There is an appalling lack of places to send children—other than the local jail. This is compounded by a severe lack of imagination on the part of judges in coping with the problem.

A Louisville, Ky., juvenile-court official says that in some parts of his state some youngsters are held "in the basement of the sheriff's home." Even in progressive states like Ohio many cities hold children in jail because there are no other facilities.

In Carlsbad, N.M., a boy who ran away from home was held in the county jail. The juvenile probation officer, who does not have a college degree, and is considered qualified for the job because he has experience in the personnel department of a corporation and a police department, wrote in his report:

"Since spending two weeks in detention ______ ______ is ready to go home." But home problems—apparently an unbalanced mother—made that an unwise choice. A psychological examination indicated that the boy was not retarded. So the officer wrote:

> It is unfortunate he is not eligible for treatment at Los Lunas institution [for the mentally retarded]. The [New Mexico] Boys' School [for delinquents] is not the place for this boy. I am sure there is a problem in the home that is not conducive to this boy's welfare. Quite frankly, a placement for this boy has me as puzzled as I have been with any youngster for a long time.

What did the judge do?

Committed the youngster to the New Mexico Boys' School at Springer, N.M.

Yet John F. X. Irving, executive director of the National Council of Juvenile Court Judges, told me in an interview in Chicago that one study shows these correctional facilities may do little for the child. Two groups were studied. One group spent 18 months or more in an institution. Another group had never been committed after violations. There was "no real difference" in the two groups, Mr. Irving said.

The day I visited the Los Angeles Juvenile Court, I found more than 200 children had no beds in the juvenile home. They were sleeping on mats on the floor.

Mr. Irving estimates that "100,000 children wind up in police lockups or jails every year—jails that are substandard for adults."

In South Carolina a corrections official estimates 30 percent of those held in institutions (for adults and children) are mentally retarded and should be in special facilities.

If you wonder why these dilemmas exist, consider the following typical cases I observed and consider how you would resolve them, keeping in mind that the law requires the court to do what is best for the child.

• Miami: A 15-year-old Spanish-speaking youngster is sentenced to 10 days in jail for driving without a valid license. Sheriff's officials admit they have no place to put him, except with teen-agers charged with crimes like robbery, murder, and rape.

Later, accompanied by the public defender, I questioned Judge D——. Judge D—— said he processed the case without knowing much about it because of a large volume of court business. He also partly excused his actions by explaining that the boy was "only" a migrant worker's son.

The following day, after an investigation of the case, Judge D—— let the boy go, for he had a valid beginner's permit (though he should have had an adult along) and was driving the family pickup to the scene of an emergency.

There had been no plan to let the youth go early until I asked the judge about the case.

• Chicago: A 14-year-old girl breaks into violent sobs and hugs a social worker when her mother and stepfather tell the judge they don't want her any more. She was drunk when police found her. The social worker indicates the girl turned to alcohol to blur dreadful home conditions and to dull her craving for parental love and understanding.

She was returned to the juvenile home pending further study of the case.

• New York City: A 19-year-old boy sits next to me awaiting sentencing in a Brooklyn court. He has been charged with possession of narcotics equipment, to which he pleads guilty. A burglary charge is then dropped after the property owner cannot be found. I ask him how long a sentence would be fair and he says six months. We continue to talk and he admits he has had a "fix" that morning because he expects to be in jail for several months. He also admits stealing to support his habit.

The judge, who is unaware that the youth is in court under the influence of narcotics, lectures to him about using dope and lets him go.

• Cincinnati: A mother collapses into unconsciousness on the courtroom floor when the judge announces he is sending her son to the industrial school for breaking rules of probation. The boy, who is 16 and husky, has ignored a court-ordered 10 P.M. curfew, and was found rough-housing with a 12-year-old girl who was baby-sitting. The girl, apparently mature for her age, had been egging him on. No sexual misconduct took place, but the boy did "playfully" choke the girl with a towel after she snapped him with it.

• Portland, Ore.: A pretty redhead and stocky stepfather ask the court to return their four-year-old boy. The child was taken from the home after the stepfather slapped him on the face as punishment, and neighbors complained. Because the boy bruises easily the case was thought worse than it actually was. The stepfather says he has learned his lesson. The child has been in a foster home several months.

The judge increases visitation rights and tells the parents they will get their child back in a few months if they continue to show a proper attitude.

• Chicago: An attractive young blonde stands before the juvenile-court judge and asks him for the return of her child. Beside her stands an older man who says he is the father of the child and wants to help rear it. But the couple cannot marry because the blonde is still married to another man.

She is vague about two other children whose custody she has lost, but she says one was through adoption. She is an admitted narcotics addict and worked as a part-time prostitute to support the drug habit. But she tells the judge she has reformed and needs the child to give her something to do and help her keep away from drugs.

The judge asks a social worker to check on the home and gives the woman visitation rights at the foster home. He then asks her to bare her arm so he can see if there are recent needle marks. There are bruises, but she insists they came from playing with her dog.

• Los Angeles: Young girls are brought before the judge without parents to stand beside them. One, 14, ran away from home and lived with a girl friend in an abandoned car for three weeks. She was drunk when picked up.

The judge has her held in the juvenile home for another hearing.

• Los Angeles: A 15-year-old boy who hasn't seen his father in years was arrested driving a stolen car. He says two friends stole the auto and invited him for a ride. He says he took over the driving after they had trouble controlling the car. He knew it was stolen. He had been picked up previously for a curfew violation.

The judge—actually a woman social worker who was a court-appointed referee—tells the youth he must remain in Juvenile Hall until an investigation is completed. Hearing set for two weeks later.

• Denver: Two little boys from a broken home appear with their mother. All are well dressed. The boys are charged with breaking off 50 auto antennas to use in playing "swords."

The mother and her boys appear eager to make amends. They agree that the boys will pay for the damage from their paper routes. The court, impressed with the evidence of sincerity, will mail out checks so the children will not get a bad reputation in their neighborhood.

• Cincinnati: A little girl accused of being constantly truant by school officials breaks down and cries and tells the judge she feels dreadfully uncomfortable at school and around other children. Now her younger brother and sister are skipping school for the same reason.

The judge tells the girl she will be "the death of your mother, and you will have that on your conscience the rest of your life." Then he orders a psychiatric exam to see "if you are faking."

• Philadelphia: A 17-year-old boy, teased by a 16-year-old girl, gets angry and hits her on the head with a broken bottle. At the hospital she needs 15 stitches. Now she testifies that "he really didn't mean it." The boy has been kicked out of school, has a long record of minor offenses. But he is holding down a job now. Both parents are in court.

The judge says that sending the boy to reform school or prison could do more harm than good. The judge, contending that the youth would lose his job and might even turn to a life of crime, gives him "one more chance: keep on a straight line, son."

• Denver: A little fellow about eight tells the judge he has no father, has trouble with his mother but likes her, and sometimes just feels like leaving home. On Sunday night he "stayed out late" and then was "scared to come home," so he slept on street corners and walked around. The mother wants the boy committed.

As the child hangs his head and cries, the judge sentences the youth to "the home for 30 days."

The problems are roughly the same in Atlanta, Battle Creek, Durango, Eugene, Flagstaff, Gainesville, Helena, Indianapolis, and on through Zanesville.

There can be little doubt that these juvenile problems are complex. Or even that our best judges find it hard to make right decisions when they are overloaded with work, are short on help and information, and lack proper facilities for a child who must be held.

But what of the other children who are tangled up with the "law" but do not go to court?

The Supreme Court, in the Gault decision, did not rule on what it called the "pre-judicial states of the juvenile process." This was undoubtedly to keep the door open for the use of social workers, psychiatrists, and other professionals who work with the courts in some cities. They try to help the child without going to court.

But it also leaves the door ajar on another practice, one that may well be dangerous, called "station adjustment." I found it in widespread use. And I am concerned because it takes place in the police department, behind closed doors, and without any outside supervision or criticism, and usually without the help of nonpolice professionals.

Take Wheaton, Ill., a wealthy bedroom suburb 25 miles west of Chicago.

For several years Sergeant Ralph Fortman, a conscientious 17-year veteran of the force, was the community's only juvenile officer.

Wheaton is county seat for prosperous Du Page County, where the per capita income is about the highest in the nation. It is located less than six miles from the site selected by the Atomic Energy Commission for the coveted new accelerator, much to the outrage of a dozen other states.

Finally, with 500 youngsters a year being picked up, the juvenile officer's job became too large for one man. The solution to the problem does not seem a logical one under the circumstances. The detective bureau was merged with the juvenile bureau to form a three-man "bureau of investigation and juveniles." Sergeant Fortman was placed in charge.

These three men are expected to handle both jobs 24 hours a day, seven days a week, in a community that in the next census will probably hit the 30,000 mark, and is ringed by other suburban communities, pushing the population far higher.

To add to the burden, the circuit-court judges in Du Page County have designated juvenile officers as probation officers —giving the Wheaton officers a third job.

Using what surely must be considered a flaw in the much-touted Illinois Juvenile Court Act, passed in 1965, these three officers are charged with what amounts to finding youngsters guilty, sentencing them, and correcting them—all without any formal court process taking place.

It works this way:

A child is accused of shoplifting. If he is a first offender, and has not argued with the arresting officer, he is put on "station adjustment."

This means, according to Sergeant Ray Schnurstein, one of the two men working with Sergeant Fortman, that the child has a police record, "must report to us on a certain day at a certain time" for an indefinite period of time, and has his "school record and his home record checked" by the police.

It is also used for youngsters accused of curfew violations, smoking, making too much noise on a street corner and not moving when told to by a policeman, minor liquor violations (one can of beer was the example used), and other minor offenses.

In spite of their heavy workload, the three Wheaton officers may be quite capable of doing an excellent job. Sergeant Fortman says he had to take his name out of the telephone directory so many parents were calling him at night when children did not show up, had been drinking, or refused to follow the orders of a parent.

But the practice raises many questions. For none of the men has any special training beyond a few seminars put on by Northern Illinois University and the Illinois Youth Commission. And there are many smaller police departments in the area. Sergeant Fortman admits each juvenile officer and police chief has his own concept of how to handle youngsters.

The President's commission suggests that Youth Service

Bureaus be established to help youngsters in trouble. These agencies would be staffed with professionals who could provide "group and individual counseling, placement in foster homes, work and recreation programs, employment counseling, and special education (remedial, vocational)." The report concludes:

> Police forces should make full use of the central diagnosing and coordinating services of the Youth Services Bureau. Station adjustment should be limited to release and referral; it should not include hearings or the imposition of sanctions by the police. Court referral by the police should be restricted to those cases involving serious criminal conduct or repeated misconduct of a more than trivial nature.

No one knows how many million youngsters have had police contact without court action. But juvenile-court officials know the number is high. Nor do these figures include the tens of thousands of young people over 17 who are in trouble.

Prison officials interviewed indicate that adults in trouble usually had their first collision with society's standards when they were young, graduating from probation to reform school to jail to prison.

The more candid among juvenile-court and corrections officials admit that the present police-court-corrections approach to solving problems of children may even help create criminals.

At least several assert that throwing a boy in jail with experienced hoodlums becomes an education in crime for the youngster. This is being done in almost every state.

It is not uncommon for one police officer to throw a child in jail for the same offense that nets a lecture from another policeman.

The very fact that the police often are inconsistent adds to the problem. A common question from those arrested (also heard in adult traffic cases) is: "Why me?"

And as the President's commission reports, skin color and the economic status of the parents may often affect what happens to the child who comes in contact with the police.

"Slum offenders are more likely than suburban offenders to

be arrested and referred to juvenile court," the report asserts. "In fact, recent self-report studies reveal suburban and middle-class delinquency to be a more significant problem than was once assumed."

In Denver, for example, half of the children in Juvenile Hall come from families with incomes of more than $7,200, says one spokesman.

At the same time, I found that middle-class people somehow forget that slum children are not growing up in a horrible environment by choice. Slums exist because they are tolerated by the "good people" of a community. To slum children middle-class rules don't make sense.

In Gary, Ind., one 16-year-old boy who has grown up in a neighborhood of filth, prostitution, crime, and gambling—all only three blocks from the Gary police station—was recently expelled from school. While the citizens tolerate the other corruption, school officials tossed him out because he was caught smoking on the playground.

Without pocket money, adult supervision, or the education to get a job, this boy now stands on street corners with other youngsters in the same fix. Yet one school official has told me that the youth received one of the highest IQ test scores in the city when he was in the eighth grade.

"Our great dilemma is that in this field we know so very little about causes of delinquency," says Mr. Irving of the juvenile-court-judges organization. "A judge can find statements on both sides of every theory. And he is so overburdened he does not have the opportunity to make a study in his own town.

"My personal observation, after sitting in on many cases, is that most of the children in our courts come from an environment where they do not feel wanted and loved."

This writer seldom—if ever—saw a child in court from a happy, healthy home. Dozens of parents simply didn't show up in court. Others showed personality faults—often the inability or unwillingness to control the child.

The majority of delinquents are those Milwaukee Family Court Judge Robert W. Hansen calls "half-orphans"—the thousands of children growing up in broken homes. Families in which one parent has passed on do not have the same problem, he adds, because these children have not faced the hatred and turmoil that accompany divorce.

Chicago's Judge Dahl told me "only 15 percent of the kids we get come from a home with two natural parents where only the father is working."

Lawyers in divorce courts know the problems.

They tell of the hatred in homes of battling parents—how a child is torn between his mother and father, mentally jerked from one side to the other in a dispute. Many children have trouble both concentrating and getting along with others at school. Older lawyers report that many children of divorced parents come to them in later years for divorces.

"The discipline in the home breaks down," says Leonard L. Loeb, of Milwaukee, one of several lawyers interviewed in family court. "The children are set adrift. They cannot accept basic social values, even religious values. Because of the feuding, their parental images are all fouled up.

"And children in divorced families generally don't have the [material] things they need because few men can support two households."

Says Judge George B. Richter of Waukon, Iowa: "Children are most affected and least protected in divorce proceedings, and many wind up on ADC [aid to dependent children]."

To help ease the problem for children, Judge Hansen has established a policy of hiring lawyers for the children in cases where custody is at issue, or other problems develop. Here is a case I saw:

The husband was a stocky man in a dark suit. The wife was a small woman with glasses, wearing a black raincoat and blue chiffon head scarf.

They sat properly apart. Already their home had been sold, the furniture divided, the $160 bank account spent.

The husband was accused of drinking too much, making statements about his lack of love for the wife, "running around," and not properly supporting the children. As I frequently observed in other cases, the wife's contribution to the problem was not discussed.

Both had come before the court's conciliation service (which was criticized by some lawyers as being too ready to say a divorce was the only answer). There one brief interview had indicated that the marriage probably could not be saved. But the divorce was held up.

For, during proceedings, Judge Hansen found that the turmoil in the home was having a serious effect on Jimmy, the oldest boy. His grades were dropping. And he was fighting with other youngsters. School officials indicated they might send the youth to a psychiatrist.

At this point (in the fall of 1966) Judge Hansen appointed a lawyer-guardian for the children and asked court social workers to investigate. It was found the father had not visited the youngsters in more than a year. Jimmy felt his father disliked him, and the boy was deeply hurt.

With the help of the father's own lawyer, the appointed guardian, and the social worker, the father began to recognize he had more than his own selfish interests to think about.

Since then he has been visiting the children regularly, giving them the attention they wanted. And Jimmy's problem has eased: Teachers say his marks are up and he is getting along better.

A social worker testified that the three children now had no greater problems than "most children with this kind of domestic turmoil in the home." In this case the divorce was granted—but free of the parental hatred I saw in other courts.

Unfortunately, most states pay little attention to the rights of children. As one lawyer told me: "The courts simply act as a butcher, whacking the marriage into pieces."

Those who bother to think about these problems, and too few Americans do, conclude that there must be better answers. Judge Hansen suggests one solution is the Milwaukee Family Court's "Bill of Rights of Children." Those rights include:

1. The right to be treated as an interested and affected person and not as a pawn, possession, or chattel of either or both parents.
2. The right to grow to maturity in the home environment

which will best guarantee an opportunity for the child to grow to mature and responsible citizenship.

3. The right to the day-by-day love, care, discipline, and protection of the parent having custody of the children.

4. The right to know the noncustodian parent and to have the benefit of such parent's love and guidance through adequate visitations.

5. The right to a positive and constructive relationship with both parents, with neither parent permitted to degrade or downgrade the other in the mind of the child.

6. The right to have moral and ethical values developed by precept and practice and to have limits set for behavior so that the child early in life may develop self-discipline and self-control.

7. The right to the most adequate level of economic support that can be provided by the best efforts of both parents.

8. The right to the same opportunities for education that the child would have had if the family unit had not been broken.

9. The right to periodic review of custodial arrangements and child-support orders as the circumstances of the parents and the benefit of the child may require.

10. The right to recognition that children involved in a divorce are always disadvantaged parties and that the law must take affirmative steps to protect their welfare, including, where indicated, a social investigation to determine, and the appointment of a guardian ad litem, to protect their interests.

Milwaukee's Family Court is more of a family court in name than in fact. Judge Hansen agrees that another step is needed. This kind of solution was discussed at a meeting of Juvenile Court Judges in June of 1967 in Fort Lauderdale, Fla. One speaker, Judge Bertram Polow, of the New Jersey Juvenile and Domestic Relations Court in Morris County, asked, "Is there a need to unify the work of all those various independent departments, agencies, tribunals, branches of the judicial, and other facilities treating the problems that arise out of marital difficulties and family controversies?"

Then he answered his own question: "There is unquestionably substantial support" to include all the family problems "within a single family court. And this family court should be a division or department of a trial court of general jurisdiction."

The American Bar Association, "at least as long as I can remember, for at least 23 years . . . has constantly supported the creation of family courts in every jurisdiction," he added—along with most other organizations concerned with family, juvenile, or court problems.

"As a matter of fact," he said, "I know of no nationally organized group that has ever opposed this family-court concept."

Yet the need is clear. In almost any city in the nation, a single family may be involved in hearings in several different courts. Judge Polow's example: "First, a juvenile court passes on a charge involving delinquency of children; second, the divorce court entertains a suit for divorce, alimony, and custody; third, a court of civil jurisdiction perhaps entertains an action for necessaries which were furnished to an abandoned wife by a grocer or some other tradesman; and fourth, a criminal or domestic-relations court deals with charges of desertion and nonsupport."

It is difficult to understand in an era of family conflict, easy divorce, a growing crime rate, and mounting juvenile problems how the nation continues to ignore this partial solution, but it does. Yet both the need and the logic are clear.

Perhaps it is the same problem that confronts our entire system of justice: Too few care.

Perhaps that is why, in Du Page County west of Chicago, a county with a reputation for good schools and an average income per person which is near the top, if not the highest in the nation, there is no juvenile home. Teen-agers 14 and over are held in the county jail. In the fall of 1967 Wheaton police found it necessary to wait for an opening in a juvenile home in neighboring Kane County for a 13-year-old who was in persistent trouble.

I found many juvenile-court judges conscientious and sincere, doing the best they could with limited skills and information and with the tools society has provided them. But what I saw in the nation's juvenile courts can only be described as shocking. Remedies are needed.

• Americans need to learn a lot more about the cause of delinquency and its cures. More effective classification of delinquents is vital. Should the runaway be handled the same as the purse snatcher?

• Courts should be established that treat the family as a unit, for the child's problems are usually the family's problems.

• Juvenile-court judges should be selected for their skill and knowledge in handling young people. They should be backed up with a competent staff of social workers and other professionals.

For the first time, 32 new judges—out of 200 applicants—attended a month-long summer school at the University of Colorado last year. But this is only a drop of water in an arid desert.

• Citizen committees should work with the courts, oversee procedures, and encourage the community to provide funds for staff and for new and better facilities—foster homes, halfway houses, probation staffs, diagnostic centers. Some progressive courts—but too few—rely heavily on relative and foster homes instead of rooms with bars on the windows.

The problems the juvenile courts face are huge. They are supposed to give children special rehabilitative treatment. It appears that most do not. Too often the delinquent child is buffeted between his own and the adult's world.

As Associate Justice Abe Fortas of the Supreme Court wrote recently: "There is evidence . . . that there may be grounds for concern that the child receives the worst of both worlds: that he gets neither the protection accorded to adults nor the solicitous care and regenerative treatment postulated for children."

We have hardly begun to resolve this problem.

CHAPTER V

How the Game Is Played

Having run this far without a pause, perhaps it is time to stop and catch our breath and discuss a nagging question:

If the crime rate keeps climbing, and if we cannot keep up with auto-accident suits filed, and if we cannot get competent judges, and if our juvenile courts are groping in the dark, and if all the other problems discussed so far exist, have our courts totally failed?

The answer can only be No!

In a society that emphasizes material wealth and supports a nearly no-holds-barred battle for it; in a society that has moved from rutted trails to high-speed highways and jet airlines in little more than 50 years; in a society that is industrialized, mechanized, urbanized, but never pasteurized (that would, to use a dictionary definition, destroy the "vitality of the ferment"); in a society that has developed instant communications to communicate drivel, sex, materialism, and gunplay 18 hours a day; in a society that does not really know how to use power without war; in a society that lives on the edge of fear of a nuclear holocaust; in a society that hardly tamed its wilderness before the population explosion set in, our courts do surprisingly well.

It is a little like grandpa picking up grandson's new math book. Times have changed. There is some catching up to do.

We expect far too much of a system of courts geared to farm towns and a pace of life that was little faster than a horse could trot.

Add to this the fact that in an age of hard-nosed science and exacting mathematics most of our people remain romantics.

Ask a man or woman on the street why we hold trials in court and you may get a chocolate-coated answer like: "To maintain law and order. To discover truth. Or to bring about justice."

The more practical answer is probably: "It is the most civilized way of settling disputes that we have so far discovered."

It is hard to get most Americans to buy this answer. Romanticizing has become a way of life. Even the tissues we buy at the store must come in seven decorator colors and feel as soft as a kitten on a sunny, butterfly-filled, spring morning.

And so we demand truth and justice from a system that can, at best, end arguments without bloodshed.

To understand this it will help to have a little historical perspective.

Anthropologists report ancient man lived by the law of "survival of the fittest." The strong man with the big stick carried the law in his hands.

As tribes organized, religious leaders became lawgivers. Laws were "handed down" by tribal gods. Thus the people were forced to conform to tribal norm largely out of fear. Often priests could order punishment, including execution.

Sometimes tribal counsels sat in judgment. Some early systems of justice were quite advanced.

Babylonian stone and clay tablets tell of a well-developed system of legal codes some nine centuries before the Christian era. They also had courts and written evidence. Those wronged received compensation from the guilty party. A system of commercial and property law was also developed.

Law and religion have always been closely knit.

Moses is credited with making more lenient laws. His "eye-for-an-eye" concept made retribution more equal to the crime.

The American system is based on the English common law—a blending of old church law, the law of kings and feudal lords, standards of property rights, and manners and morals dating back thousands of years.

While it is not static, law does not change swiftly. To a great extent Americans today are governed by their grandfathers, great-grandfathers, and several generations before that.

But Americans, in a system that supports government "by the people," have added legislative law to common law, the former overshadowing the latter.

And each law passed must eventually be weighed against provisions of the United States Constitution and the constitution of each state.

It is easy to confuse our philosophy of justice—those ideal concepts or principles that have been the core of so many ringing Fourth of July speeches—with the machinery of justice. And with the practical application of law in a complex society.

It is common, for example, to expound on how we are a nation governed by laws, not men.

Yet anyone who has watched the pragmatic, behind-the-scenes operation of local, state, and federal lawmaking bodies must call this concept naïve.

Too many lawmakers want to be re-elected, collect campaign contributions, secure the cooperation of other lawmakers in passing legislation they sponsor, or win favor with the press. Because the bulk of Americans are apathetic, these lawmakers listen to the selfish interests of small segments of our society, are wined and dined and rewarded by lobbyists, compromise and cooperate, and fight for pet projects.

The gun lobby has, for years, blocked legislation that might keep guns out of the hands of the irresponsible. The gun does not care who holds it, who uses it, or how it is used. Nor does the law care.

Men care. And men bring about the passage or rejection of laws.

A handful of store owners on the fringe of the slums argue they are doing the poor a favor by extending them credit. Interest rates may be 100 or 200 percent or more. I have *seen* this in our slums. Then these store owners, under law, can go to court and take the wages of these people when they have trouble paying—even when it means the man will be fired by his employer and the family becomes a burden to taxpayers by going on welfare.

Our legislatures are filled with lawyers. They are supposed to respond to the will of the electorate. Whether they do or not is constantly debated. Yet the final decisions on our laws are not left up to legislators, or even the people.

As Charles Evans Hughes, a Chief Justice of the Supreme Court of the United States, once said: "We are under a Constitution, but the Constitution is what the judges say it is."

The courts interpret not only state and national constitutions. They also determine the intent of the lawmakers in statutes that are passed.

Justice Oliver Wendell Holmes said in a speech in Boston 70 years ago that some legal scholars contend the law "is a deduction from principles of ethics or admitted axioms or what not," and thus the law is considered to be something apart from what takes place in courtrooms. Yet the man who runs afoul of the law "does not care two straws for the axioms or deductions, but . . . he does want to know what the . . . courts are likely to do . . . [and that is] what I mean by law."

As already noted in the prologue, to a slum child, "the law" may mean a man in a blue shirt, or even a squad car with a light on top.

To understand the point that men, rather than laws, control our lives, note the many trial judges who interpret our laws from their own political, moral, or social views. It was Associate Justice Hugo L. Black who said in an opinion he wrote, that "for judges to rest their interpretation of statutes on nothing but their own conceptions of 'morals' and 'ethics' is, to say the least, dangerous business."

Two paragraphs from the report of the President's commission help back this up:

> A judge's attitude toward prosecutions for certain offenses also affects arrest practices of the police. In one large city, for example, it was noted that the number of arrests for prostitution and solicitation declined sharply during the months that a judge who routinely dismissed such cases was sitting in the misdemeanor division.
>
> [And] . . . it is not uncommon for individual judges to regard certain offenses as too trivial to merit any substantial penalty or even to merit the court's time in hearing them. An experienced prosecutor

is reluctant to antagonize the judge by bringing these cases to court despite the availability of sufficient evidence to convict the defendant.

I have watched judges berate youngsters for wearing long hair (what the length of the hair has to do with the law is hard to understand); throw out marijuana cases ("Smoking marijuana is safer than smoking cigarettes," one judge explained in a California court); and otherwise bend the law to fit their own opinions.

Yet part of the problem is that we are nearly overwhelmed with law. Not only does it tell us how to use our guns (at least one mile from the city limits; only during hunting season; not against our neighbor), but how to build our garages, get rid of our garbage, store our gasoline, drive our gas-buggies, give gifts (tax laws), and get married.

The hours we work, the unions we join, the businesses we own, the food we sell, and almost every other human activity is sanctioned, controlled, regulated, or supervised by the government, all in the name of law.

Laws are filled with paradoxes. Some stand on the books for years and are not enforced. We simply ignore them. We are selective about enforcement of other laws. When the friendly neighbor's child smashes our window, we call the parent. When the child of someone we dislike smashes the same window, we call the police. If it is the boss's son, we pretend it never happened.

If our state *needs* water, it is injust and immoral if other states refuse to let us rechannel a river or siphon water from the Great Lakes and not return it. If our state *has* water, we go to court to block other states from "stealing" it.

Our laws are dispute settlers, and our lawyers, judges, and courts have been designated to do the job. These men and institutions are not law and justice, although they may serve as the plumbers and carpenters who help build the systems and framework of justice.

It is impossible to separate men from government, from our laws, from our courts, or court-related agencies. Even in this era of electronic computers we dare not feed laws and other information into machines and hope that machines will provide our justice.

The law remains fallible because those who break, use, and administer laws are fallible. As Dr. Charles Gordon Post, chairman of the department of political science at Vassar College, wrote in his book, *An Introduction to the Law,* the law is an "inexact science."

"The truth is," he writes, "that lawyers deal in probabilities, not certainties."

But what of the machinery of justice in America, now that we have pointed accusing fingers at some of the men who labor in the field of law?

Is it the men or the *system* that needs correcting?

There can be little doubt that the answer must be *both.*

As pointed out at the start of this chapter, our law and our system of justice follow that of England of centuries ago.

It emerged from a system that saw disputes settled first by feud, and later by combat or ordeal. Now we use words instead of weapons. But for the average citizen the combat and ordeal go on.

Verbal thrusts and parries have replaced spears and swords, as the field of combat has been moved from the courtyard to the courthouse.

The ordeal, where a man could be bound and tossed into a stream to determine truth (if he sank, the "pure waters accepted him" and he was innocent; if he floated, the waters rejected him and he was guilty), no longer is the burden of the defendant. For he cannot be forced to testify against himself. Instead the witnesses are subjected to the ordeal as they are bound by the rules of court and are tossed into the swift, dangerous currents of cross-examination.

This, then, is what is known as the adversary system—the core of our legal system. There is little wonder that dictionary definitions of "ordeal" and "trial" have much in common.

The trial has often been under attack. Roscoe Pound, the late dean emeritus of the Harvard Law School, at one time was considered a heretic by many of his fellow lawyers. For in 1906 he had the courage to speak out in opposition to what he called the "sporting theory of justice." In his controversial speech to the ABA he said:

> So far from being a fundamental fact of jurisprudence, it is peculiar to Anglo-American law; and it has been strongly curbed in modern English practice. With us, it is not merely in full acceptance, it has been developed and its collateral possibilities have been cultivated to the furthest extent. Hence in America we take it as a matter of course that a judge should be a mere umpire, to pass upon objections and hold counsel to the rules of the game, and that the parties should fight out their own game in their own way without judicial interference. We resent such interference as unfair, even when in the interest of justice. The idea that procedure must of necessity be wholly contentious disfigures our judicial administration at every point. It leads the most conscientious judge to feel that he is merely to decide the contest, as counsel present it, according to the rules of the game, not to search independently for truth and justice. It leads counsel to forget that they are officers of the court and to deal with the rules of law and procedure exactly as the professional football coach with the rules of the sport. It leads to exertion to "get error into the record" rather than to dispose of the controversy finally and upon its merits. It turns witnesses, and especially expert witnesses, into partisans pure and simple. It leads to senational cross-examinations "to affect credit," which have made the witness stand "the slaughter house of reputations." It prevents the trial court from restraining the bullying of witnesses and creates a general dislike, if not fear, of the witness function which impairs the administration of justice. It keeps alive the unfortunate exchequer rule, dead in the country of its origin, according to which errors in the admission or rejection of evidence are presumed to be prejudicial and hence demand a new trial. It grants new trials because by inability to procure a bill of exceptions a party has lost the chance to play another inning in the game of justice. It creates vested rights in errors of procedure, of the benefit whereof parties are not to be deprived. The inquiry is not, What do substantive law and justice require? Instead, the inquiry is, Have the rules of the game been carried out strictly? If any material infraction is discovered, just as the football rules put back the offending team five or ten or fifteen yards, as the case may be, our sporting theory of

justice awards new trials, or reverses judgements, or sustains demurrers in the interest of regular play.

The effect of our exaggerated contentious procedure is not only to irritate parties, witnesses and jurors in particular cases, but to give to the whole community a false notion of the purpose and end of law. Hence comes, in large measure, the modern American race to beat the law. If the law is a mere game, neither the players who take part in it nor the public who witness it can be expected to yield to its spirit when their interests are served by evading it. And this is doubly true in a time which requires all institutions to be economically efficient and socially useful. We need not wonder that one part of the community strain their oaths in the jury box and find verdicts against unpopular litigants in the teeth of law and evidence, while another part retains lawyers by the year to advise how to evade what to them are unintelligent and unreasonable restrictions upon necessary modes of doing business. Thus the courts, instituted to administer justice according to law, are made agents or abettors of lawlessness.

Perhaps, as in professional football, the rules and players have changed since 1906. But the game is the same in 1968, if not worse than in 1906.

The game is to win, and it may mean some of the participants will be knocked nearly senseless by skilled legal quarterbacks, but this matters little.

The late Jerome Frank, a judge of the United States Circuit Court of Appeals for the Second Circuit, and professor of law at the Yale School of Law, wrote in 1949 in *Courts on Trial* that if a trial were really a search for truth we would try to remove those things that cause errors in the witness's testimony. Yet, he said, "we do almost the exact opposite."

Judge Frank contended that a businessman would never gather his information before building a new plant "by putting his informants through the bewildering experience of witnesses at a trial." Nor would generals base an attack on data gathered in this way, he added.

He quoted Henry Taft, a distinguished lawyer and brother of Chief Justice and President William Howard Taft, who wrote:

> Counsel and court find it necessary through examination and instruction to induce a witness to abandon for an hour or two his habitual method of thought and expression, and conform to the rigid ceremonialism of court procedure. It is not strange that frequently truthful witnesses are . . . misunderstood, that they nervously react in such a way as to create the impression that they are either evading or intentionally falsifying. It is interesting to account for some of the things that witnesses do under such circumstances. An honest witness testifies on direct examination. He answers questions promptly and candidly and makes a good impression. On cross-examination [by the other side's lawyer], his attitude changes. He suspects that traps are being laid for him. He hesitates; he ponders the answer to a simple question; he seems to "spar" for time by asking that questions be repeated; perhaps he protests that counsel is not fair; he may even appeal to the court for protection. Altogether the contrast with his attitude on direct examination is obvious; and he creates the impression that he is evading or withholding.

Why do we continue with this system if it is so badly flawed?

Partly because we resist change.

Partly because so few of us go to court there is no loud cry for improvements. We don't care.

Partly because lawyers and judges have led us to believe the courts belong to *them*—not to the people. The present system is profitable. Most fear the unknown. It is like convincing union plumbers we should convert to plastic pipe, or housewives who have always used gas stoves to try electric ones.

It is partly because we have learned, from elementary school up, that this is how the courts work, and that the system is the best of all possible systems.

And it is partly because, as Prentice H. Marshall, a trial lawyer for 13 years and now a professor of law at the University of Illinois, suggests, we don't know of anything that will work better.

"It is the best possible system," he argues. "The likelihood of arriving at truth is enhanced when the truth-seeking process is an adversary process.

"The only other approach is the use of the inquisitorial or

unilateral system, and what if you have a clod for a judge? What of his human frailties? The judge or inquisitor, as he undertakes the examination, gets an initial impression of the case. He is subject to the same prejudices as other human beings. Prejudgment begins to arise, and when he concludes this particular line of inquiry he considers the dispute resolved."

Not so, at least in a jury trial, says Professor Marshall, who tried both civil and criminal cases while a member of a 50-man Chicago law firm.

In the adversary process, he contends, "there must be a greater combination of human failings" to ignore truth. For not only must one of the lawyers "be a dolt, but the judge must be a dolt." And in a jury trial all 12 members of the jury must be hoodwinked.

"From the logical standpoint, when you have two sides presenting the evidence, arguing the strength of your own evidence and the weakness of the opposition's, the likelihood of truth emerging is greater than when the responsibility is placed on one person."

And he contends that criticism of the adversary system should really be aimed at the men who participate—the judges, lawyers, and witnesses.

Too many lawyers fail to keep abreast of the rule changes that take place, partly because it is human nature to be lazy, he explains.

Yet he concedes that if change comes, a panel of judges might provide the best solution—taking the burden off one inquisitor. This is, of course, how state and federal appellate courts operate, although they do not conduct trials. And we are establishing more and more governmental boards that conduct inquiries and hand down decisions.

There is little question that our adversary process is flawed. As I traveled the nation I found many incompetent or lazy lawyers, along with others who are dishonest, bend the facts, or withhold truth to assist their clients.

If Professor Marshall and the dozens of other trial lawyers and judges I have interviewed are right when they say there is no better way of administering justice than the adversary process, then our greatest hope is in improving the caliber of the men who labor in our courts, and in improving the laws passed by our legislative bodies.

Perhaps our greatest problems lie in the criminal courts, rather than in the civil, because we are dealing with the lives of men instead of with property.

In an address delivered at the 11th annual homecoming of the St. John's University School of Law on April 2, 1966, then Associate Supreme Court Justice Tom C. Clark said:

> The practice of criminal law has been degraded for half a century. Today it is at such a low level that few good legal minds will enter upon it. Indeed, in most metropolitan areas you can count the top criminal law practitioners on the fingers of one hand and in some places lose a finger or so.... The average lawyer in the practice keeps away from the criminal law like a plague. It hurts his practice, he says. The public associates him with his clients.
>
> I have a healthy respect for the criminal law practitioner and his devotion to the law.... He is the backbone of the adversary system —and it is the genius of the judicial process.

F. Lee Bailey, one of the best-known criminal trial lawyers of the decade, told me in an interview that he thinks the problem exists largely because our "law schools are wholly inadequate."

"The practice of trial law should be made a specialty," he says. "There should be another year of law school. There should be an apprenticeship. With our present teaching techniques you can never learn to be a competent trial lawyer in a classroom."

Former Justice Clark, who retired from the high bench in the summer of 1967, agrees. Commenting on the shortage of trial lawyers and the impact it has on the profession, he says:

> [T]he law schools have aided and abetted in this deterioration. [There are] six of them in New York City. I dare say that most, if not all, merely require the study of one course in criminal law, and sometimes for only one term of four or five months during the freshman year. Moreover, from what my law clerks [have told] me, over the past 17 years, the law schools have generally downgraded the

practice of criminal law. The professors suggest a specialty such as tax, labor relations, antitrust, and the like.

He contends that effective counsel in the adversary process "is a better lie detector than a polygraph."

Commenting on the fact common law emerges from trials—from decisions handed down by judges and juries—and that "the tribe of advocates is a diminishing one," he calls it "highly regrettable" that we have reached our present low point.

While the adversary process is under attack in our criminal courts because of the shortage of competent lawyers, it is in more obvious trouble in the civil courts. As I pointed out in Chapter II, civil courts have a huge backlog of auto-accident cases.

Judges across the country complained that lawyers must shoulder much of the blame, while lawyers pointed accusing fingers at the judges.

Here conditions have become so extreme that there is growing talk about replacing the adversary system with boards or arbitration panels. This, much to the alarm of lawyers who make a handsome living handling auto-accident cases. But it has happened in workmen's compensation, and it could happen again.

One thing is clear. The lawyers are making large sums under the present system. Nor are judges being hurt.

It is the people of America who are being hurt—even if they never go to court—by climbing insurance rates, by the crime explosion, by the delays, and by other court-related problems.

The solution seems clear: let the people put the lawyers and judges on notice.

Either improve the adversary process through better rules of procedure, by assuring the nation that competent men are available to try the suits, and through fair, just decisions, or the people of America will change the system through pressure on our legislative bodies.

CHAPTER VI

Prosecutors, Police, and Power

Suppose:

• The nation's airlines turned their jets over to young men who, as college students, had studied flying a semester or two, could pass an exam on aerodynamics, but had little or no actual flight experience.

• Each young pilot was allowed to select or reject his passengers arbitrarily. Could choose his own flight times and routes. Used an often-conflicting rule book to chart the way. Consulted the tower only when he wanted to land. Dumped some passengers off en route, and carried others too far.

• Pilot pay was so poor most found it necessary to hold down a second job and waited for the day when they were skilled enough to quit the airline and strike out on their own.

• That ground crews—those with nuts-and-bolts responsibility for keeping things running smoothly—were also often underskilled, underpaid, and overworked.

• And that after passengers were unloaded, accommodations were usually horrible, service nearly nil and there was little sure way of returning them safely home.

Absurd?

Not when it becomes clear that in the face of a soaring crime rate the American system of criminal justice closely parallels this.

The pilot is the prosecutor—fresh out of college; the ground crew, the police; the man supervising from the tower, the judge; men and women who are accused by police, the passengers. Many are dumped off at fourth-rate jails or third-rate penal institutions that are underfinanced and poorly equipped to help lawbreakers return to a useful place in society.

This reporter has learned after touring the nation's courts for months that the role of the trial judge is crucial. Yet the man on the bench has meaningful contact with only part of those who become entangled in the state system of criminal justice.

In practice both police and prosecutor function as judge and jury at the start of every case. Then the court must approve or disapprove of their actions by finding a man guilty or not guilty—if the case reaches court.

The traffic officer who stops you for speeding makes a "judicial decision" when he gives you a ticket. He may let the next man off with a warning. By shooting a fleeing burglar, the detective may hand out a capital penalty for a crime that might otherwise have netted probation, or at worst, 5 to 10 years in prison.

When the youngster next door is brought home in a squad car and your child is held in jail for the same offense (an estimated half-million youths were jailed last year), the policeman involved is in a sense acting as a judge. For without holding a hearing—beyond his listening to or ignoring your child's protests—that officer has "sentenced" your youngster to one or more nights in jail.

It is common practice for a prosecutor to try a few men for assault with intent to kill, drunken driving, or murder. Then, for the sake of expedience or for other reasons, he reduces charges for others (who have broken the same law) to simple assault, reckless driving, or manslaughter. Still others are released by the prosecutor, who may be convinced of their guilt but feels he lacks evidence to convict.

As the President's Commission on Law Enforcement and Administration of Justice has pointed out, the prosecutor "decides whether to press a case or drop it. He determines the specific charges against the defendant. When the charge is reduced, as it is in as many as two-thirds of all cases in some cities, the prosecutor is usually the official who reduces it." And "he is particularly able to influence police operations."

The report also asserts:

> Law-enforcement policy is made by policemen. For policemen cannot and do not arrest all the offenders they encounter. It is doubtful they arrest most of them. A criminal code, in practice, is not a set of specific instructions to policemen but a more or less rough map of the territory in which policemen work. . . . Every policeman, however complete or sketchy his education, is an interpreter of the law.

The National Council on Crime and Delinquency reports that there are "some 420,000 law enforcement officers employed by 40,000 separate" police departments in the United States!

While policemen make the arrests, it is the prosecutor who holds the controls in his hands and guides the ship. Because his decisions touch more lives, many lawyers assert that he is more important than the judge.

Yet thousands of prosecutors are men fresh out of law school who are learning their craft at state expense. Some have studied trial procedures for one semester at best. Because of recent innovations a few have spent time in court while still law students. Others have practiced law a few months or years and take the prosecutor's job while their practice builds and to gain experience.

Because so many of the nation's prominent trial lawyers have learned their trade via this route, it is widely defended—not so much for the service it renders to society as for the value of the experience to a beginning lawyer.

"Most prosecutors are young men with little trial experience because few experienced lawyers want the job," says Robert E. West, president of the Vermont State's Attorney's Association.

"At least two in our state were elected before they passed the bar exam. The pay is so low most have a civil practice on the side, so the public isn't always properly represented. Often being prosecutor comes second.

"I was astounded to find that, except in the large cities, nearly every prosecutor in the United States is part time."

The office of district attorney is often a springboard for higher office. For example, Thomas E. Dewey, former Governor of New York and onetime Republican presidential candidate, gained his reputation as a prosecutor. Earl Warren, too, was a prosecutor before he became Governor of California and later Chief Justice of the United States. Other prosecutors have had varying degrees of subsequent political success.

Given the right circumstances the supposedly sacrosanct system of justice can come under the control of one determined man. So I learned in a conversation that ended in the early morning hours of Feb. 7, 1967, in the expensive Oklahoma City home of Curtis P. Harris, Oklahoma County District Attorney.

Until a few years ago Mr. Harris was a condemnation lawyer earning between $50,000 and $150,000 a year. He decided to take the $15,500 post as prosecutor when his daughter's home—"She lives right back of us here"—was twice burglarized.

The first time, while his daughter was away from home and the grandchildren were staying with Mr. and Mrs. Harris, "somebody cleaned it out." But it was the second incident that convinced Mr. Harris to take action—action that has had a subtle but meaningful impact on the lives of all who live in Oklahoma County.

He tells it this way:

"About 2 o'clock one afternoon my daughter, who was pregnant at the time, heard a noise at one of the screens. Then she heard a window going up and saw a man coming in with another right behind."

She frightened the men away and was unharmed. But Mr. Harris, stewing about the two events, decided to "investigate" what the police were doing. He went down to police headquarters.

"The police told me, 'We catch 'em, but they're not being prosecuted very often,' " he says. "And they showed me how one man had been released on 41 different bail bonds."

As soon as he could, he ran for the prosecutor's office and was elected.

Determined to stamp out crime by taking a hard line, he has urged citizens to pack guns and shoot to kill if someone attempts to rob or molest them.

"This is war!" he says emphatically.

While thousands praise what he is doing, other Oklahomans assert he is fighting crime by creating a police state, with Curtis Harris sitting on top of the heap calling the shots.

Mr. Harris contends:

- Few if any criminals can be rehabilitated, so the best solution is to lock them up and throw away the key.

- Police do not arrest "innocent" people, although some are found not guilty in courtrooms. The difference between guilt and innocence, he asserts, is the inability to win a conviction through lack of evidence or because a lost witness cannot be found.

Mr. Harris has harsh words for his fellow lawyers.

"The legal profession can cut crime by 50 percent overnight simply by telling the truth" about their clients, he says.

When a nationally known attorney came to town and told the bar "how he uses chicanery" to free defendants, the lawyers "stood up and applauded."

"I can only ask what kind of bar we've got when lawyers give this kind of thing a standing ovation," he says.

Mr. Harris does not oppose leaking of information to the press that would be inadmissible as evidence in court. For example, he says he is not bothered when prospective jurors read about a defendant's prior criminal record—although it cannot be mentioned during a trial.

"A man's criminal record is the truth, isn't it?" he argues. "To say publicity prejudices jurors is saying that jurors lie when they tell the court that what they have read or heard will not influence them."

Yet when a jury refuses to convict a man, Mr. Harris says he sometimes "checks up" on members of the jury to find out why they voted as they did.

One wonders if this practice could not lead to jurors growing afraid to decide cases in favor of the defendant and against the prosecution.

In *State Trials* by Cobbett and Howell it is related how, in 1554, a jury found a celebrated lord not guilty of high treason, and so the whole jury was clapped into prison—apparently a common practice of that era. It was more than a century later that this was outlawed.

Mr. Harris also tells of jailing 110 men from "Friday to Monday" in an attempt to "solve" the killing of a little liquor store owner." While none of the men jailed had anything to do with the crime, he says, it helped the police find the guilty parties. As further justification, he adds: "On that weekend we had only one little Coke machine break-in."

A measure of his control: Last year when certain judges failed to measure up to his standards, he took his case to the voters—"naming names" at luncheons, club meetings, and other gatherings.

"I got out and campaigned to beat 'em, and they were beaten," he says. "Now I don't have a judge down there who won't say I'm right."

Some say he has less power than is generally believed. But power is vested by the voters.

"I was just re-elected to a second term, and I beat my opponent eight to one," he says.

His crackdown includes misdemeanors as well as more serious crimes. In his first year misdemeanor fines collected jumped from $3,000 or $4,000 a year to $65,000. Drunken drivers "used to pay $10 and get 10 days," but now they are fined $300 to $500 and six months to a year in jail, he says.

Some old cases, "six or seven years old," have been brought to trial.

"We try as many cases in a month as the prosecutor used to try in a year," Mr. Harris asserts. "In my first year in office we cut the over-all crime rate 24 percent while it was going up across the country. Last year we cut it another 3 or 4 percent."

There is little question but that Mr. Harris is conviction-minded or that his methods are effective. Many Oklahomans say his approach is right. Others contend that a prosecutor with so much political power and with a police force to back him up could—in the guise of crime fighter—do great harm to a system of justice that depends on balance.

Some judges and lawyers interviewed agreed that such practices as those used by Mr. Harris could lay the foundation for a police state.

Convictions are only one side of the coin, moreover. Screening of cases before they get to the trial state is vital to justice, too.

The President's commission points out that the law makes prosecutors and judges responsible for meting out rigorous treatment for dangerous offenders or for offering remedial opportunities to offenders who seem likely to benefit.

> ... The law gives wide latitude to police and prosecutors in making arrests and in bringing charges, judges in imposing penalties....
>
> Almost half of all arrests are on charges of drunkenness, disorderly conduct, vagrancy, gambling, and minor sexual violations.
>
> Such behavior is generally considered too serious to be ignored, but its inclusion in the criminal justice system raises questions deserving examination.... The investigation and prosecution of such cases ties up police and clogs courts at the expense of their capacity to deal with more threatening crimes....
>
> In some cities the enforcement of these laws has been unhappily associated with police, prosecutor, and court venality and corruption, which in turn have led to a general decline in respect for law.

In Pittsburgh I saw a man jailed by a nonlawyer-judge on charges of rape. No prosecutor or defense lawyer was present. The arrest was made on a middle-aged woman's signature.

"I understand the fellow didn't pay her the 10 bucks she asked for," a police sergeant told the judge later. "What do you want to do?"

"Well, maybe he'll pay off next time he fools with a prostitute," the judge said, laughing. "The warrant is signed, and there's not much we can do about it now."

In a Houston criminal hearing, an auto owner and used-car dealer wrangled for nearly an hour over a complicated deal that might have involved fraud. Finally the judge, whose docket was jammed, threw the cases out, explaining it was "a civil action" and "should never have been filed in this court."

This is an all-too-familiar complaint. I heard it in courts in almost every city I visited, even when prosecutors piously insisted they were doing a "good job of screening." One prominent district attorney who said this, was refuted later by an assistant who had to handle the DA's cases at the lowest level. The assistant indicated that his boss had higher political plans and didn't want to offend the public by throwing out cases and getting the reputation for being soft on criminals.

After sitting in courtrooms and talking to judges and lawyers across the country, I also found:

• That in thousands of lower courts (and this is where 90 percent of all defendants appear) a policeman or judge acts as prosecutor, though neither has legal training. Policemen too often are trying to justify the arrest instead of seeing that justice is done.

• That politically ambitious prosecutors are too often "conviction-happy," as one West Coast judge put it. This can result in the "little guy" being pressured into pleading guilty to a charge that probably would be reduced if he knew enough to demand a trial. In some cities where justice is dispensed assembly-line fashion, 95 percent of those convicted plead guilty without ever going to trial.

(This is not to say that lawbreakers shouldn't admit their guilt and accept their penalty. Rather it is a commentary on inequality. The complaint most often heard is that the "little guy" who is a first offender goes to jail or pays a fine while the professional criminal with the right lawyer and enough money wins.)

• In dozens of courtrooms the prosecutor has never seen the case before a folder is thrust into his hands for a preliminary hearing or for trial by a lower-court magistrate. Too often no consideration has been given to the validity of the charge or evidence. Even in more serious cases the prosecutor has a limited amount of time to prepare his case, unless it is a spectacular crime that will make page 1 in the newspapers.

Generalizations, of course, bring up exceptions. Just as there are many good judges in the United States, so there are also competent prosecutors and excellent policemen. As is usually the case, a state or community simply gets what it asks for.

Several years of watching the Michigan State Police in action gave me an insight into the kind of job a carefully trained force of first-class men can do.

On the other hand, experience with several police departments and sheriffs' offices has indicated a drastic need for upgrading those departments.

The police problem has been much discussed in recent months. Thousands of men with little training, limited education, and often from the lower economic levels of society make decisions daily that would tax experienced judges.

The President's commission report points out that parts of our system of justice—"magistrates' courts, trial by jury, bail—are of great antiquity. Other parts—juvenile courts, probation and parole, professional policemen—are relatively new."

Stanley Schrotel, former Cincinnati police chief, and a lawyer, told me in an interview in 1966 that policemen are sometimes criticized by those who fail to understand the role of the police in our society.

"The police department was created by society to maintain law and order," he explains. It is up to the people to decide what laws they want, and how the laws should be enforced. Making laws is not within the police province.

"Too many communities forget this. Through indifference, or for other reasons, they permit the police agency to proceed in its own direction. Then they criticize the results."

Yet the police have formed a common front across the country to oppose civilian review boards. It is easy to understand why. No one, including those who labor on the public payroll, wants big-brother agencies looking over his shoulder or second-guessing him.

It is a curious fact that some governmental officials are angered by the press when it serves in a watchdog role and exposes wrongdoing. Certainly there will be opposition to agencies of government that monitor police activities. But just as judges and lawyers hesitate to enforce the canons of ethics, so policemen are often slow to eliminate the bad eggs.

For years there have been reports of police bribe-taking. More recently, scattered departments have had police working with burglars and crime-syndicate hoodlums.

It was this kind of scandal that brought Orlando W. Wilson to Chicago in 1960. He admitted to me, before his retirement in the summer of 1967, that it was impossible to weed out all bad or corrupt policemen.

The least we can do is improve the training of policemen. More often than not we hire a man because he is over 5′8″ tall, has no criminal record, and is willing to take the job. Pay is so low and the job of finding men so difficult that some cities have now lowered educational standards, and it is not even necessary to have finished high school.

Chief Schrotel was deeply concerned over this growing problem. "You invest in the police officer almost plenary [absolute] powers," he told me. "An officer is able to take property from an individual—a decision based only on his judgment of the circumstances. He says, 'Tow that car away.'

"He is able to deprive people of their liberty. In extreme circumstances he can take a human life. We can only hope that he has sound judgment. That he has done it on moral grounds. On legal grounds.

"We must see that we place this authority in extremely competent hands. I quake every time we ask a young kid to raise his right hand, when we put a uniform on him and turn him loose on society. As a citizen, as well as a policeman, I want to be sure the man carrying that gun and wearing that badge has the highest qualifications to carry out such awesome duties."

Chief Schrotel points out that the FBI has won such wide

respect and has succeeded in its law-enforcement role because of high standards.

"A special agent is highly educated, well grounded, socially graceful, and a man who never violates your trust," he explains.

But how do you find men like that when most communities are only willing to pay $5,000 or $6,000 a year—and often less? I have been told by police officials around the nation that they compete directly with factories for men.

No wonder there is a conflict when Negroes and Spanish-speaking Americans are confronted daily by white policemen.

"We are calling on policemen to make judgments in situations highly charged with racial overtones," Mr. Schrotel says. "Yet that white policeman is originally from a socioeconomic level a cut below the mean. From a group that has strong negative feelings about Negroes.

"We put him into this highly charged situation and expect him to understand what is happening, why it is happening, and how to handle it when he is ill equipped in experience to do the job."

Policemen are often alienated from others in our legal system, except, perhaps, the prosecutor. I found that it is a rare city where policemen praise the courts.

Most often I heard complaints that the judges refuse to crack down on habitual criminals. Some are arrested time and again, only to be released to prey on the public again.

Crammed dockets, where "deals" are made with those who have been arrested, lower police morale. A policeman who has spent days gathering evidence, or who has caught a man red-handed, only to find he is allowed to plead guilty to a lesser offense because it will save the time of a trial, can become bitter.

And officers complain that they spend "too much time twiddling our thumbs in courtrooms" as lawyers maneuver, ask for continuances, or otherwise delay justice. Too often the policeman goes to court on his own time—when he could be sleeping, relaxing, or doing chores around the house for his wife.

Recent Supreme Court rulings have had a serious impact on

the administration of criminal justice—and on the police and prosecutors.

In one split decision, *Escobedo* vs. *Illinois,* the High Court reversed a two-year sentence given to a man convicted as a hired killer. Police had refused to let the suspect consult his lawyer until they finished questioning him.

Subsequent rulings have made it even more difficult to get a man to confess, police complain.

In a letter to this writer Denver Police Chief Harold A. Dill summed up the police stand when he said: "Our laws are all right. Interpretation is poor."

Orlando Wilson told me that the only answer is for the Supreme Court to reverse itself because "we simply cannot live with their recent decisions."

Yet others have milder views.

Captain Raymond H. McConnell, who heads the detective division of the Michigan State Police, points out that these High Court decisions are, at least in part, the result of poor police work. And while the decisions are hard to live with, cities are being forced to upgrade their police departments.

"We must become better, more professional officers to get the job done," says Curtis Broston, St. Louis police chief.

While policemen and prosecutors must work together as a team, the prosecutor should keep tabs on the police department and on the jailer. And on citizens who file complaints.

In Carlsbad, N.M., I met J. Lee Cathey, an assistant district attorney. He keeps weekly check on who is in jail, and makes sure they are moved through the courts as swiftly as possible. Everyone charged with a felony (a serious crime that can bring a prison term of one year or more) must have a lawyer at preliminary hearings.

And no charges are made against a man without Mr. Cathey's specific approval, after carefully reviewing the case.

In courts across the nation I heard complaints that a badly bruised wife will file a criminal action against her husband, have him arrested, and then come in a few days later begging to have charges dropped.

When Mr. Cathey is confronted with such a case, he tries to

reason with the woman and, where it is advisable, keep such a complaint out of the court system—or at least give the woman time to cool down and make her decision at a calmer moment.

Unfortunately, the best prosecutors usually leave office as soon as they can for private practice. Men in every section of the country complained that pay is poor—often $5,000 to $7,000 a year, or less, in a field that can yield $25,000, $30,000, or more for a competent lawyer.

It should be noted from my interviews with lawyers and judges that, as in other professions, many men who attend law school—perhaps too many—do so because the profession can be profitable, not primarily out of a "love of justice" or because they have a burning "social worker's" philosophy. This may explain why more top lawyers don't take low-paying jobs as prosecutors and judges.

Nor is the problem limited to lower courts. Robert C. Finley, Chief Justice of the Supreme Court of Washington State, told me that even if the governor of his state walked into the office of a leading attorney to tap him for a seat on the Supreme Court, he would probably hear a long list of excuses as to why the man could not accept.

Low pay is a problem in the cities, too. Philadelphia's colorful prosecutor Arlen Specter, recently a candidate for mayor, told me the pay for his staff is "abominable."

Philadelphia starts a district attorney at $6,954, which means that only men fresh out of law school will apply. Even experienced men get only about $15,000—certainly less than men of equal skill might get in their own law firm or as a good trial lawyer in a city of comparable size.

Mr. Specter says that while he was authorized to have 51 men, he had only 49. He said 76 were needed.

"Our men average in excess of 60 hours a week, and none are working less than 48," he asserts.

There can be little doubt that we should give our prosecutors more men and enlarge most police departments. And we must give them more training and more pay.

I am convinced that policemen—the members of the justice team who too often come from the lowest social levels of our society, with the least education and the poorest pay—have the most difficult job. Only those who run our prisons have nearly comparable problems of low pay and incompetent staffs. And the prisons handle only guilty men, while the police must sort the guilty from the innocent, sometimes tracking them down and subduing them under the most trying conditions and at the risk of their own safety, always wondering if they will be charged with "police brutality."

In a speech before the West Virginia Trial Lawyers Association, Inspector Dwight Dalbey of the FBI pointed out that while "the facts of the case often are obscure and difficult of ascertainment . . . the law requires, and the public expects, that the officer will act quickly, decisively, and accurately."

His decisions involve constitutional law. And "We expect of a police officer the wisdom of Solomon in understanding the law, the strength of Sampson in arresting a criminal, the gentleness of St. Francis of Assisi in repelling a riot, the patience of Job in dealing with each of us, and the moral purity of Caesar's wife in a nation whose public and private morals in areas outside police work are sometimes open to legitimate question."

What are the answers?

"The problem of crime must be solved by society," says Orlando Wilson. "We must correct fundamental things wrong in our society—things that cause criminality beyond the scope of police activity. I am talking about economic problems—slums—people with educational deficiencies—lack of training—lack of vocational skills—large numbers of unemployably disadvantaged people."

But if my tour of the nation made me certain of anything, it is that while we are doing these things we must also hire better men to run the first stages of our system of criminal justice. We must have better policemen, and experienced, full-time prosecutors.

CHAPTER VII

The Courtroom Team

There are some who discount the importance of the rest of the courtroom team—the clerks, bailiffs, court reporters, and, in the past few years, the court administrators.

But they, too, have an impact on the quality of justice we find in our state courts. Changes are in order in some areas.

The bailiff is the uniformed man who sits in almost every courtroom—criminal and civil—to keep order. Usually he is under the control of the sheriff rather than the judge, and may well be too close to retirement to track down criminals or chase speeders.

His presence in criminal courtrooms is useful. But in civil courts many assert that he is little more than the man who keeps the coffee hot for the judge, runs a few errands, and, in more polite courts, opens the swinging gate for witnesses.

Says one former big-city bailiff:

> I spent my days sleeping on the couch in the judges' chambers. If he wanted me to run an errand the clerk would buzz and I came out carrying a lawbook so that it looked like I had been working.
>
> My main job was to tell everyone in the courtroom to stand when the judge came in each morning and again after the noon recess. I also took juries to lunch at a local restaurant. Bailiffs make a nice profit on this. We got a free steak dinner. And the restaurant, to encourage us to bring juries in, served us all the free martinis we could drink in coffee cups. The meals usually would cost only half what we had been given, so we kept the rest.

In Los Angeles, where pay is above average ($500 to $700 a month) and the caliber of men as high as any around the country, I watched one Los Angeles Superior Court bailiff fuss with his stamp collection for hours during a jury trial. He would, with considerable rustling and crackling, remove stamps from one glassine envelope, study them, and then transfer them to another glassine envelope. Several jurors seemed distracted by the noise, and I found it hard to hear witnesses with soft voices.

This reporter found that these men may serve to bolster a judge's ego—especially when the judge's pay is low. As a practical matter, the bailiff's duties could be easily handled by the clerk of the court, who is always present.

Court clerks and court reporters (stenographers) are necessary, and have varying degrees of skill. Some judges complain that deputy clerks are political hacks appointed by the elected chief clerk of the court. Judges too often have little or no say in the selection or firing of these deputies. In some cities clerks lose records and create other unnecessary delays.

It is not uncommon to hear a client asking his lawyer in the corridor outside a courtroom, "Why aren't we going to court today?" The lawyer then explains that some clerk or other court employee has fouled up the records and they will have to come back later.

Or the lawyer may be frantically calling witnesses on the phone because his client's case has come up a day early or because subpoenas were not properly issued or served.

Court critics, including lawyers and judges, say too many judges let clerks or bailiffs control their courtrooms. And as often as not, when corruption is found in the court, a clerk or bailiff has a hand in it. This is especially true in traffic court.

Nearly every large city with a strong, watchdog newspaper has unearthed scandals in courts in recent years. One Indianapolis judge told me of several instances of court personnel involved in illegal court practices. Chicago's traffic court has often been hit with ticket-fixing scandals.

But court jobs are usually political. Too often the "fixers" are shifted to another job rather than fired.

Some Chicago lawyers assert it is still possible to get your case moved up the civil docket by paying off certain clerks.

Others say payoffs may be necessary to get court records from some clerks.

Not much attention is focused on clerks and other court workers in the professional legal journals. Little research on court personnel has been done. When there is research, more often than not it is ignored.

A Midwestern judge gave me a typical answer on this point: "I have so many things to think about, I simply haven't given court personnel a thought."

The few cities with full-time court administrators have been able to make some headway in unsnarling nonjudicial problems. But progress is slow, and most court administrators lack the power to make sweeping improvements. Judges balk. County or state officials may block progress by refusing to appropriate funds to make the improvements needed.

Hiring a court administrator is a growing trend, and in states like New Jersey, Washington, Illinois, and California these men are providing badly needed services. In some states at least someone has been designated to keep statistics, so problem areas (and problem judges) can be identified, if not eliminated.

I was especially impressed with what I found in Los Angeles, where growth of court business has been beyond belief. Not too many years ago the dockets began swelling up like a balloon. Without an administrator, it finally exploded, throwing cases into old Army barracks, the halls, hotel rooms, and trailers.

In 1959 the courts moved into a huge new building, but six months later the load became too great again and splattered back out into warehouses and hotel rooms and trailers.

Now the administrator's office has charge of construction of new buildings in several regions of Los Angeles County, and by 1970 will have all multicourtroom courthouses with unfinished courtrooms in each for future needs.

Each building is being constructed with smooth operation in mind, including the orderly flow of prisoners, public, judges, and jurors, in some instances through separate entrances and corridors.

Little things, like making it possible for all spectators to hear what is being said, are being taken into consideration.

Yet if what one Eastern court administrator says is true, most of the nation will have a long wait before it reaches the point where we now find Los Angeles. For he said L.A. is now "15 years ahead of the rest of the nation."

Several cities are using computers to keep track of cases and to assemble dockets, as well as to keep track of verdicts and prisoners. Systems to look up the law for judges and lawyers are being perfected, and when in operation, thousands of man-hours will be saved. Administrators are usually responsible for bringing this new equipment into the courts.

But in some cities judges remain unaware of the importance of hiring men with special skills for the administrator's job. Too often some struggling lawyer is tapped. These men may be "safe" choices—no threat to the old way of doing things. Or the judge may not understand that almost any bright business administrator can learn the operation of a court, but not every lawyer can be transformed into a bright business administrator. Like arguing a case before a jury, court administration takes special skills.

As a group, the most competent court personnel, including judges, are the court reporters—at least in the larger cities. The reason: Judges worry about higher courts reversing their decisions and want to make sure the record is accurate. So do lawyers who may appeal. Thus those who are charged with keeping an accurate record of proceedings must be competent. And unlike the job of judge, prosecutor, policeman, or corrections officer, the court reporter's performance can be objectively measured and evaluated.

Julian J. Covel, of Jamaica, N.Y., president of the National Shorthand Reporters Association, says there are "approximately 11,000 shorthand reporters in the United States . . . the vast majority court reporters," though others take depositions or work in legislatures and other similar bodies.

"Earnings begin at about $8,500 to $10,000 and can reach $20,000 or more," he says.

Yet only 10 states—California, Colorado, Florida, Illinois,

Iowa, Kansas, New Jersey, New York, Oklahoma, and Utah—have legislation that assures courts of having reporters that measure up to Mr. Covel's standards: "Able to record accurately a minimum of 200 words per minute, have high intelligence, a fairly extensive vocabulary, a good knowledge of the English language, and good hearing."

Like a brilliant judge or outstanding lawyer, a skilled reporter is a pleasure to watch. This writer sat in on a complex medical-malpractice trial in San Francisco's Superior Court. A doctor rattled on for two hours in machine-gun fashion, firing off volleys of high-powered medical terms, and the reporter took it all down with ease—while the jury looked dismayed, clearly not comprehending.

But what do you do in rural areas, where few people have the necessary shorthand skills?

Frank R. Kenison, the Chief Justice of the New Hampshire Supreme Court, and Robert B. Williamson, Chief Justice of the Maine Supreme Judicial Court, told me that the "good life" of the small towns often entices competent court reporters to the New England states.

In states like Indiana and South Carolina, this reporter saw proceedings recorded electronically, at first blush the best possible way to make an accurate record.

But Mr. Covel, who has well-founded pride in his profession, argues:

> Attempts to record court proceedings electronically have failed to achieve the desired result in all impartial tests made, since tape recorders cannot distinguish between similar sounds, but pick up all the noises in the courtroom. This frequently results in an undecipherable jumble. Voices overlap. A truck rumbles past. A chair scrapes the floor. A juror clears his throat.

Yet as I visited courts across the country, I found that this very inability to filter out "unwanted" sounds can be an advantage over the shorthand method.

For instance, when a judge loses his temper or commits some other breach of courtroom decorum, the court reporter simply stopped taking shorthand, picking up again when procedures returned to normal. It is clear that a judge who gets an appeal in a higher court may never know what really went on in the lower court even though the appeal may be based on mistakes make by the lower-court judge.

Slowly, with considerable resistance from some judges and lawyers, we are starting to bring other skills into our courthouses. We are, for example, hiring more psychiatrists and social workers.

In a growing number of large cities nonlawyers are actually hearing cases in juvenile courts, not because of flaws in the law, but because they have special skills and training. I watched Jane S. Almassy sit as a "referee" in juvenile cases in Los Angeles.

In one case a boy charged with possession of marijuana had a lawyer, hired by his parents. She handled it with the skill of the best juvenile judges—perhaps with more. Yet her background is not in the law, but rather in social work and probation. As is the custom in Los Angeles, the youth was told he would not be made a ward of the court if, for six months, he had "no more trouble with the police."

In other family matters nonlawyers are used. In Pittsburgh a special department has been established to try to head off divorces, as well as collect support money. Patrick Tamilia, who heads the section, showed me a computer now in use. It makes up thousands of support checks and keeps the records for an annual distribution of over $6 million, he said.

In trying to save Pittsburgh marriages, "15 college-trained people" are employed as counselors. They are not required to be lawyers.

These changes are taking place mainly in the large cities, but business goes on as it has for decades in the hundreds of single-judge courts scattered across the nation.

One solution to this problem is the formation of court districts, with judges riding circuit. Yet in most districts there is a separate clerk in each courthouse—often with little to do between terms of court.

Many court jobs are rather mundane—not really different from those found in business and industry.

If International Harvester can keep track of thousands of tractor parts; if American Airlines can keep tabs on flight schedules, weather conditions, and the hours of pilots, mechanics, stewardesses, ticket-sellers, ticket sales, the connecting flights of other airlines, and tens of thousands of passengers; and if Ford Motor Company has a pretty fair idea of how many cars to produce without going broke, it seems certain that some of these same techniques can be applied to our courts.

This may require changes, like giving judges or the court administrator control over clerks and bailiffs.

But to bring about needed improvements judges and lawyers themselves must stop fighting change. They must recognize that the courts belong to the people. And that it is the responsibility of judges and lawyers to see that improvements are made—quickly.

CHAPTER VIII

Jail or Bail?

It was a mild evening in January when I visited a night session of Pittsburgh's municipal court.

Because the new night court had been lauded as an important improvement in Pittsburgh's system, I was poorly prepared for what I found there.

Business was slow, so the judge was indulging in horseplay, rollicking around the courtroom. This went on for about a half-hour before he finally took the bench. A handful of people, waiting for a hearing, watched silently while he wisecracked with a bystander.

Equally casual were the comings and goings of a man who from time to time walked to the bull pen where prisoners were kept. Sometimes he disappeared into another room. When I walked into the room, he was standing near the safe, chatting with the two policemen assigned to the court. Occasionally he would go into the restricted area where the judges' chambers are found.

The man was a bail bondsman, and from all appearances he was using the courtroom to conduct his business—hardly in keeping with accepted court practices.

My immediate impression was that the judge was setting high bails for the profit of this bail bondsman. When I questioned the judge, he denied it. But he did admit that he set one bail high to help detectives extract a "voluntary" confession from a man accused of burglary.

Police told the defendant the judge would set a high bail

unless the man admitted to the crime. When he did, the judge said, "That's how it's supposed to work."

Despite the questions raised by the conduct in that Pittsburgh courtroom, the idea of having a judge on duty after hours is considered by some court officials as a step forward in expediting justice.

In many cities defendants arrested in the afternoon or evening (and most are) sit in jail at least until the following morning. Sometimes days pass before they get a hearing or make bail. Men lose their jobs and their families go on welfare because of this.

Even though the defendant is later released on bail, freed for lack of evidence, or even acquitted, the damage has been done.

New York and Philadelphia now have 24-hour courts. Pittsburgh's is open until about 2 A.M.

Many thoughtful lawyers and judges interviewed are concerned over bail-bond practices. Few Americans realize how involved and costly getting out on bail can be. (The professional criminal knows: He retains a standing bail bondsman and writes off the bondsman's fee and the bail as a "business expense.")

It has been estimated that there are more than 3,000 bail bondsmen across the United States. Most of these operate out of shabby little offices and are backed by little more than 10 of the nation's surety firms.

"A central fault of the existing system is that it detains too many people, with serious consequences for defendants, the criminal process, and the community," asserts the President's Commission on Law Enforcement and Administration of Justice. "The first step of reform is to introduce fact-finding procedures which will furnish immediately after arrest verified information about the accused and his community ties.

"With this information a rational assessment of the risks can be made, and where there is no significant risk the defendant can be released without bail."

I was appalled to find, as I traveled the nation, how easy it is for a citizen (or policeman) to have someone thrown in jail.

Either can swear out a warrant and have a person arrested on a grudge. The charge may be totally unfounded and ultimately dismissed. But the arrest takes place. And the law provides little practical recourse for the arrested person.

A problem involving police-initiated arrests arises from the difficulty of getting the arresting officer to appear in court to testify. There are at least two reasons for this:

- Usually a policeman must testify on his own time—taking the morning or afternoon off from work and making it up later or simply spending part or all of his day off in court. Obviously such a system does not encourage the officer to appear.

- But sometimes an officer is vindictive and wants to see the defendant punished. So the officer deliberately fails to show up in court. (This is especially true when the policeman knows he is short on evidence.) The result is that the defendant must keep coming back to court until his accuser shows up. Such police-caused delays can cost a man money in time off from work. He may even be held in jail if unable to make bail. The taxpayer foots the bill for his "room and board."

The abuse of the arrest-jail-bail system by police to usurp the authority of the court and punish those arrested remains widespread. I found evidence of the practice in every section of the nation.

In Des Moines policemen used to be under orders to arrest men for OMVI—operating a motor vehicle while intoxicated. Under this order officers would arrest for OMVI even when they knew they lacked evidence to obtain a conviction.

"The boys figured the defendant would at least be rapped for the bond [defendants pay a bail bondsman $25 to write a $300 bond for OMVI] and also spend a night in jail," said Captain Wendell Nichols. The OMVI charge was probably valid in 9 out of 10 cases, he added.

In effect the police were using some arrests as punishment, knowing they wouldn't stick.

It was the penalty imposed on "that 10th fellow," plus a recent upgrading of the police department, that finally brought about a change in the Des Moines arrest philosophy.

Many agree with Pittsburgh's noted Common Pleas Judge, Ruggero J. Aldisert, when he says bail bondsmen are "vultures." In some states bondsmen demand payment of up to 10 or 20 percent of the bail. The defendant loses this money—even if charges are later found false.

On a good night an unethical bondsman, with the cooperation of a judge, police, or lawyers, can pocket a sizable sum—all in the name of "service to humanity." And this type of judge, policeman, or lawyer often gets "gifts" or outright kickbacks for services rendered.

On that night in Pittsburgh the judge was setting bail of between $500 and $5,000. Bail bondsmen in Pennsylvania are supposed to receive a 6 percent fee. But as Judge Aldisert said: "Who knows what a poor devil may pay? These fellows collect whatever the traffic will bear."

During the evening I also found some men unable to make bond.

The next day I asked other Pittsburgh judges about what I observed in the night court.

One of them, Ernest C. Jones, who had been promoted to chief magistrate by the Mayor a few days earlier to clean up the city courts, said he was disturbed by what I had found.

Immediately after our conversation he ordered a crackdown.

He banned bail bondsmen from the courtroom. Now prisoners select a bondsman's name from a printed list and make the contact by telephone. Mr. Jones said that the amounts of bail have been reduced: Those charged with misdemeanors (less serious crimes) now get out on $500 bail, instead of $1,000 as in the past.

Among other security measures, Mr. Jones has also installed a lock system with a master push-button that controls the doors to the courtroom. (Shortly before my visit, a policeman was shot with his own revolver in a corner of the courtroom complex.)

Mr. Jones pointed out he was cracking down on delays in bringing defendants from outlying areas into court—delays apparently caused by the ties that exist between policemen and certain bail bondsmen.

The effect of the changes—and the need for them—were immediately made apparent.

The night I left Pittsburgh I flew to Philadelphia. When I walked into the night court in that city, I had expected to quietly blend into the crowd unnoticed.

To my surprise, an assistant district attorney, Ned Wolf, walked over and shook my hand, saying, "You must be the reporter from *The Christian Science Monitor.*"

When I asked him how he knew, he said someone from the Pittsburgh court had called (without Mr. Jones's knowledge or permission) to tell them to watch for me. The Pittsburgh informant even gave out a description. The Pittsburgh court shake-up had already begun, even though I had not as yet written a word.

Some of the shortcomings of the Philadelphia court system have already been covered in this book. There, as in other cities, abuse of the bail-bond system is reported to be widespread.

The new 24-hour court had difficulties almost before it started. There were reports that bail bondsmen put pressure on lower-court magistrates to stay off the job. Whether or not there was such pressure, some of the magistrates refused to sit. They were subsequently ordered to by Chief Administrative Judge Vincent A. Carroll.

According to Edward J. Blake, court administrator, there has been significant improvement. All bail transactions have been ordered out of the courtroom and must now take place in the office of the clerk of courts. Fines are no longer paid directly to the magistrate.

As Mr. Blake put it: "The time had come for the money-changers to get out of the temple of justice."

District Attorney Arlen Specter, who supported the new court, had said earlier that it would help eliminate the "opportunity for bail bondsmen to profiteer."

Bondsmen assert that their greatest service is going after the man who jumps bail. This to avoid paying the forfeiture.

"The person on bail actually belongs to us," said an Indianapolis bondsman I interviewed at length. "We don't have to go through all that legal stuff like extradition.

"One fellow drove to Florida. He was on $5,000 bail. We picked up the man, put handcuffs on him, and brought him back. The law says we can use whatever force it takes to bring him back."

A sharp bail bondsman can, without too much effort, make "at least $10,000 to $15,000 a year," he added.

In Indiana he must "have a clean record, pass a test, and put up collateral of $2,500." The actual risk is usually taken by a surety company—although in several states visited I found that cash in the bank, property, or even thin air are used by bail bondsmen to back up their bonds. Some write more bonds than they can cover.

In Indianapolis I found that some bondsmen and lawyers may work hand and glove, referring business to each other.

"What court are you going to be in?" one bail bondsman asked a client as I listened. (The man named the judge.) "Then call Frank," he said. "He can take care of you."

As the discussion continued, the implication was clear that the lawyer had the judge "in his pocket."

In Oklahoma City the law was changed after it was found lawyers and shady characters were in the bond business. As one court official put it: "A bondsman might own a lot that wasn't worth $100, yet he would list the lot in a $100,000 bond. We had over a million dollars in forfeitures on fake paper. The bonds weren't worth the paper they were written on."

A former bootlegger was writing bail bonds on real estate actually owned by the Roman Catholic Church of Tulsa and Oklahoma City diocese.

This resulted in bail reform there. Bail bondsmen are now registered with the state insurance commissioner. They work through surety companies, and post cash or securities to back up their business.

Yet on one of the days I visited Oklahoma City a former bondsman was in court for getting a defendant released on phony papers.

The picture is grim. The problems nationwide.

In calling for changes, President Johnson has said: "The defendant with means can afford to pay bail. He can afford to buy his freedom. But the poorer defendant cannot pay the price. He languishes in jail weeks, months, and perhaps even years before trial."

The President's Commission on Law Enforcement and the Administration of Justice cited these examples of the problem:

> A man was jailed on a serious charge brought last Christmas Eve. He could not afford bail and spent 101 days in jail until a hearing. Then the complainant admitted the charge was false.
>
> Another man spent two months in jail before being acquitted. In that period he lost his job and his car and his family was split up. He did not find another job for four months.

Sometimes, too, if there is a great public hue and cry about a particular crime, bail may be set so high as to become meaningless as a protection to the defendant.

For the reader not familiar with the work and the words of the criminal court I will pause here for a brief glossary:

Bail—A sum of money put up by the defendant to secure his freedom until the date of his trial. If the defendant does not appear at the trial, this money is forfeited to the court. The amount is set by the judge depending on the severity of the crime and the defendant's reputation.

Bail bond—A document which obligates the signer to pay the face value (bail) if the defendant fails to appear for trial.

Bail bondsman—A person who signs a bond that guarantees the amount of bail if the defendant fails to appear for trial. The bondsman works on a fee basis. Say the judge sets bail at $1,000. If the defendant can't raise it, he may contact a bail bondsman who agrees to stand good for the money. For this service the bondsman charges the defendants a fee—perhaps 10 percent of the bail, or $100. That is the bondsman's fee for risking loss of $1,000 if the defendant "jumps bail" (fails to show up for trial). In some states the fees and activities of the bondsman are regulated by statute.

Recognizance—Release of a defendant without bail. This is known as ROR (released on recognizance) or OR (own recognizance). It means the court is reasonably sure the defendant will show up for trial. No money is involved.

In a few states the judge has guidelines for setting bail, or works out an agreement with his fellow judges. In most states this is not so, and whim guides the judge as much as fact.

Despite the dark picture, much of the court-related reform that has taken place has nevertheless been in the area of the bail bond.

Much of the credit goes to Louis Schweitzer, a New York City industrialist and engineer. Learning that a man could sit in jail for a year or more in New York because he lacked money to pay a bail bondsman, Mr. Schweitzer formed the Vera Foundation (named for his wife) in 1961.

Foundation employees began screening defendants for the courts to see how many could qualify for release on their own recognizance—or signature.

The plan was so successful that now more than 100 cities use it to some degree.

Yet I found none that begin to measure up to the New York plan.

In 1964 the Vera Foundation (now the Vera Institute of Justice) turned its release-on-recognizance (ROR) research project over to the Probation Department of the City of New York.

Last year that department, with 40-plus employees, screened 64,458 defendants and found 35,458 qualified for interviews. Of these, 20,937 received favorable recommendations. And 9,938 were actually released. Another 3,226 were released by judges on information provided by the ROR staff without the favorable recommendation.

New York City budgeted $298,000 for the program in the last fiscal year, which ended June 30, 1967. With the 24-hour court now in operation the staff has jumped from 40 to 83.

New York officials estimate that millions of dollars have already been saved in New York by this system—both in taxpayers' money and in money that might be paid to professional bail bondsmen. For it costs $7 a day to hold a man in jail, and it is estimated each man is held an average of 15 days.

"Under ROR he is allowed to go back to his job," said Henry H. Smith, chief of the ROR program in New York. "Before, his family probably had to go on welfare to eat. And it has helped solve a very serious housing problem in the Corrections Department, where there is a great shortage of space."

He also asserts that perhaps up to 65 percent of those who are involved in the program have charges dismissed or are found not guilty when they have their day in court.

How many fail to show up in court?

A 1965 study shows about 1.8 percent, an average that approximates or betters that of professional bondsmen.

Yet a more recent report shows that the figure may be closer to 4 percent in New York City. This may reflect flaws in the court system rather than in the ROR program.

Mr. Smith gives this example:

A young man was arrested for possession of burglary tools. Living at home with his parents and working full time, he was released under the ROR program.

This young man showed up in court 15 times on the charge. Each time the arresting policeman failed to show up in court.

On the 16th court date the young man failed to appear. He was fed up with the whole thing, Mr. Smith says. Then the man was arrested on a bench warrant. The ROR program chalked up a "failure." Yet the officer still did not appear in court.

Finally, with the help of ROR people, the judge dismissed the charges against the young man.

It is hoped that in New York City the 24-hour court will resolve some of the police failure-to-show problems.

Des Moines has a program called pretrial release. In a metropolitan area of more than 200,000 persons it operates on a budget of $15,000 by using six students from Drake University Law School. Each works part-time.

It was launched by the Hawley Welfare Foundation in 1964. Since then 3,116 interviews were held and 2,595 (83 percent) persons were found qualified for release. Of these, 2,269 (73 percent) were released, with a no-show rate of 1.3 per cent.

Figures on the total number arrested in the period are not really meaningful. For although city police arrest roughly 9,000 persons a year, 4,612 were charged with being drunk in 1966, and 1,709 were picked up for moving-traffic violations. Add to this the number of those charged with disorderly conduct and vagrancy and those with out-of-town addresses (thus not eligible for ROR) and the indication is that a high percentage of those who might spend several days or weeks in jail are being released.

There is a side benefit, says Captain Nichols: Letting a man out on his own signature helps reduce bitterness toward the police.

Los Angeles officials also tell how bail bondsmen abuse their position to take advantage of an inexperienced public:

> New York relatives of a man charged with a felony (serious crime) called a bail bondsman to ask how they could get the relative out of jail. He told them to send him (the bondsman) a check for $1,650, although he knew full well that the bail was set at $1,100. (Normally this would require surrendering only $100 to the bail bondsman.)
>
> After sending the bondsman $1,100, "he ran up over $400 in expenses" before the defendant realized what had happened, a court spokesman asserted.

Since 1963 Los Angeles has had an OR (own recognizance) program. It is headed by Bill Box, who has a staff of five investigators and one clerical assistant.

All defendants are now given an OR application when they are arraigned in municipal court, he says. The following morning those who make application are interviewed.

"All we do is evaluate a person's character," Mr. Box says.

"We look at his past record and check with schools, neighbors, employers, and other references he may give out."

But the tiny staff means that "we don't have time to get to everybody." To solve that problem "we put those with the best possibility of getting OR'ed on top of the pile and those with the least possibility on the bottom."

The office handles only about "a dozen a day—favorable and unfavorable."

And a man may remain in jail two or three days or more before he is released under the system. Others are able to post cash bond. And others get out when charges are dropped.

"Many defendants are never brought to arraignment," Mr. Box says. "They are held 48 hours, and they find something is wrong (lack of evidence, for example) or the complaining witness changes his mind."

Only felonies are covered.

"This program was offered to Municipal Court, but it was turned down," Mr. Box explains. "Each judge makes his own decision there."

Other advantages? In January of 1967 taxpayers of Los Angeles County were saved at least $43,000 in jail costs, according to Mr. Box's records. This saving was in addition to welfare payments to a defendant's family, income taxes he pays on earnings the defendant would otherwise lose, and other side benefits.

Perhaps the most liberal program I saw was in San Francisco.

John Ballestrasse, a bail bondsman, complained that "hippies" are being OR'ed left and right. He said 95 percent of them are arrested for narcotics violations. Those who peddle narcotics always have plenty of money and can well afford bail, he said, yet they are OR'ed.

I was in the office with Mr. Ballestrasse when he returned from jail with a young Negro he had bailed. The Negro had been "arrested for loitering," said Mr. Ballestrasse. "All he was doing was watching the hippies."

Incidentally, Mr. Ballestrasse's office was not the sleazy type of office out of which most bail bondsmen operate. It was well appointed and presided over by an attractive blonde.

The OR program has put some bail bondsmen out of business. It is operated by 12 VISTA workers under the federal antipoverty program, 25 law student volunteers, plus youngsters working in the Neighborhood Youth Corps.

Between Aug. 26, 1964, and Feb. 28, 1967, a total of 18,731 prisoners talked to staff members. Of these, 13,475 were processed, and favorable recommendations presented in 4,226 cases. And 3,196 were OR'ed.

This can be compared with Los Angeles, a far larger city, where between January, 1965, and January, 1967, only 4,954 applications were processed and 1,228 prisoners released.

Yet San Francisco's "failure to show" record is better than that of Los Angeles. For San Francisco's program shows 2 percent of those released did not come to court. In Los Angeles the rate was 2.9 percent.

And a spokesman for the San Francisco OR project asserts that bail bondsmen have a failure-to-show rate of 6 percent.

Cuyahoga County (Cleveland), with a population more than double that of San Francisco County, launched its bail-reform project in April, 1965.

In two years a total of 716 persons were released, with a failure-to-show rate of 1.9 percent. Of those released, 88 were charged with carrying concealed weapons, 76 for burglary, 65 for auto theft, 64 for forgery, 49 for poor-relief (welfare) fraud, and 43 for grand larceny.

No recent study has been made of the expansion of the Vera Institute's Manhattan Bail Project, which has successfully extended OR to the "little guy," Vera officials say. The best estimate is "over 100 cities."

It has also been found that those released on bail are more often acquitted or put on probation by judges than are those who stay in jail pending trial. This is partly because a free defendant can build a better defense. In jail he cannot help his lawyer find witnesses, and his ability to confer with his lawyer is limited.

Also, a judge may be more inclined to rule against a man who cannot raise bail or secure release under the new recognizance programs.

I found widespread national interest in the plan, but bail bondsmen and others who oppose it have successfully blocked it in hundreds of other communities.

Illinois is credited with coming up with one of the best systems. A recently passed state law permits a defendant to post 10 percent of the bail in cash with the court—the amount once paid to the bondsman. Under the new law the defendant will get back 90 percent of the money posted if he appears as required.

He may also post 100 percent in cash (also acceptable in most other states) or in securities. Or he may pledge double the bond in local real-estate holdings.

While this has curbed abuses by bail bondsmen, new problems have popped up.

In the spring of 1967 two Chicago judges—a Republican and a Democrat—were suspended by Chief Judge John S. Boyle. One of them, Louis W. Kizas, facing charges by the state attorney general as well as possible dismissal, resigned.

Judge Boyle said the two men had written hundreds of bonds at odd hours, sometimes when they should have been in their courtrooms, and often on weekends, at night, and during the early morning hours.

It was also charged that a "tight little group" of policemen and lawyers was involved.

The investigations indicate the need for more supervision and control in the system.

In other cities aggressive newspapers have uncovered other bond scandals. Yet too often abuses continue unchecked.

Meanwhile, many bail bondsmen make huge profits. They justify the old bonding system as "the American way" or the "free enterprise way."

I found other bail problems.

In some states motorists are permitted to post "bail" for traffic offenses, then forfeit the bail instead of appearing in court or paying the fine.

"This all-too-common procedure smacks of enforcement for revenue—a sad commentary on the integrity of our judicial system," one official of the Traffic Institute at Northwestern University writes.

As I found disparity in sentencing, so also I noted widespread inequities in bail—both in traffic and in criminal cases.

A study released in March of 1967 by the judicial council in the State of Washington shows, for example:

In Yakima County a motorist charged with a hit-and-run death must raise $1,100, while on Mercer Island the bail is $150, and in White Salmon $250.

"Following too close" requires a $44 payment in Yakima County and $10 in Union Gap.

Disregarding a flagman has a bail requirement of $104 in Clallam County and $10 on Mercer Island.

Efforts are being made to bring about more uniformity in Washington.

Bail reform is slowly gaining headway. More progress can be found here than in other court problems. Yet most courts still operate under the old system.

CHAPTER IX

If You Are Poor

On an average working day William P. Gibson sits in his corner office on the 11th floor of the Texaco Building in Houston. From his window he can look out on the city. The Astrodome gleams in the hot Texas sunshine.

Mr. Gibson's job is to ponder the thorny legal problems that confront a large corporation leasing land, drilling wells, and selling oil and natural gas.

Like many big-city lawyers, he had never had a reason to enter a criminal courtroom. That is, not until the day I met him at a preliminary hearing in a justice-of-the-peace court. Mr. Gibson was there to defend a young man charged with armed robbery.

Neither he nor his company had heard of the youth until a few days before. Yet, as a court-appointed defense attorney, Mr. Gibson was in court on company time. And the young man was charged with, of all things, holding up a rival firm's gas station.

How did this come about?

The story begins with the Supreme Court of the United States and its often criticized recent decisions on criminal law.

What the High Court has done, among other things, is to make it clear to the nation's state courts that "equal justice under law" is more than a nice slogan to chisel over the courthouse door. It is now a mandate.

In 1963 the court held (*Gideon* v. *Wainwright*) that a man is entitled to legal representation whether he can afford a lawyer or not. The High Court reasoned that "any person hailed into court who is too poor to hire a lawyer cannot be assured a fair trial unless counsel is provided for him. This seems an obvious truth."

It explained that states spend millions of dollars to "establish machinery to try defendants accused of crime." Every man who can afford to hires the best lawyer he can get when charged with a crime. "The government hires lawyers to prosecute." Thus lawyers must be considered "necessities, not luxuries" in the United States.

Yet this position, I found, is still opposed by some police, prosecutors, and those unfamiliar with the field of criminal law, who see it as another way to raise taxes, take business from private law firms, or move toward socialism or worse.

Those who defend providing lawyers to the poor point out that the Sixth Amendment to the United States Constitution states: "In all criminal prosecutions, the accused shall enjoy the right to . . . have the assistance of counsel for his defense."

Too often when judges comply with the Supreme Court mandate, methods of compliance circumvent the court's intent.

Take the young Negro arrested in a neighbor's apartment in the building in New York City. He entered the apartment through a window from a fire escape. Police charged him with burglary. On the surface it looked like an open-and-shut case.

When he got his day in court, the judge asked him if he had a lawyer. The youth said no, so a member of the public defender's staff was assigned. The defender took the youth aside and in a brief conference told the young man, "I can get you off on a misdemeanor [less serious crime], and the judge will probably give you a break if you plead guilty." The lawyer made almost no effort to find out the facts.

The next thing the young man knew he was pronounced guilty. While he sat in jail for three weeks for a presentence investigation, his mother entered the office of Henry B. Rothblatt, widely known Bronx lawyer, and asked for help.

Mr. Rothblatt checked the record and found that the judge had not advised the youth he had a right to hire his own lawyer. Nor had he been told he could have a postponement to hire that lawyer. Mr. Rothblatt also contended that the youth was not in the apartment to commit burglary. Rather, he said, he was on a secret visit to his girl friend, who was afraid to tell her mother or the police the truth.

"The judge," said Mr. Rothblatt, "had no choice but to set the conviction aside. The young man was obviously denied effective counsel. It cannot be just nominal: Counsel must be effective. It is clear that the courts are responsible for the competency of the counsel they assign."

There long has been a shortage of competent criminal lawyers. And as I traveled I found that the recent Supreme Court rulings have made this shortage even more acute by increasing the need for lawyers at least tenfold.

To many the work remains "unclean" compared with corporate law, and the pay is low. Only attorneys retained by professional criminals and a few name lawyers like F. Lee Bailey of Boston, who are hired by the wealthy when accused of murder or some other serious crime, find the field really profitable.

Further, the criminal process is exceedingly complicated. A man caught up in it—whether guilty or not—feels bewildered and alone.

He faces investigation; arrest; police questioning; possible publicity in the press, financial chaos at home, and loss of his job; jail unless he can raise bail; a preliminary hearing before a minor-court judge; the grand jury (in some states); arraignment before another judge; strong prosecution accusations and arguments couched in unfamiliar legal jargon, along with the strange and seemingly stilted formalism of the court procedure; sometimes an indifference or disdain toward him as a human being; witnesses who swear to his guilt—sometimes falsely; and a skeptical judge or jury.

If he enters a guilty plea, it may be the result of a plea-bargaining session which merely served expediency—saving the court's time. Or he may be found guilty by a jury—in rare cases unjustly.

In either case, he then faces a sentence that too often does not rehabilitate him. He can appeal to a series of higher state and federal courts—if he has the money or can convince a judge that he is entitled to free counsel for the appeal.

Without a lawyer that defendant may have little hope of justice in such a complex system.

The system could, of course, be simplified. But at present this seems unlikely.

Under the Supreme Court rulings, free counsel to the indigent is the only solution. It is provided in several ways.

In urban areas I found that the public-defender system, which can best be described as a parallel system to the prosecutor's office, is growing in popularity. At last count 272 agencies are operating in the nation's 3,100 counties.

Many are tax-supported. Others operate as charitable agencies known as legal-aid societies (usually the name for the 398 agencies that handle civil cases for the poor).

These charitable agencies are often criticized. Ellery E. Cuff, when public defender of Los Angeles County, put it this way:

> While it is true that a legal aid organization may have one or two highly capable and experienced men at the top, the individuals destined to carry the brunt of the workload are young attorneys who are starting out and who will be affiliated with the organization for only a short period of time. A new lawyer is hardly qualified to meet career men steeped in the art of criminal trial work, such as are found in [some large city] prosecutors' offices.
>
> Experience aside, most legal aid organizations suffer from a chronic lack of funds; certainly few such organizations can afford to maintain a staff of skilled investigators—a growing practice of defender offices.

Ironically, this reporter heard similar complaints about many of the public defenders' offices around the nation.

In Philadelphia, for example, I watched several public defenders at work in night court. All were pleasant, conscientious young men. In a few years they will undoubtedly become skilled trial lawyers. But they were obviously doing their clients more harm than good.

One was shy, inarticulate, and badly bullied by the magistrate. Every three or four minutes he had a new client assigned to him. After hurried, whispered conferences with them, he would stand before the magistrate and argue their cases.

Some were charged with felonies (serious offenses) and would have another chance in a higher court. For them this was the preliminary-hearing step in the judicial process.

But many others were accused of only misdemeanors. The magistrate would hear the argument and then, if they were found guilty, fine them or send them to jail, and enter their names on the criminal record.

In each case the young defender held a lawbook and leafed through it—like a weekend handyman trying to find out how to repair a faulty air conditioner or television set.

Later, when I interviewed the young lawyer, he told me he was just five months out of school. I found a similar pattern across the country, with many a defender's office simply a do-it-yourself training ground for would-be trial lawyers.

Assigning inexperienced men is supposed to satisfy the "law" and make the client believe he is getting "justice."

These beginners are often assigned to lower courts because they "can't do too much harm there," I was told.

The federal antipoverty program is providing some funds for legal defense of the poor in criminal cases, although these lawyers normally deal in civil matters.

In some 2,700 of the nation's 3,100 counties, judges simply appoint a local lawyer when a defendant cannot afford one.

I have watched this system in operation. Some appointed lawyers are both skilled and conscientious. But all too often the judge, knowing he must appoint an attorney to satisfy the higher courts in case of later appeal, points his finger at the nearest available lawyer.

This may either be a young and inexperienced man hoping for such an assignment or a skilled attorney who figures his time is worth $35 or $40 an hour and wonders why the judge is picking on him.

Often as not, this skilled lawyer spends five minutes whispering in a corner of the courtroom with his "client," then—without any investigation in the man's behalf—offers to plead him guilty.

Judge Temple Driver, a noted judge from Witchita Falls, Tex., sums it up for much of the nation when he says, "Appointed counsel can be about the same as no counsel at all."

Norman G. Kittel, of the department of political science at Wisconsin State University, opposes assigned counsel for other reasons, the "foremost" being the "dependence created by this means of appointment."

In June, 1967, he wrote in the *Legal Aid Briefcase,* the magazine published by the National Legal Aid and Defender Association:

> Attorneys appointed by trial judges cannot represent the accused with the single-minded devotion and independence necessary to an adequate defense. The American legal system is an adversary system requiring a determined partisan as a defense attorney. Counsel appointed by the trial judge is forced to consider his relations with the judge throughout the handling of his cases. To do otherwise is to risk his source of livelihood.

Some cities operate with a combination of systems. They may depend upon public defenders or legal aid for run-of-the-court cases. They select name lawyers from the trial bar for cases that catch the attention of the press and public.

Whatever the system, there is a growing shortage of competent criminal trial lawyers. Because of recent Supreme Court rulings—especially the decision that says children, for the first time, are entitled to lawyers—I found a great deal of concern over this shortage.

The National Council of Juvenile Court Judges, in its newsletter, put it this way:

> The right to counsel raises for juvenile courts a question with which criminal courts have been dealing since the Gideon decision: Where will lawyers be found to represent the juvenile from an indigent family who requests counsel?
>
> Certainly the right to counsel means—as the [Gault] decision indicates—the right to [have] counsel assigned by the court without cost if desired and if there is an inability to pay for legal services. Otherwise two systems of justice develop: one for affluent people

who utilize lawyers; the other for poor.... If this does not put a price tag on justice, it at least renders justice unequal and therefore discriminatory.

Of all the defender systems in the United States, it is the Houston plan that is most often cited as the one with the greatest promise.

The criminal bar, until this plan was launched there some two years ago, was made up of between 100 and 150 lawyers of varying skill. Too many drifted into criminal practice because they couldn't make it elsewhere.

Now, under the supervision of the Houston Legal Foundation, all lawyers under 50—and this means roughly 2,800 of the 4,000 lawyers in Harris County—are appointed as counsel in criminal court. This regardless of their normal practice: auto-accident cases, real estate, corporate law, patents, tax matters, or a dozen other specialties.

The foundation is headed by Judge Sam Johnson. The Ford Foundation has split the $250,000 annual costs with five local groups.

Among other things, it supplies lawyers with an investigative staff—something most volunteer systems lack. And for the lawyer inexperienced in criminal court, experts in criminal law provide instructions or even a cram course in criminal-court procedure.

Equally important, most Legal Foundation lawyers work in pairs.

Mr. Gibson's partner (in the case mentioned at the beginning of this chapter) is Louis J. Andrews, an experienced civil trial lawyer. This is Mr. Andrews's second case since the program was launched.

Because lawyers in other cities who had heard about the Houston plan expressed skepticism, I told no one in Houston that I planned to watch foundation lawyers in action. I even picked the courtroom at random, and found Mr. Andrews and Mr. Gibson at work.

They were as skilled as any public defender I have seen, and probably better than the average trial lawyer hired by a client.

Later I asked them about the program and their role in it. Mr. Gibson's corporation supports it. So does Mr. Andrews's. Their enthusiasm was obvious.

"I want to give [the young man] the same representation he would get if he were a paying client," asserts Mr. Andrews.

The young man gets better-than-average help from Mr. Gibson because this corporate-lawyer-turned-defense-attorney is determined to prove to his company that he can handle cases not normally in his area of law.

But benefits go far beyond helping the poor find justice in the criminal courts of Houston. Judge Johnson puts it this way:

> This program has helped lawyers understand their basic obligation as lawyers. Originally there were three professions—the ministry, medicine, and the law. A person called to one of these professions expected to make sacrifices.
>
> This has been largely put aside, until now. Most attorneys have looked on the law as a profitmaking enterprise. As a business. Our plan has helped bring about a reawakening. Lawyers are beginning to understand they have a basic obligation to mankind.
>
> And attorneys are taking pride in what they are doing. For many who practice corporate law, this is the first time they have had clients with eyes and arms and legs—alive and breathing. This has been a real awakening for them.

It has also resulted in better performances on the part of judges and prosecutors—a total upgrading of the Houston system of justice.

Now the word gets around quickly if judges or prosecutors are lazy or incompetent. For they must face a cross section of the entire bar—including some of the highest-paid corporate lawyers in the Southwest. This keeps them alert and busy, Judge Johnson asserts.

This growing involvement of all lawyers in criminal law has also helped stimulate interest among members of the bar in crime legislation for the first time, he says.

He adds that for the first time many lawyers begin to understand that the people who end up in criminal court are fellow human beings.

This new view may help improve jails, the state corrections system, and other court-related agencies and institutions, he says.

"It has already resulted in the awakening of the law schools here and elsewhere to the need to look at criminal law and the whole problem of legal ethics," he adds.

The Houston plan is one solution. What of the others?

Many lawyers and judges interviewed feel the public-defender system is the best solution to the right-to-counsel problem. Yet they also raise questions.

"What kind of lawyer can you hire for $7,000 or $8,000 a year?" is a complaint often heard around the nation.

"Our county can't afford a defender's office," is another common argument.

Which may be a strong reason for adopting the Houston plan.

Judge Johnson estimates that an adequate public-defender system in Houston could easily cost $1 million a year or more, since it would parallel the Harris County prosecutor's office in staff.

The Legal Foundation operates on $250,000 a year. In addition to this, as in many sections of the nation, lawyers are paid a token amount from county funds when they appear in court. In Houston this amounts to $25 a day.

The real saving, he quickly adds, comes from the thousands of dollars in free time donated by the high-priced lawyers who serve under the plan.

There is little question that a public-defender system is costly—although in almost no cities does it have a staff comparable to that of the prosecutor's office.

Los Angeles County is credited with the first defender's office (operating as it is known today) in the United States. That office was created in 1914.

A half-century later (the 1964-65 fiscal year), the county budgeted $1,180,992 for the public defender. And that was before the full impact of the federal Supreme Court rulings was felt.

Last year more than twice that amount—$2.5 million—was

budgeted. And the staff has jumped from 66 to 166 lawyers in a four-year period. It includes 15 investigators and 32 clerical workers, plus an executive assistant with business experience, pushing the total to 214.

To make sure first-class lawyers are signed on, the pay has been improved. The beginning lawyer (there are 47 young lawyers) is paid $10,000 a year. As quickly as possible he is jumped to the rating of Deputy Public Defender II, which pays $14,800. There are 54 men in this category. Twenty-nine others have advanced to Category III, which pays $18,500. And 27 are in Category IV, earning $20,500 a year.

This is more than judges make in many of the states surveyed by this newspaper. It means young men can sign on without feeling they will short-change their families. And it helps assure the office of finding young men like Peter Paul Gamer, a recent graduate of Harvard Law School.

I watched him handle three lengthy preliminary hearings before Judge David J. Aisenson. He won two out of three for his clients.

Later, when I interviewed Mr. Gamer, I learned he had gained some courtroom experience while a student at Harvard under a new program in the municipal courts of Boston.

Los Angeles is also pioneering in selecting clients who do not usually fall under the classification of hard-core poor. For example, a man earning $10,000 a year but who has 10 children and stacks of unpaid bills may be as much in need of a free attorney, in the eyes of the Los Angeles public defender's office, as a Watts Negro.

Miami (Dade County) also has a public defender's office. With a population of one-sixth that of Los Angeles, Dade County has only nine assistant public defenders—one-sixteenth the number found in the West Coast city. And with a top salary of $8,800 a year, Miami defenders may maintain a private law practice on the side.

Because of a lack of funds, Miami's defender has no investigators, says Robert L. Koeppel, who has held the elective office 10 years.

Despite the existence of a public defender's office, the court still appoints the defense attorney in a capital case. I interviewed one of these, Irwin Block, who says an appointed lawyer is paid up to $500. He was defending a young Negro in a rape case.

"I've already spent $350 of that for the investigation," he said. "And the trial hasn't even started."

This is the kind of problem that bothers men like F. Lee Bailey, who gained national recognition in his defense of Dr. Sam Sheppard in the second trial in Cleveland. Mr. Bailey places great emphasis on investigation. When a man's life is at stake, he contends, $50,000 isn't too much to spend on that part of the case alone.

In Cook County, Ill., where the population is roughly five-sixths that of Los Angeles, the defender's office operates with only a quarter of the attorneys—39. On August 1, 1967, that figure increased to 42, says Defender Gerald W. Getty, who handled the Speck murder case. He is also short on other staff, operating with four investigators and seven clerical workers.

Lawyers in the Chicago defender's office start at $7,200 a year and can work up to $15,600, he says—depending upon turnover at the top. Most are young men with limited trial experience.

Only 30 percent of defendants facing felony charges go to trial. The rest plead guilty under the plea-bargaining process described in Chapter X.

"Of the 30 percent we contest, we win about half," Mr. Getty says.

Oklahoma County, with a population of 545,000, has three full-time lawyers on the defender's staff. Don Anderson, who has a Phi Beta Kappa key, is paid $10,200 a year. Each of his two assistants earns $9,000.

The prosecutor's salary is over $15,000 a year, with 14 assistants receiving salaries up to $12,000, plus "three or four investigators," says Mr. Anderson. In what must be an understatement, he asserts his office could use "at least three more" defenders.

New Jersey's new public-defender system began operation

on July 1, 1967. The office has cabinet-level status and is appointed by the governor with advice and consent of the Senate for a five-year term.

The public defender has a deputy, assistant deputy, and office staff. He sets up regional offices in major urban areas.

The public defender may use his own legal staff or farm out work under contract to private law firms. In such cases, he retains supervision of cases. Previously lawyers volunteered for public-defender work. They may continue to do so, giving the public defender a pool of talent to draw on.

The public defender determines who is eligible for such defense aid. Previously the judge on the case made that determination. If a defendant cannot pay costs now but later becomes able to do so, the state can collect the value of services rendered.

There are no official estimates of the cost to the state, but expectation is it may run around $2 million for the first year. Cost of the system will be financed out of general state revenues.

Many of the recently opened defenders' offices operate, or had their start, through Ford Foundation grants and the formation of the National Defender Project of the National Legal Aid and Defender Association. The Ford Foundation's grants to the national defender projects totaled $6.1 million.

In the past five years, the number of defender offices has increased from roughly 100 to the present 272. Most have local matching funds.

One of the most recent was started up in Clarke County (Athens), Ga.—the first in the state. A full-time defender attorney is assisted by law students at the University of Georgia.

Similar programs have been under way for some time at other schools, and some have expired. The Wyoming Defender Aid Program was launched in 1965 in cooperation with the Wyoming bar and the University of Wyoming. Other cooperating schools include Boston University, the University of Chicago, University of Missouri, Stetson University, University of Virginia. In each the schools agreed to expand instruction in criminal defense.

Public defenders should be more skilled than those who represent the paying clients, says Junius L. Allison, executive director of the National Legal Aid and Defender Association. He points out: "These clients will always be poor, often confused, many times frightened by the 'law,' and inarticulate in telling their stories. A higher degree of interviewing skill and a greater amount of patience will be needed than usually required for private clients."

And many areas are slow to adopt a system of legal aid for the poor. Dean Russell N. Sullivan of the University of Illinois Law School notes that in his state there still are "many counties in which there is no public defender and no formalized method of securing counsel."

Seattle, Wash., remains one of the largest urban areas without a public-defender system.

In 1966 322 indigent defendants—carefully screened as to need by King County (Seattle) Superior Court judges—received appointed counsel.

These appointed lawyers are paid $75 for each day of trial as long as the total cost is less than $325. In first-degree murder trials and other serious or complicated cases the fee may be fixed higher by the court. Total cost in 1966, including 15 juvenile cases, reached $39,295.76, says Robert C. Wetherholt, the court administrator.

In Seattle there is interest but also some opposition—perhaps widespread—to a public-defender system, because it would increase city costs considerably. A defender would need a full-time staff, office space, furniture, and clerical help, it is pointed out.

Other states continue to back the old system of appointing lawyers to defend the poor.

Maine has "many former county prosecutors who are out of office and willing to accept the assignment" of defending indigents, says Superior Court Judge Thomas E. Delahanty of Auburn.

He adds that if there is a shortcoming, it is that "counsel for the indigent feel they have an unusually heavy burden . . . and are deeply concerned with the complete protection of the individual rights of the accused as well as protecting themselves from a charge [after the case is tried] of incompetency."

This may result, he contends, in the appointed lawyer's going to trial even when he might advise a paying client to plead guilty because the evidence is strong against him.

Regardless of the system, the Supreme Court ruling is being circumvented in some areas—this through the defendant's waiving his right to a lawyer.

Some officials, like Judge J. Skelly Wright of the Federal Court of Appeals in Washington, D.C., wonder if the same kind of pressure used on defendants to confess may not be used to get the defendant to waive his right to an attorney.

The system also falters when less serious crimes are involved. Even the best defender systems are unable to staff every case in every courtroom—although I found some cities (San Francisco, for example) providing counsel for minors in traffic court.

And too often defenders and appointed counsel enter the case too late—after the defendant has been in jail for days or weeks, and has had a preliminary hearing. By then the defendant may have lost his job, and his family is probably on welfare. The defense lawyer has missed the "discovery" opportunity of the pretrial hearing, where the prosecution attempts to convince the judge that it has enough evidence to put the man on trial. It is at this point that the defense lawyer should be able to find out how strong the case against his client is.

While interest has been growing in the criminal field, the civil area is not being neglected either.

It is easy for the poor to find a lawyer who will take a case that will yield a large judgment. This is usually in the auto-accident field, where the lawyer takes the case on a contingency basis—if he wins he gets a third or more of any settlement or judgment.

But what does the newcomer to Chicago do when he finds himself trapped into paying three times the going rate of interest under a contract with a Shylock used-car dealer—and the car probably ready to fall apart?

There are many lawyers who say they will take a case without charge when an indigent defendant walks in the door.

Interviews indicate that lawyers today take few free cases voluntarily. But there is great variation from region to region and lawyer to lawyer.

Albert A. Ehrenzweig, a professor of law at the University of California, wrote after reading the *Monitor* series, telling his own story which makes this point.

"When I came to this country 28 years ago," he writes, "I was penniless, did not speak English, had to support wife, children, and parents, and was unable to use anything that I had learned and done as a judge and law teacher in my first life. And yet I was permitted and encouraged to rejoin my own profession for a life in freedom and dignity. I knew, I knew deep in my heart, that there was no other country in the world in which this could have happened."

When a moving firm "cheated us out of our last belongings" shortly after arrival here, "I was directed to a fine lawyer."

"'Sure,' [the lawyer] said, 'you have an airtight claim, and I shall take your case, but you will understand, I must have one hundred dollars as a retainer.'"

Professor Ehrenzweig adds, in an article published by the *California Law Review*, "I did *not* understand.

"Would he not get his fees from the defendant, as he would anywhere else in the world? I did not have the hundred dollars. . . . I did not sue."

He contends that even if he had sued and won, "I would not have been made whole for I had to pay my own lawyer." His research shows that "as early as 40 years ago, the Massachusetts Judicial Council pleaded for reform, asking: 'On what principle of justice can a plaintiff wrongfully run down on a public highway recover his doctor's bill but not his lawyer's bill?'"

Then he answers his own question, and that of the Massachusetts Judicial Council, by explaining:

"How often have I heard my [law] colleagues' chiding: 'You simply have not grasped the American sense of fairness. It is bad enough to see one lose who in justice should have prevailed. To make him pay the winner's counsel would add injustice to injustice, would mean stepping on one who is down, and it would make honest men unwilling to go to court, be it as plaintiffs or as defendants.' "

To which he replies, using the words of Sir Arthur Goodhart, ". . . if justice is so much a matter of luck, it hardly seems worthwhile to have courts and lawyers; it would be cheaper, and certainly less dilatory, to spin a coin."

To some extent traditional legal-aid societies have helped fill this gap—but even these agencies have not really done the job.

Legal-aid societies in large cities often have been located inconveniently for those they are designed to help. The trend now—especially under the antipoverty program—has changed to put these offices in the neighborhoods where the poor live.

These traditional legal-aid societies have also been very selective in choosing their cases to avoid being overrun by indigent applicants. These societies are also selective for fear of treading on the toes of private lawyers, who complain that the legal-aid people are taking business away from them.

The civil-law field really began blossoming with the arrival of the Office of Economic Opportunity's antipoverty program. Currently its budget is $47 million, says Earl Johnson, who heads the legal-services program.

Antipoverty legal offices have moved into areas of law—such as divorces and other family problems—which have been avoided by the traditional legal-aid groups.

Wisconsin has one of the more interesting programs. In the 26 sparsely populated northern counties where a half-million people live a "judicare" program has been launched. There 37,000 families with annual incomes of less than $3,000 a year have had no formal legal aid available to them. They either went without legal help or asked lawyers to take their cases without pay.

Now they can hire the lawyer of their choice and have the fee paid by the government upon presentation of a wallet-sized card. The fee is computed on the basis of $16 an hour, or 80 percent of the minimum local bar fee schedule, whichever is lower. Without special permission, lawyers must charge less than $300. Most have kept the figure under $100. And no attorney is allowed to bill more than $3,000 in any one year.

The advantages, according to those who support the program, include allowing the person using the service to feel he is not singled out and getting less than the best possible legal help.

The need is so great, however (it is estimated that there are between 14 and 20 million potential legal cases a year throughout the United States), that the OEO is concentrating on changing laws—local, state, and national—that affect the poor.

This may come as a shock to some citizens, for it is not a widely publicized fact. The law, explains Mr. Johnson, has been on the side of slum landlords, greedy moneylenders, and others who exploit the indigent. So the OEO hopes to push the balance back toward the middle of the scale.

New legal areas keep cropping up as a result. In New York, for example, a federal judge has held that a student being disciplined by a public school has the right to counsel!

And the government now is supporting suits against itself in the field of welfare. Public-aid recipients are gaining new legal rights.

In Philadelphia the occupants of one apartment building scheduled for urban renewal demolition found that there were no plans to replace their old building with low-income housing. So they went to court, had the building declared a historic monument, and continue to live there while urban renewal goes on around them.

Extending legal aid to the poor—both civil and criminal—is a growing field. But many assert it is in keeping with the philosophy of individual rights.

It was Judge Learned Hand who said, "If we are to keep our democracy, there must be one commandment: Thou shall not ration justice."

CHAPTER X

The Sentencing Wonderland

It was after 1 A.M. in a darkened tire store when Chicago police pointed their revolvers at Leo W—— and told him to come out quietly.

Court records describe him as 30, white, a skilled tradesman, and three-time "loser"—always for burglary.

In 1955 he was put on probation with no jail time. In 1961 he got probation again. Two years later he was sentenced to the county jail for a year.

On trial for the fourth time while I visited the Cook County Criminal Court, he admitted his guilt and was sentenced to five years' probation with the first six months in the county jail. (The law says he could have been sent up for from one to life.)

About the same time Leo W—— was caught in the tire store, another young man, Archie S——, 26, a Negro, was picked up by Chicago police in a stolen car.

Also a three-time "loser," always for auto theft, he too was given straight probation on his first two trips to court. The third time he "borrowed" a car he was sentenced to one to four years in prison. (The law says he could have been sent up for a maximum of 10 years.)

On this, his fourth time in court, Archie S—— was sent to prison for a two-to-four-year stretch—four to eight times longer than Leo W—— will serve for burglary, an offense usually considered more serious than auto theft.

The same judge handed down both sentences.

Not too many blocks away other men accused of burglary—and equally guilty—had charges reduced by a deputy state's attorney to petty theft or criminal damage to property—offenses classified in Illinois as less serious crimes.

In rural Illinois counties judges were sentencing burglars with less criminal experience than Leo W—— to 5, 10, or more years in prison.

What happens in Illinois is typical of most states. Nationally I found the arrest-jail-bail-trial-sentencing-probation-or-prison-parole system to be a grim wonderland. And it can make justice seem a sorry joke.

Except for police practices, sentencing may be the most flawed of all. More often than not it is based on tradition rather than on reason, and on whim rather than on fact.

Across the nation I asked prison officials what they considered the most pressing court-related problem at the prison. "Disparity in sentencing," they replied. I asked them for examples—cases which involved roughly comparable circumstances. They offered several.

Take Dave ——, a young man from northern Wyoming. Dave is serving from 10 to 12 years in the Wyoming State Penitentiary at Rawlings for a $7.50 armed robbery.

John ——, who committed the same crime and got $124 in the southern part of the state, was sentenced to two to three years in the prison.

"A crime like robbery shocks the people in northern Wyoming," says Warden Leonard Meacham. "Those who live along U.S. 30 in southern Wyoming are a lot more blasé about it."

In Minnesota the State Legislature has established the penalty for aggravated robbery (where a weapon has been used) at 0 to 20 years.

Jack Young, superintendent of the reformatory in St. Cloud, reports Peter S—— was sentenced to five years in a Minneapolis court. Yet Roger P——, of Duluth, is serving 20 years for the same offense—although this can be balanced out by the parole system. Minnesota judges set maximum, not minimum, sentences.

Yet in the majority of states the trial judge, who probably has little or no information about the defendant or the correctional institutions, has final say. The President's commission reports: "In most jurisdictions today the trial judge's sentence cannot be adjusted by an appellate court if it is within the statutory limits, no matter how harsh or arbitrary it appears to be."

At the Georgia Industrial Institute at Alto, I found prisoners between 14 and 19 years old. Many were first offenders.

James W—— was sentenced to life from a court in Taylor County, after being charged with rape. Harvey J—— is serving three years for the same offense from Paulding County. David J—— was accused of *attempted* rape in Bibb County and is in for three years. Elmer E——, from Baldwin County, is also serving time for attempted rape—17 years.

Yet about 100 miles east, in Greenville, S.C., almost nobody is charged with rape, according to B. O. Tomason Jr., the county solicitor. He asserts that very few grown girls or women are really raped, and that in most cases the act is the result of the girl's leading the man on and then regretting it later.

In the Georgia institute John B—— is serving six years for auto theft in Richmond County. Kenneth B——, sentenced for stealing two cars, in Dougherty County, is in for a third of that—two years.

Don B—— of Fulton County is serving two years for stealing a car. And Arthur W—— is serving six years for stealing a car in Muscogee County.

Melvin M——, also from Muscogee County, was sentenced to 15 years for burglary. John B——, of Glynn County, is serving 10 years. And a Wayne County judge sent Jackie C—— to prison for one year for the same offense.

But Melvin B—— is a real "winner" among the "losers." Found guilty of two robberies, one rape, and one auto theft, he was sentenced to only three years in prison.

Says Georgia's State Corrections Director, Asa D. Kelley Jr.: "One of our great needs is uniform sentencing. It varies from judge to judge and from rural to urban communities."

Sitting in courtrooms across the nation, checking jail and prison records, and interviewing judges, lawyers, police officials, and prisoners, I found:

• The United States has merely graduated from the hanging tree, whipping post, and town-square stocks to ugly prisons. There society hides its problem children behind thick granite walls.

This has done little to solve the crime problem.

"We put a boy in a training school and hope something nice will happen to him," says Paul W. Keve, who heads Minnesota's Corrections Department. "We hope that by some magic he will be transformed into a better person. Then we turn him loose a year later and he gets in trouble again, and everyone wants to know why the institution has failed."

Too many prisons and so-called training schools usually provide a system of rewards, punishment, and regimentation that tends to dehumanize the inmate. It is hardly designed to rehabilitate him.

• Criminal justice often involves more retribution than rehabilitation (although it is rehabilitation that society likes to talk about). Many judges, prosecutors, and other court officials interviewed agree with Chicago's Robert D. Boyle, deputy chief of the criminal division of the Cook County state's attorney's office, who says, "We believe we should take from the defendant what he owes society."

• No one, not even the best judge, really knows how long to sentence a man to prison or whether probation is the best answer.

He does not know, at the time the crime was committed, whether the man was hostile or hungry, drunk or discouraged, resentful or retarded, goaded by a greedy wife or by a desire to get something for nothing.

Nor does he know if just the shock of being caught will bring about reform in one man while 10 years in prison will only make another man more hostile.

Judge Elvin J. Brown of Norman, Okla., one of the nation's leading state trial judges, told me: "I never feel so inadequate as when I'm passing sentence. I don't think the courts and judges should have anything to do with sentencing. I don't have any way of knowing how long [the man who stands before me] should go to the penitentiary."

Says the President's commission:

> The difficulty of the sentencing decision is due in part to the fact that criminal law enforcement has a number of varied and often conflicting goals: the rehabilitation of offenders, the isolation of offenders who pose a threat to community safety, the discouragement of potential offenders, the expression of the community's condemnation of the offender's conduct, and the reinforcement of the values of law abiding citizens.

How do sentences come about?

"It depends upon how a judge feels about a crime," explains Mr. Boyle, of Cook County. "Some judges are hard on those charged with serious crimes against the person, like rape and robbery. Another judge—he would be in the minority—may be incensed when property rights are violated. So he may be tough on men charged with burglary and auto theft and lenient on those accused of rape and robbery."

Mr. Boyle might have added that decisions are sometimes also based on the judge's reaction to the way a man is dressed, his age, the length of his hair, the color of his skin, his nationality, or even his religion.

Paul W. Keve of Minnesota points out that knowing a policeman can often help a defendant.

"I have seen policemen come into court and complain on one day that the court is too easy on criminals," he says. "A few days later, when someone the officer knows is in trouble, he will be back in court asking the judge to give the fellow a break because he has problems at home."

The public reaction to crime is often the same—outrage when a stranger commits an act but understanding when it is a son or neighbor who has stolen the car or broken into the building. Knowing the judge or prosecutor can help. And where judges owe their jobs to political leaders, a telephone call can change things.

Unfortunately, there are too many judges who pass sentence

according to how the wind is blowing from a press or public angered by a crime.

Justice William Grimes, recently elevated from the trial bench to the New Hampshire Supreme Court, points out that the founding fathers said the American system of justice should, among other things, protect the minority from the aroused majority. It should bring reason and balance to impassioned, emotional situations.

"The citizens have no idea what a sentence should be," adds Chicago's Mr. Boyle. "There are no guidelines to sentencing, other than statutory limitations. So we try to figure out the sentence based on our experience."

What Mr. Boyle means is that prosecutors and experienced criminal court judges have a better idea of what is "fair" in length of time for a given crime than do angry citizens. This sense of fairness is in answer to complaints about disparity—not in terms of rehabilitation.

In several states, especially in the Midwest and Southwest, I found judges rely heavily on the prosecutor's recommendation. This is a dangerous practice, especially when a prosecutor is trying to build a record so that he can run for higher office.

• As I toured the country, I was told that when judges pass sentence, they often do not realize what a prison sentence means to the man convicted.

In several states judges are becoming aware of this shortcoming. Last summer, reports New York State Commissioner of Correction Paul D. McGinnis, judges in his state visited prisons.

More judges should do this and, during the visits, ask hard questions and demand honest answers.

• Both prosecutors and defense lawyers can influence the outcome of a trial, the sentence, and other court business by "getting next to a judge."

Influence can be so subtle that sometimes the judge is unaware of it.

Judge Brown notes, for example, that now and then a lawyer will casually mention that he (Judge Brown) would make a good prospect for the federal bench.

"I feel kind of unclean when that happens," he says.

In Los Angeles County all one-judge courts are being phased out. But in two areas, San Fernando and Glendale, I found members of the bar fighting to prevent that from happening.

"The local lawyers love to have a one-judge court," says Andrew L. Schultz, executive assistant administrator of the Los Angeles Superior Court. "They set the judge up on a pedestal. They invite him to all the functions. They honor him and bow to him. They know this personal relationship or friendship gives them an edge over outside lawyers, and they get continuances and other advantages when they want them."

• Influence works the other way, too. Nearly all of the lawyers I interviewed asked me not to use their names "because it would hurt my clients before the judge." The point is clear. Lawyers felt if they made honest criticisms of a judge or court they could not get a fair trial. One New York City lawyer summed it up when he said, "Look, I can tell you a lot, but you want me to let you use my name. You're asking me to crucify myself and my clients."

• Unfairness on the part of judges, the inequities caused by police and prosecutors in selection of who is charged with a crime and who goes free, and disparity in sentencing all hinder rehabilitation.

Several corrections officials interviewed agree with Warden Meacham of Wyoming, who told me:

"We have men in our prison who shouldn't be here. They could be better handled by local community resources—mental health clinics and welfare departments, for example.

"Once a man leaves a community for prison, rehabilitation becomes increasingly difficult," Warden Meacham says. "Disparity in sentencing causes bitterness and makes it harder to work with these fellows.

"When he gets out, the community will shun him. I'm an

ex-policeman, and I know that he will become a regular target for police investigations when he gets out. You don't check on the mayor or minister when a crime is committed.

"So he gets discouraged and says, 'I've got the name so I might as well have the game,' and winds up back in the institution."

• The recidivism rate (number of men who go back to prison) is high, although I found it as difficult to get reliable figures from prisons as to get them from police, prosecutors, and judges.

There are estimates that 70 percent of those who are jailed as young men will spend more time in jail or prison. I found that usually the prisons report from 40 to 60 percent recidivism. But variations in record-keeping, sometimes to obscure the truth, make most statistics questionable.

Whatever the figure, it is clear that the present court system isn't doing its job since even competent judges admit it.

• The cost of this faulty system of justice is unbelievably high, considering what the citizen gets for his money.

"On any given day [the nation's corrections system] is responsible for approximately 1.3 million offenders," reports the President's Commission on Law Enforcement and Administration of Justice.

"In the course of a year [this system] handles nearly 2.5 million [men, women, and children] and spends over a billion dollars doing so."

No one knows how much is paid out in welfare benefits to the families of these prisoners; how much is lost in income taxes, local sales taxes, property taxes, or in man-hours. But the figure is undoubtedly staggering.

• Arrest by local police or sheriff can have the same effect on a man and his family as conviction in court: this constitutes another "sentencing" inequity.

Take the case of a man in northwestern South Carolina.

He was arrested in connection with handling stolen goods. Though he was arrested on Monday, he swore he was not told of the charges against him until Tuesday. The warrant for his arrest was not signed till 4 P.M. Wednesday.

When he got out on bond (set at $5,000), he had to agree to pay the bondsman $400 at $25 a week. Even if acquitted, he will never get the $400 back.

The company for which he worked fired him. At last check he was unable to get a court hearing. Yet no one will hire him until his name is cleared. Friends have stopped talking to him, he says, and he is in tight financial straits, for the state unemployment office refuses to pay him because of the criminal charges pending against him.

There are similar men in the United States in jail or on bail and out of work. Even if they are eventually freed, future employers may well turn them down because of the arrest record.

The power society gives police is huge. How it is used has a direct effect on taxes, both in welfare and jail costs, and on the crime problem.

Too often the men selected to enforce the laws are of low caliber. The average small-town policeman is paid $5,000 a year. Yet he is often called upon to make decisions that would cause the highest-paid lawyers to spend sleepless nights.

And far too little is spent on the nation's 4,000-plus county and city jails. Many are dank and filthy.

And there are always the reports of innocent men going to jail. Sam P. McKenzie of Atlanta, considered by many to be one of nation's leading trial judges, had a Negro youth released after he had served almost a year in prison. (Another judge had sentenced him there.)

A white boy had accused the youth of committing an indecent act. A court-appointed lawyer, William Jessee, fought for months to get him free. The young Negro was working after school in a grocery store to save money to go to college and had never been in trouble.

Judge McKenzie says it was subsequently discovered that it was a case of mistaken identity.

Every year newspapers print accounts of men who have served time in prison for crimes others have committed.

Innocent men have gone to prison because someone lied on the witness stand. The President's Commission on Law Enforcement and Administration of Justice asserts that perjury is widespread. It also asserts that the requirements to prove perjury are so complicated that perjury convictions are hard to obtain.

It is significant to note that the commission urges abolition of the rigid two-witness and direct-evidence rules of common law that must be followed in order to prove a statement false.

Thoughtful judges point out that policemen, prosecutors, and judges too often do not see those ensnared in the system of justice as fellow men and women. As in prison, they become mere numbers, or, as one law professor put it, "simply blanks."

The laws also are badly flawed.

"We must redefine sections of the criminal law," says Hans W. Mattick, associate director of the Center for Studies in Criminal Justice at the University of Chicago Law School.

"A whole series of offenses that presently clog the machinery of criminal justice from police through parole can be handled by alternative means.

"I'm talking about drunkenness, traffic offenders, narcotics addicts, vagrancy, gambling, and private sexual conduct between consenting adults.

"These may well be better handled by such agencies as the department of welfare, department of public health, and the bureau of streets and highways. And this would free the police to deal with serious crime."

"We have too many old laws that don't mean a thing," says Judge J. Edward Lumbard, of the United States Circuit Court of Appeals in New York. "Legislatures keep passing laws on top of laws."

This, too, leads to inequities.

A report by the Colorado Research Council points out that in that state

A person convicted of murder in the first degree, if the sentence of death is not imposed, becomes eligible for parole after serving

10 years; but a person convicted of second-degree murder, a lesser grade of murder, may have to serve 15, 20, or more years before becoming so eligible. The maximum penalty for destroying a house with fire is 20 years; with explosives, 10 years. The maximum sentence for stealing a dog is 10 years; and for killing the dog, six months and a $500 fine.

A system known as plea bargaining is common in many larger cities. Too often it involves the kind of haggling that goes on in a used-car lot. It takes place in secret in the judge's chambers with the prosecutor and defense attorney bidding against each other.

In Chicago when a judge hears the defense lawyer ask for a "conference," he can assume that the lawyer means a plea-bargaining session. It happens every day.

In a typical case it worked this way:

The prosecutor recommended a one-to-three-year prison term for a man involved in a laundry-company swindle. The defense lawyer said it was too high. After wheeling and dealing the man was given five years' probation with 90 days in the county jail. And that was delayed so that the man could take part in his daughter's wedding a few weeks later.

The judge lectured the man and warned him that he could be sentenced to 10 years for the crime. But it was all cut and dried—decided behind the closed doors. The lecture and warning were simply for appearance's sake and to fulfill the law.

While the United States Constitution guarantees a man the right to a trial by jury, experienced Chicago defense lawyers warn their clients that demanding a trial can be foolhardy.

Says Stanton Bloom of the Cook County Public Defender's office:

> A man may be offered a 1-to-3-year term [by the prosecutor with the judge's approval] if he pleads guilty.
>
> If he demands a trial before the bench [the judge] and is found guilty, he can expect a 2-to-5-year sentence. If a jury finds him guilty, the prison term will probably be 4 to 8 years.
>
> That's the penalty imposed for taking up the court's time.

States with better court systems frown on plea bargaining. Superior Court Judge James L. Reid of Portland, Me., says he is certain there is "no case in Maine where this is done." One reason the practice can be avoided, he added, is that "we have no appreciable backlog of unfinished business."

Sentencing is a controversial area. It has been suggested that sentencing boards, such as those found in California and Washington, may be one solution.

Some states use a system of review by higher courts. Yet Sol Rubin, of the National Council on Crime and Delinquency, asserts that "it at best achieves a small reduction of the most excessive sentences, but in no jurisdiction does it appear to have substantially altered sentencing patterns."

Other areas call judges together from time to time to discuss sentences, but Mr. Rubin contends they seldom "alter attitudes of judges, and they do not change sentencing systems at all."

"Requiring the judge to give the reason for his sentence is a device used in some jurisdictions," he adds. But he finds that this may simply lead to rationalization, rather than change.

He sees, as does the President's commission, a plan used by federal judges in eastern Michigan and also used by two other federal court districts as useful. There judges meet in the morning before getting involved in other court business, and discuss presentence reports.

But single-judge courts and those in large cities with many judges would find the system impractical, Mr. Rubin adds.

So he presents an interesting suggestion: He would have the Supreme Court of the United States act as it did in the case of school segregation and order the states—under the Fourteenth Amendment to the Constitution—to end sentencing inequities.

But this seems to be only part of the answer.

What is needed? This writer found confusion so great that it becomes clear that we should completely review the criminal process.

Should criminal laws be changed and simplified? Should we more carefully define what is crime and what is mental illness? The answer seems to be yes to both questions. It is up to our state legislatures to bring this about, but it will undoubtedly require strong citizen pressure.

And what of our methods of enforcing laws—should these be changed? Again the answer is yes.

Police should not have subtle sentencing power—holding men for days, weeks, or months in jail, only to have the case tossed out in court. We must work toward eliminating the disparity in the arrest stage of our criminal process as well as disparity in sentencing by judges. One man should not be freed at the whim of a policeman, and another charged and jailed when offenses are similar or identical.

If we are determined to let policemen decide who goes to court, then policemen should be better trained and more highly educated. And prosecutors, working full time, and judges should have greater interest in and control over this phase of the criminal process.

Policemen, prosecutors, and judges should have a great deal more understanding of the philosophy that underlies criminal law.

If our goal is really rehabilitation—a process that involves changing a man's way of thinking about himself, other men, and their lives and property—we should work toward that goal.

This means the law must be fair and applicable to all. That all policemen, prosecutors, judges, and juries are fair and honest. That in convicting and sentencing a man, we use fact and reason rather than emotion, tradition, or whim.

If we continue to depend on punishment to bring about change in the thinking of criminals, that punishment must be clearly defined, and it must serve some purpose. A man contemplating a crime must understand he will be institutionalized, and cannot get away with the crime—if he is caught—by paying someone off or by making a deal with an overbusy prosecutor or judge.

At the same time, judges must have more information when they pass sentence. It must be accurate, useful information, and judges must be trained to understand it and to understand what a sentence to a correctional institution means to the man, his family, and to society.

Far too many judges turn to some overworked probation officer in this—a man who more often than not lacks the skill, training, or understanding to make a meaningful evaluation. And I discovered many of these judges believe they are "bending over backwards" if they take the time to study these reports before passing sentence.

While a valid presentence investigation has merit, one study shows that it is used in only a dozen states for all defendants. And my survey for *The Christian Science Monitor* raises questions about the reliability of the reports, other than providing information about the man's prior police record.

The solution probably lies elsewhere—perhaps in a sentencing commission separate from the courts.

In two states, California and Washington, a board fixes the sentence of any man who has been convicted in the courts—after a series of tests are given and the man's background checked. The length of time a convict spends in prison is tied to his "needs" and to progress made while there.

Court officials know so little about why men commit crimes, and how we can alter the criminal mentality and thus prevent crimes, that more basic research is needed. In time we may well look at prison sentences and executions as being as primitive and inhuman as the witch hunts or the removal of a man's hand or foot or head as punishment—practices that were common only a few centuries ago.

There is interest in some states in reviewing sentences to end disparity. Oklahoma has long had this system. In December of 1965 Maine established a special appellate court—made up of three members of the Supreme Judicial Court—to handle this chore.

The defendant in Maine must file notice of appeal within 30 days after being sentenced. Those in prison when the law went into effect were given until Nov. 30, 1967, to file. Forms are available at both prisons and courthouses, and court clerks are required to notify each person who is sentenced of his right to appeal.

The special appellate court may also *increase* sentences, although at last check none had been increased. And only those sentences obviously too long were being considered, although the Massachusetts plan, where all appeals resulted in hearings, may soon be used.

While this may help make sentences for similar crimes more equal, it does not get at the root problem. It does not change our system of "serving time" into true rehabilitation. In one Maine case, where a man tried to burn down an occupied theater, the sentence was severe—50 to 100 years. Earlier he had been sentenced to 1½ to 3 years for arson, and he admitted to the appellate court that he was worried about his compulsion to set fires.

Perhaps only a change in our laws will put him where he must belong—in a mental hospital. The very test of sanity in our courts may well be considered a little insane.

The judge's job in all of this is difficult, if not impossible. As Judge McKenzie of Atlanta points out: "To the trial judge's care is entrusted an awesome power. He may, by the exercise of this power, separate a person from his family, destroy his good name and reputation. He may wreck his career, and in fact he may, by his act, deprive a person ultimately of life itself. . . . A trial judge must be ever conscious of the fact that power can be misused. . . . Consequently he must accept the responsibility of his office with humility and must exercise the power of his office with caution. In other words, he must constantly keep in mind that as with all power and privileges there is a corresponding responsibility. That is, a responsibility to use his power prudently, soberly, and intelligently."

It is in this same spirit that policemen and prosecutors should labor.

And it is something all citizens must understand in this search for justice in a free society.

CHAPTER XI

Corrections: A Misnomer

It was while I was touring a prison for young men in Georgia —the Industrial Institute near Alto—that I saw a guard kick a youth.

The first explanation given was that the guard was just playing around. Later I was told the man who did the kicking had been hired at $196 a month. Under the new pay scale of $326 a month, which went into effect in January of 1967, it was hoped better men could be found.

In the spring of 1967 a man died in Chicago's House of Corrections. It was charged that sadistic guards and tough prisoners teamed up to administer beatings.

In "drunk tanks" across the nation teen-age boys, some in jail for minor offenses or even traffic charges, are seriously injured while being forced by older prisoners to submit to unnatural sexual acts. Some are hospitalized. A few die—perhaps more than publicly admitted.

While visiting the modern East Facility of the California Men's Colony near San Luis Obispo, I was told one of the four wings was reserved for prisoners with "no record of homosexual activity." Officials were proud of this experiment.

In St. Louis a private consulting firm from Chicago, hired to look at the county jail, reported that it was dirty, the food "unpleasant," prisoner supervision inadequate, employee morale low, and that the prisoners had little to do besides watch television or talk with each other.

In one Texas town I visited a barber was appointed probation officer by district judges. The barber resigned and moved away when one of the men he was supervising complained that the barber was trying to force him to commit immoral acts.

Experienced probation officers admitted to me that when male officers have women under their supervision, the more attractive girls may be forced to let the officers "visit" them at night from time to time.

In Greenville, S.C., a generally enlightened town, the jail I toured was so old and overcrowded that prisoners were sleeping on the cement floor without blankets—including youngsters in their teens who spend days listening to hardened criminals brag about their exploits.

Little wonder that our so-called "corrections" system does so little to correct, and that 40 to 60 percent of those who spend time in prison return to jail. With so much injustice in our system of justice, little wonder that those who tangle with the law become bitter at an early age and take their anger out on innocent members of society.

This is not to excuse crime and violence. Neither can be tolerated if the goal of our society is to achieve freedom from fear for all citizens.

Rather it is to point up the hypocrisy in our present system of justice, and to alert our citizens of the need for reform as the crime rate soars.

For I discovered, as I interviewed judges and lawyers, policemen and prosecutors, corrections officials and prisoners, that even if other court problems are resolved, judges will still have a difficult time knowing what to do with men who are found guilty.

Says the President's commission report:

> The institutions in which about a third of the corrections population lives are situated for the most part in remote rural areas, or in the basements of police stations or courthouses. The other two-thirds of the corrections population are on probation and parole, and so are widely, and on the whole invisibly, dispersed in the community. Corrections is not only hard to see; traditionally society has been reluctant to look at it. Many of the people, juvenile and adult, with whom corrections deals are the most troublesome and troubling members of society: The misfits and the failures, the unrespectable

and the irresponsible. Society has been well content to keep them out of sight.

Its invisibility belies the system's size, complexity, and crucial importance to the control of crime.... On any given day it is responsible for approximately 1.3 million offenders. In the course of a year it handles nearly 2.5 million admissions, and spends over a billion dollars doing so. If it could restore all or even most of these people to the community as responsible citizens, America's crime rate would drop significantly....

For a great many offenders ... corrections does not correct. Indeed, experts are increasingly coming to feel that the conditions under which many offenders are handled, particularly in institutions, are often a positive detriment to rehabilitation.

Life in many institutions is at best barren and futile, at worst unspeakably brutal and degrading.... The conditions in which [prisoners] live are the poorest possible preparation for their successful reentry into society, and often merely reinforce in them a pattern of manipulation or destructiveness.

As I have pointed out, it is impossible to chop our system of justice into separate chunks and pieces if it is to be understood and improved. The crisis in our courts is directly tied to the crisis in our prisons, and the growing crisis of crime in our society.

One feeds on the other, and all are part of the whole. Judges who sentence offenders to horrible holes for years carry a burden of guilt not really different from legislators who let these conditions exist. And citizens are to blame for not bringing pressure on the lawmakers.

If a dozen trial-court judges in each state refused to sentence men and women to prison until conditions were improved, we might see relief in six months. But it would take courage to do this. It would take an understanding of the problem. And it would take the joint effort of the judges because, with our present way of thinking, a single judge would be written off as a "nut."

Steps must be taken to help the people of America understand the corrections-system problems so that even without courageous judges improvements can be made. Until the President's commission began looking at the nation's growing crime problem there was little information available—a flaw that runs through the entire system of justice.

To get some idea of the scope of the corrections field, the Commission hired the National Council on Crime and Delinquency (NCCD) to survey the nation. It found that:

> Eighty percent of the $1 billion expenditure for corrections goes to operate institutions which employ 87 percent of all correctional personnel. Yet only 3.6 percent of all institutional workers are classified as "treatment" practitioners.
>
> Community-based services such as probation, parole and juvenile aftercare receive only 20 percent of all corrections funds. On an average day community services are responsible for two-thirds of all offenders handled by the correction system, yet these services employ only 13 percent of all correctional personnel.

The NCCD sees the imbalance growing as more prisons are expanded and new prisons built.

As is the case for police departments and courts, there are thousands of separate jails and prisons in the United States, "each administered by different branches and levels of government and each competing for funds and manpower at all governmental levels."

The New York based organization estimates that "at least twice as much treatment manpower is needed to bring loads down to manageable limits and to provide services for offenders who are now excluded." Yet "few students in universities and colleges are being prepared for the correctional field. Without major assistance the schools cannot begin to meet the professional manpower needs of the correctional field. Only half the correctional agencies have regular in-service training programs of any kind. Moreover, many of these programs are limited to administrative matters, not improving skills."

Too often, the report adds, "correctional planning depends upon blind chance." Little is done to gather statistical information to help future planning and to evaluate present methods of handling prisoners.

But there is a deeper problem, as pointed out by Dr. Karl

Menninger, chairman of the Menninger Foundation, in an article in *The New Era,* a prison-published magazine supervised by the Federal Bureau of Prisons. For the "treatment" prescribed by society is "punishment," a "course of treatment which psychiatrists do not use," he explains.

Yet this punishment is not as severe as it once was. We have turned our backs on, and walked a few steps away from, the day when men, women, and children gathered round to enjoy a public hanging or beheading.

In 1966, when Norval R. Morris gave the Julius Kreeger Professorship inaugural lecture at the Law School of the University of Chicago, he discussed this change, explaining that in his view, "the mainspring of penal reform has been neither empirically validated knowledge nor a developed theory."

"Decency, empathy, the ability to feel at least to a degree the lash on another's back, the removal occasionally of our customary blinkers to human suffering, a respect for each individual springing from religious or humanitarian beliefs—these have been the motive forces of penal reform," he said.

Then he added: "One does not have to travel far from this place today to find thousands of convicted persons, adult and juvenile, subjected needlessly to such suffering and for grossly protracted periods. . . . Moreover, such suffering is more than useless; it is harmful to us. It tends to increase the social alienation of those we punish beyond our social needs, and it is highly probable that we pay a penalty in increased recidivism and increased severity of the crimes committed by those who do return from such punishment to crime."

Paul W. Keve, the highly creative corrections director in Minnesota, asserts the solution to the crime problem, and thus the answer for penal institutions, involves changing the thinking or self-concept of those who break society's standards.

"We are dealing with people who have had a lifetime of seeing themselves defeated," he says. They never had the experience of helping somebody else. They have always been helped. They have had to go to the welfare department. They are always filling out a form. Always getting arrested. Always on the receiving end.

"They have developed extremely poor opinions of themselves. They are not motivated to improve themselves. We put them in prison and reinforce this by dehumanizing regimentation. We make all the decisions for them—even the little decisions like what hallways to walk in."

Yet there is scattered evidence of change.

In Minneapolis a dozen boys study aviation every Saturday morning. All have been in trouble with the law. All, he says, were "raised without the understanding they have ability or worth. They don't believe in themselves."

At the airport they first take a flight—just for the experience. Then for 15 weeks they study the principles of aerodynamics, navigation, cloud formations, weather, and other navigational basics.

As their final exam they act as navigators in all-day flights to the Canadian border in several light planes.

"They do all the planning and navigation," he says. "They call the weather bureau. The pilots fly exactly as the boys tell them. The kids didn't think they could do anything. Yet in 15 weeks, starting from scratch, they can actually navigate a plane all day by themselves."

Mr. Keve also points out that in Washington, D.C., a federal corrections project copies the capitalistic, competitive living that goes on outside the institution.

"They furnish a boy with only the opportunity to make money. He pays for everything—his meals, room rent, everything. There is a cafeteria where he can make choices. He doesn't eat what everybody else eats. He can buy a salad or not. A dessert or not. He can save his money or squander it. If he does not use his money responsibly, he goes on relief and sleeps on a cot in the hall."

Mr. Keve calls this a "magnificent step toward breaking away from the old institutional habits." It helps the inmate adapt to normal life when he comes out.

The Highfields program in New Jersey is also high on his list. There a "synthetic culture" has been developed to change the inmate's way of solving problems.

"If he has been fighting in the streets with his fists, he learns to fight with words. Instead of taking things that don't belong to him, he learns to work for them. Instead of taking the criticism of an employer personally, he learns to take it constructively."

Mr. Keve believes that after short periods of this round-the-clock synthetic culture the inmate should be returned to the streets—but should be given support while there.

A California experiment is also worth watching, he says. Selected prisoners are being taught sociology, research, and related subjects. When they leave the institution they work with professionals in disadvantaged areas.

Like reformed alcoholics, these prisoners learn to turn the experience they have gained through the years in crime, delinquency, and being poor into something useful. They help bring about changes in others who are in trouble or at the edge of trouble, and they can do it better than anyone because they have "been there." They identify. They understand. They know the language.

More than that, it helps rehabilitate the men doing the helping because it gives them a goal or mission they have never had before.

One solution that is considered effective has been around for years. Known as the Huber Law because it was backed by Wisconsin State Senator Henry Huber, it was passed in that state in 1913, and permits prisoners in county jails to serve their sentences at night and work during the day. In Wisconsin in 1965 the law was finally extended to the state prisons and men serving time for felonies.

Explains Sanger B. Powers, director of corrections in Wisconsin: "Many people end up in jail for 15 days, 30 days, or 6 months. They were employed before being arrested. They have families to support. And very little is accomplished when you lock them in jail and force their families to go on public aid."

Senator Huber was shocked by the idleness he found in Wisconsin jails in 1913. Although at last count about half of the states have adopted similar laws, he would be shocked today if he visited some other states. Even in Wisconsin the law is not followed in some counties. In 1964 a total of 58 Wisconsin counties, out of 72, had one or more prisoners working days, and earnings totaled nearly $1 million.

Taxpayers gain because those working under the Huber Law also pay the sheriff board. Under the law the prisoner may:

- seek work;
- work at his regular job;
- attend school or college;
- conduct his regular business if self-employed;
- go home and keep house for the family if a woman;
- receive medical treatment.

And the sheriff also looks for work for those who do not have jobs or cannot find them.

Earnings go for the prisoner's board; for travel and other work expenses; for support of the prisoner's family as ordered by the court; for payment of the prisoner's bills and his fines and court costs. Whatever is left when the prisoner is released goes to the prisoner.

Professor Morris of the University of Chicago proposes use of the Swedish adult correctional system. This, he says, includes: "an attempt to preserve his social ties, and, if it should be necessary to incarcerate him, to do so briefly and in conditions of reasonable comfort with little disruption of those social ties as possible." He also lists: "no large penal institutions; regular home leave; over a third of prisoners held in open conditions lacking bolts, bars and walls; adequate work and vocational training; a sense of near equality in the relationships between prisoners and staff."

In the United States halfway houses help reduce prison time and ease the convict back into society.

Yet society continues to reject the ex-con. He is feared; picked up by policemen at every turn because "you don't arrest the mayor or suspect the superintendent of schools—you pick up the guy who has the record"; finds it hard to get a job; and may have had no job training in prison except making license plates—and if he tries making plates in civilian life, he is thrown back into prison.

Many Americans believe that punishment can be used to prevent people from committing crimes. It is the reason capital punishment remains on the books in many states. Yet statistics show the murder rate is just as high in states where there is a death penalty as in states where it has been abolished.

A year in prison or a $1,000 fine might keep housewives from parking longer than their nickel permits in a downtown area, but it probably would not keep an alcoholic from drink or even a kleptomaniac from filling her pockets at the five and ten. Nor would it keep a teen-age boy from driving too fast, at least if he thought he could get away with it.

Yet this is the stuff our laws are made of.

It is hard to decide which is worse: our prisons or our jails. Many I visited are horrible beyond belief. A good farmer has far better conditions for his cows than we maintain for many of our prisoners.

There is a trend away from this, a trend toward highly impersonal jails with electrical locking devices and canned music to soothe the prisoners and keep them calm and safe. I have been in these jails and have found them, in their way, nearly as bad as the old kind. And too little planning for the growing number of arrests being made is evident.

In Miami I found the new jail overcrowded. In a number of cities people sleep on the floors for lack of beds.

In Loving, N.H., the two men in jail get three meals a day, instead of two, by volunteering to work on the city garbage truck.

Some Southern states still have highway chain gangs, although most have eliminated the chains. In Northern states inmates work prison farms and forestry camps, punch out license plates, and make furniture and other articles for parks and state institutions.

I found that in several states the department of welfare and the corrections system had been merged—at least in name. I have long wondered why the next, very simple step is not taken—a step that involves treatment of environment and the family *before* crimes take place, rather than holding people in jail or prison after the fact.

In too many states social workers function more as "policemen" of the poor than helpers who want to resolve the wide spectrum of family problems that range from lack of food to poor health, from a lack of education to a shortage of clothing.

In researching the Midtown slum in Gary, Ind., for *The Christian Science Monitor* in 1966 I found children growing up surrounded by crime and violence—three blocks from the city police station. I found boys mugging strangers and children earning their spending money soliciting for the prostitutes who lived in the next apartment or a few doors down the street.

Yet we wait until these children graduate to more violent crimes, and treat the individual rather than the conditions that breed crime.

It would make the same kind of sense if state or county highway departments opened stations at the ends of roads to fix springs and tires for motorists with taxpayers' money instead of filling the holes in the roads.

As in all other areas of our system of justice, a great deal more research is needed. And perhaps a little more common sense would help.

Yet it is not a hopeless cause. Men like Mr. Keve are optimistic. He believes that by the end of the century our thinking will change and we will know how to resolve these problems now falling under the heading of corrections.

We have already taken new views toward mental retardation, venereal disease, and mental health, he says—things "you couldn't even discuss 30 or 40 years ago."

"I think the crime problem is next on the list," he adds. "I am optimistic about the next three decades."

CHAPTER XII

Lawyer Troubles

During the summer of 1967 in Chicago's suburbs a lawyer was asked by a client to go to court to straighten out a traffic offense involving a driver's license.

The attorney decided to plead his client guilty and "ask for the mercy of the court"—something he probably saw on the Late Show on television. It seemed like an easy out. The client was a responsible citizen. And car thieves and minor burglars had been known to get off with a lecture or, at worst, six months' probation.

The lawyer was stunned when the judge sentenced his client to seven days in jail. When the lawyer recovered enough to ask why, the judge explained that had the lawyer bothered to look up the law he would have known a guilty plea for that offense carries an automatic seven-day jail term.

The lawyer lost a client. The client went to jail. The story is making the rounds. And lawyers in general are being berated as stupid, lazy, greedy, or incompetent—depending upon who tells the story.

It is unfair to denounce a profession because of one man. Unfortunately, too many stories have been circulated for too many years. About too many lawyers.

After the court series began running in *The Christian Science Monitor,* calls began to come in from around the nation from people who wanted me to recommend "an honest lawyer." And a United States Congressman, a lawyer himself, wrote, urging me to investigate attorneys in the House and Senate of the United States. Others commented on lawyers in our state legislatures.

At the American Bar Association's annual meeting in Honolulu in the summer of 1967 much concern was expressed over the inability of middle-class citizens to find competent attorneys. For the average American is not poor enough to have free counsel, nor rich enough to hire top men.

Earl F. Morris, of Columbus, Ohio, ABA president for 1967-68, saw it as an important challenge. Theodore Voorhees of Philadelphia, chairman of the National Conference of Bar Presidents, said, "There is today great concern within the profession as to how its services may be made more available to middle-income brackets—to those who can afford to pay fees, but not very large ones."

And he pointed out that while local bar associations may give out lists of lawyers to inquiring citizens, "the association neither vouches for the competency of the [lawyer] nor the quality of their services."

In all of this there is a bright note. At last leading lawyers are talking openly—at least within their own ranks—about the bitter complaints aimed at their profession.

"Every president of the American Bar Association receives a considerable volume of mail complaining of conduct of lawyers, and of the unwillingness of lawyers to discipline their fellow lawyers," says Lewis F. Powell Jr., of Richmond, Va., a former ABA president, in a speech released in February of 1967 in Houston.

"There is no greater frustration than that of a layman who has a complaint against a lawyer either for neglect of duty or lack of fidelity," Mr. Powell explains. "He knows that only in the rarest case can he recover damages in court—even if he can persuade another lawyer to represent him. In the exceptional case of obvious criminal conduct there may be recourse through the prosecutor's office.

"But in the typical case of a grievance by a client against a lawyer, the only feasible recourse is through channels within the profession. This means, in too many instances, no recourse at all."

Part of the problem is that citizens don't know where to turn when they have lawyer troubles. And even when they find out, it may be hard to get the local bar association's grievance committee to do anything about it, Mr. Powell adds.

How many complaints are valid?

"A high percentage of these are no doubt without foundation," Mr. Powell says. "Many result from misunderstanding or ignorance. Others reflect the understandable resentment of disappointed litigants. And some originate from the 'nuts' who complain about everything.

"But many complaints against our brothers are not groundless, and despite diligent and dedicated work by grievance committees and the available staffs of state and local bars, many complaints are never adequately investigated or pressed to formal action. A certain number of lawyers guilty of misconduct, which discredits the entire profession, are never disciplined."

As I traveled the nation, sitting in courtrooms and talking with lawyers, judges, prosecutors, policemen, law professors, and citizens, I was surprised to find there is little agreement on what is and is not ethical.

This includes handling of clients, fees charged, use of chicanery—deception or trickery—in the courtroom, taking advantage of "loopholes" in the law to free guilty clients or break contracts, and hiding facts that would harm a client.

"I'm known as a lawyer who can find loopholes in airtight cases," says Valdahe Pitman, a well-known Oklahoma City trial lawyer. And he adds that he is proud of this reputation.

It is quite evident that corporate lawyers have different standards from criminal lawyers. An expert in trusts, real estate, or in other specialty areas also operates on different moral principles—depending upon, among other things, his background, personal philosophy, and the client he is handling.

Geoffirey C. Hazard Jr., executive director of the American Bar Foundation in Chicago, sees the conflict over ethics as caused by several interrelated problems:

• Lawyers have established for themselves a professed level of ethical aspirations that is quite high—so high that it is extremely hard to live by them.

• Few individuals in society are so exposed to huge temptation as are lawyers. Thus the opportunity for unethical practice is increased manyfold.

• What lawyers do, how they work, and how they think of themselves and their professions varies a great deal. This is directly related to their background, attitudes about work, and other attitudes.

• Lawyers' ideals are embodied in canons of ethics that are based upon a profession living in the 19th century. These canons suppose a lawyer is in a single-lawyer office, skilled in all things he takes on, judged by his reputation, and bound by very personal ties of honor.

It is assumed every lawyer in the United States lives in a town of 25,000 or less and that every lawyer relies on the canons of ethics as his guide.

In fact, "the lawyer and his work is very much transformed from that," Mr. Hazard asserts. A very high percent work in large cities, in "group settings," in large firms, or in government. Yet the "canons are based on the old model" of the lawyer.

• The apparatus for enforcing the ethical conduct of lawyers is exceedingly feeble. It is, in most cases, loosely organized, poorly staffed, and not particularly aggressive.

With lawyers coming from varied backgrounds, doing many unrelated things in their work, governed by outdated rules and a weak system of enforcing rules, and exposed to great temptations, problems arise.

"This is true of everybody in a position to exploit someone," Mr. Hazard adds. "It is as true for accountants and newspaper reporters as lawyers."

Part of the problem centers on who runs the local bar associations—those private groups presently charged with the huge, and often neglected, responsibility for policing their own ranks.

In some states the lawyers are divided into groups related to the kinds of things they do. Corporate lawyers band together. Trial lawyers form another group. In other states all operate under the same umbrella. There may be little understanding of each others' problems. And one group—as a whole—may be more ethical than the other.

The corporate lawyer almost never enters the criminal courts. He has had little or no training in law school to help him understand criminal court, since law schools generally teach how to look up the law, not how to practice it. And when a corporate lawyer finds himself in criminal court with a client—perhaps a case of income-tax evasion or price-fixing, he may want the courts to have two standards:

- A tough one for the run-of-the-mill lawbreaker who steals hubcaps and tires or a fur coat; and

- Lenient standards for the corporate executive who may take millions, but is "a solid member of the community"—a "prominent citizen."

It becomes clear that lawyers, while condemning other lawyers, may have "blind spots" in their own areas of interest where they rationalize unethical behavior.

Part of the problem is lack of information about the profession.

The American Bar Association, which forms one big tent over all kinds of lawyers (although far from all lawyers belong to the ABA), finds it difficult even to define what a lawyer is and does, says Barlow Christensen, an ABA research attorney assigned to look at these big questions.

Many jobs a lawyer performs are also handled by laymen, he points out. Real-estate brokers make property transactions and do it quite legally—although lawyers consider this within their province and warn people that not having a lawyer present is a big risk.

Accountants, bookkeepers, and everyday citizens fill out tax reports. Some lawyers make tax reports a specialty.

Someone other than a lawyer can appear before many of the semijudicial governmental boards and regulatory agencies, yet today a number of lawyers specialize in this.

It may even be more meaningful to list what a layman cannot do—like take a case for a client before the Supreme Court—to get at what a lawyer does in our society.

Thus specialization and ethics are both problem areas, and are found to be interrelated—especially when ethics must be considered in the framework of "the lawyer's work."

There are roughly 300,000 lawyers in the United States. No one really knows how many appear in court, however. I found that in large cities the civil and criminal trial bar may consist of 1 or 2 percent or less of all lawyers in that city.

Yet in rural areas almost all lawyers spend a third or more of their time in court.

In Spencer, Ind., for example, a community of about 2,600, there are six practicing lawyers, a part-time prosecutor, and a full-time judge. One father-and-son firm does a limited amount of trial work, while the other four lawyers spend much of their time in the trial field.

Use of lawyers' services varies widely. Of the 300,000 lawyers, it is estimated by the ABA that 10 percent, or 30,000, are on corporate payrolls—about 26,500 in private industry, over 2,000 working for educational institutions, and another 1,000 working for "other" private employers.

Another 10 percent work for the executive and legislative branches of government. Of these, nearly 8,000 work for cities and counties. Roughly twice that number are on the federal payroll, while about 6,500 are on the state level—many of them working in the state attorney general offices.

Some 9,000 are employed full time by the courts—federal, state, and local. An undetermined number, but several thousand, are part-time judges.

This accounts for only about a quarter of all lawyers. Another 12,000 are reported to be retired or inactive. But there is no clear explanation of what the 200,000 in the "private practice" of law do. Some are specialists, handling only defendants or only plaintiffs in auto-accident cases. Others enter a courtroom a dozen times a year, or less. And a few spend most of their working time in court.

Some specialize in divorce. Others handle only one or two divorces a year, if any. A number work in the field of real estate. How many no one knows.

In the field of auto-accident litigation specialization increases the confusion.

Take Al J. Cone of West Palm Beach. He heads a firm of 19 trial lawyers and only works in the personal-injury field.

A number of Florida lawyers accept injury cases and try to settle them out of court. When that fails (out-of-court settlements can run as high as 90 or 95 percent of all injury cases filed), these lawyers may turn the case over to Mr. Cone for trial because their field of specialization is not in the courtroom.

"I paid one West Palm Beach lawyer $38,000 in referral fees last year," Mr. Cone told me. "I'm satisfied that if he tried the same cases he wouldn't have made $6,000 or $7,000. And the clients would have been hurt far worse."

"There are dozens of other practices [fields] I don't know anything about," he adds. "I would be almost guilty of malpractice if I tried to handle a will-contest case, real-estate titles, or a patent case, for example."

Yet thousands of lawyers who may be less qualified than Mr. Cone in these specialized areas do take these cases every year.

This is especially true in a small town. Says a leading Iowa judge:

"In smaller communities the lawyer has to take all of a client's business, or the client will take his business elsewhere. This probably means handling tax matters, for example, although the lawyer may not really want to."

In large cities the large firms—some with 40, 50, or 100 lawyers—have teams of specialists. One team may prepare cases, then turn them over to the "persuaders"—lawyers who know how to be convincing with a jury or can skillfully handle a judge. And many of these firms deal largely with corporations.

Of the 200,000 lawyers in private practice, roughly 114,000 are in one-man firms. Many accept all the business that walks in the door, and they do it gratefully. Practicing law can be feast or famine, lawyers report.

But a one-man firm may have nobody to help look up law—unless he has a skilled secretary. If it is a case involving a trial, he may handle the investigation, interview witnesses, take care of the paperwork, put the pleadings in the proper form, help pick a jury, and argue the case by himself. Some do it well.

Yet too many lawyers are poorly prepared for this by the law schools.

"A typical American law-school curriculum is designed primarily for turning out associates for large-city law firms, and corporate work is undoubtedly a substantial part of that firm's work," says Professor B. J. George of the University of Michigan.

One of his colleagues, Professor Yale Kamisar, adds: "The young lawyer is much more qualified to argue a case before the Supreme Court of the United States than in the lowest police court."

A New Jersey civil trial lawyer admits that "when I was starting out in the practice of law I simply took my clients for a ride. I used them to gain experience, and they suffered horribly in the process."

"In most schools a senior gets three or four lectures on the canons of ethics," says Professor George. "That's all he gets."

Yet lawyers deal with human problems and are confronted with difficult judgments every day. Ways of handling them vary widely. Lawyers, judges, professors cite many examples:

One of the most difficult: A corporate lawyer finds, while looking over a client's books, that the firm is cheating on its taxes or hears that certain executives are engaged in price-fixing. Should he confront the company president—probably to be fired? Should he find ways to cover up for the firm? Tell the Internal Revenue Service or Justice Department?

Some lawyers and most laymen find it equally difficult to know what to do in criminal cases where the client is obviously guilty. For our system says a man is innocent until proven guilty, thus giving guilty men the same right to a fair trial as those who are innocent. Hence, many criminal lawyers will do everything possible to get their man off, even when he has—in a confidential interview—admitted his guilt.

To do anything else is "childishness," says a University of Chicago law professor.

Or take the case of a young man who admits to his lawyer that he raped a minister's daughter who is engaged to the son of a bank president. The town knows what has happened. The youth can testify he used to go steady with the girl and she voluntarily submitted to him on many other occasions. The young man faces a long prison term because the judge is tough on rape cases. Should the lawyer put the young man on the stand and ruin the girl's reputation?

Lawyers find this harder to answer, usually prefer not to put the boy on the stand. But there is some division on this, too.

More thought is being given to these problems than in the past. Monroe H. Freedman, a law professor at George Washington University, is one of those stimulating the thinking in the criminal field—although he is often criticized for it.

He asks, among other things:

Is it proper, when a witness is telling the truth, to discredit him by aggressive cross-examination? Is it proper to put a witness on the stand when you know he will commit perjury? Is it proper to give your client legal advice when you have reason to believe that the knowledge you give him will tempt him to commit perjury?

He points out that Canon 15 of the American Bar Association's canons of professional ethics tells lawyers they should give their "entire devotion to the interest of the client, warm zeal in the maintenance and defense of his rights and the exertion of his utmost learning and ability." The canons also admonish lawyers not to violate the law and require candor toward the court.

On the question of discrediting a truthful witness, Professor Freedman contends that if it serves justice and the lawyer's client is innocent, the "attorney is obligated to attack, if he can, the reliability or credibility of an opposing witness whom he knows to be truthful." But Professor Freedman carefully qualifies the circumstances.

On the question of expected perjury, he contends that lawyers soothe their consciences with phrases like "legal fiction" instead of lying. Legal fiction begins when the lawyer pleads a guilty man innocent.

Other lawyers, he says, choose to remain "selectively ignorant." This is done by insisting "in his first interview with his client that, if his client is guilty, he simply does not want to know.

"Perhaps the most common method of avoiding the ethical problem is for the lawyer to withdraw from the case, at least if there is sufficient time before trial for the client to retain another attorney."

This, however, merely passes the buck to another lawyer.

Others may tell the judge of the problem, which could result in a mistrial, says Professor Freedman. Or, he points out, a lawyer may let the client take the stand, turn his back, take no part in the story telling, and then make no reference in his closing arguments to the lies his client told.

Professor Freedman contends an attorney has no other choice than to put the defendant on the stand and let him commit perjury if the lawyer is to honor the canon of confidentiality.

On the question of giving the client legal knowledge that might tempt him to commit perjury, Professor Freedman argues that the client should know the laws that are involved in a case—even if informing the man about the law may tempt him to lie.

He contends, as do most other trial lawyers interviewed, that under the adversary system of justice "the most effective means of determining truth is to present to a judge and jury a clash between proponents of conflicting views." Anything less than a full-fledged defense effort, he says, causes this system to break down.

Because of these knotty problems the American Bar Association has a committee, headed by Edward L. Wright, of Little Rock, Ark., rewriting the canons of ethics.

The present canons were framed in 1908, Mr. Wright points out, and hardly apply to the present age. Further, they are long-winded, although often couched in beautiful language.

He hopes that by this summer a terse list of "thou shalt nots" will be ready, followed by commentary of greater length.

Already the ABA has formed a committee on evaluation of disciplinary enforcement.

Former Associate Justice Tom C. Clark of the Supreme Court, who heads the committee, said in an interview that little is known about the number of violations or the methods of disciplining lawyers who violate the canons.

"We may go around the country and hold informal regional hearings to gather information," he says. "The committee was formed to see what the states are doing—if anything—how they are doing it, and what effect it is having."

The committee will not have enforcement powers, he adds. At most it will be able to point up "horrible examples" and then offer a model system for states to adopt if they care to.

When ethics are discussed, two studies are usually mentioned.

• One is *A Study of Segments of the Legal Profession in Manhattan and the Bronx,* by Jerome Carlin. It is both condemned and praised.

Mr. Carlin points out that of a group of 20,500 lawyers, 22 percent, or 4,500, committed some serious violations during the year of his study. Yet fewer than 2 percent of lawyers who violate the canons go through disciplinary machinery, and only about .02 percent are disbarred, suspended, or censured.

• In a Missouri public-relations survey in 1962-1963 it is pointed out that 22 percent of the lawyers surveyed believe that half of the Missouri lawyers break the code of ethics and 5 percent of the lawyers believe "few lawyers" observe the code.

Sometimes lawyers harm the interests of clients because of pressures and problems related to the courts. This is especially true in the criminal field.

One nationally known New York attorney complains that judges induce lawyers to plead clients guilty because "they don't take cases in the order they appear on the docket."

"I got to court at 9:23 this morning and my case wasn't called until 3:21," the lawyer explains. "In criminal court the client isn't like a fat, rich corporation and can't afford to pay a lawyer for the waiting time. And the criminal lawyer isn't making enough to spend all that time standing in the corridor.

"With the poor calendar control here we might have our witnesses assembled and be ready to go to trial and they don't get to my case at all. It's easier to plead guilty and get out of there."

Former Dean Erwin N. Griswold of the Harvard Law School has often said there are too many lawyers in the United States, but not enough good lawyers.

This has long been true in the criminal field, although that is starting to change. The brightest young lawyers from the prestige schools are usually snapped up by the nation's big law firms.

Criminal fees lawyers charge can vary, too. Says one Washington lawyer: "Here they vary from $10 to $100,000. Often a criminal lawyer—unless he is a 'name' lawyer like F. Lee Bailey—takes what he can get. And in advance." Many of these problems have been covered earlier in this book.

Recent Supreme Court rulings that bring the right of legal counsel to those who need it most—the poor—have been discussed in Chapter IX.

Meanwhile, calls for self-policing by the legal profession continue to mount.

As Orison S. Marden, past president of the American Bar Association, says:

> I am convinced most lawyers want a vigorous disciplinary program. We can have it only if the profession at large supports the effort. I earnestly solicit that support.
>
> Let us get rid of the bad apples—who bring undeserved discredit upon the great body of ethical practitioners—and let us curb certain dangerous tendencies among fringe elements in the profession.
>
> Let us always remember that we are members of an honorable profession—dedicated to service of the public. There should be no room in our ranks for those who practice law as a business, rather than as a profession—with morals no higher than those tolerated in the marketplace.

CHAPTER XIII

Why Witnesses Lie

Tuesday. Los Angeles Superior Court.

In one of the busy courtrooms a woman social worker has sworn to tell the truth, the whole truth, and nothing but the truth, and is now telling her story to the jury in a civil suit.

More than four years earlier, she says, she was leaving a parking lot one morning when an expensive new car crashed into her auto. Only the bumpers hit, so there was no damage to the car. But she was badly shaken.

A few years before the parking-lot crash she had been involved in a severe accident. Although she recovered from the physical injuries in that first crash, for months afterward she had trouble sleeping, was extremely nervous, and suffered from other complaints.

When the businessman slammed into her car, the vision of the first accident filled her thoughts, and all her old troubles came back. She was unable to work. She had a stack of medical bills to show to the jury to prove how ill she was.

Now she wanted the businessman to pay (actually his insurance company, although you cannot mention insurance in a trial in most states without a mistrial).

An hour and 10 minutes later, when the businessman took the stand, he denied there had been an accident. He had been in the parking lot, he said. But nothing had happened there. Later a policeman knocked on his door and looked at his car, but found no physical evidence of an accident.

Both had sworn to tell the truth.

Obviously one of them had not.

Deliberate lying in court while under oath is perjury. And perjury is a felony—a serious crime.

Because trials take so long and I had only a week to study the Los Angeles court system, I was unable to wait for the jury's verdict. But one thing is certain: neither the man or woman was charged with perjury. Very, very few people are.

In searching for reasons for this, I found:

• Perjury is hard to prove. Even witnesses under oath are permitted mistakes or mental blocks.

• Prosecutors have more than enough to do processing criminals hauled in by the police.

• Prosecutors, who are elected to office, might find it politically dangerous to press perjury charges—especially in civil suits involving businessmen.

• Perjury is tangled up with the entire court process, which is a "search for truth," according to those that defend it. This leads to confusion over what constitutes lying and what is just "part of the game."

• There is also confusion over this and its tie to the Fifth Amendment to the Constitution, which protects a man from testifying against himself.

Beyond this, I found that we rely heavily on the words of witnesses—often more heavily than on evidence like measured skid marks, the extent of damage, position of the cars after impact, and mathematical calculations.

In many courtrooms the word of a punch-press operator, housewife, or grandmother who doesn't even drive can weigh more than three expert investigators with a tape measure, charts, and scientific evidence. Even when that witness is some distance from the scene, was thinking about something else at the time, and "just happened to glance up" when the cars hit.

This reliance on witnesses, coupled with what has been described as "vagaries of the human mind," indicates that our temple of justice is flawed.

It is repeatedly weakened when two, three, four, or five years pass before the witnesses are called.

As one judge pointed out to me, "An hour after the accident ask one of the witnesses whether the man in the black jacket or the man in the tan jacket was driving the blue car.

"The witness scratches his head, closes one eye, squints at the ground, and finally says it was the 'fellow in black.' Then he explains why he picked that man as the driver, and even if he is wrong he will stick to his story."

Throw in the emotional impact of being involved, say in the back seat, and the problem of getting factual testimony grows worse. But if you are the driver, may lose your driver's license and your insurance, or your insurance company won't pay the bills, or someone near and dear to you was critically hurt, the possibility of getting reliable information grows very doubtful.

Geoffrey C. Hazard Jr. uses this example to explain the problem: "It took my wife four years to get me to understand that when I asked my son to tell the truth, and the boy knew he was going to be punished if he did, that I would get something less than truth."

The problem becomes more complex for the adult.

Professor Hazard contends that "lying and distortion are propelled by fear, greed, pride, and social pressures."

This is true of not only the defendant in a civil or criminal case, but also the injured party or plaintiff in the civil suit, or the victim in a criminal proceeding

The parents of the girl who was raped think of their daughter as their "sweet little baby," while the boy in the case is at least a "monster." Yet the boy's parents may well see him as the "victim" of a girl who "flaunted it in his face," a no-good "tramp."

Or take another example that seems fairly common. A man has been in an accident. His lawyer asks him how he feels. The client says "fine." The lawyer (who, you must remember, gets between a third and a half of the award in most cases)

may ask again, pointing out that "we have a $5,000 case now, but if you are still putting up with pain and suffering, it might be a $15,000 case."

At this point the man recalls that the once-injured knee ached during the last cold snap, and that he really should give up golf because swinging the club bothers his back.

Yet, according to Professor Hazard and several other lawyers and judges I have talked to, this may not really be a deliberate lie.

"If you are reminded of a pain, the suffering begins," Professor Hazard explains. "The doctors tell us if you believe you have a back pain, you will *have* a back pain."

Actually, I found that lawyers and judges are bothered by perjury and the related areas of gray: the coaching of witnesses; exaggerated pleadings; and the deliberate omission of essential facts, even under the pressure of cross-examination. They are bothered, but most dislike talking about these problems.

This is, in part, because of the nature of the lawyer's job, explains Monroe H. Freedman, of George Washington University's Law School.

"A great deal of litigation is disposed of before trial," he explains. "One lawyer will call another up, comment on the figure that has been mentioned in the suit, and then ask, 'How much does the client *really* want? What *were* the doctor bills?' "

With 90 percent or more of all auto-accident cases settled before the jury reaches a verdict, it is obvious bargaining goes on. The lawyer for the plaintiff puts the figure high—rather than a true figure—like a car dealer who starts out bargaining at the "sticker price" and comes down for the haggling buyer.

This problem (and I am not sure a hard-nosed lawyer would call it a problem; rather he would be inclined to say it is "strategy") has been eased a little by what is known as pretrial "discovery." Lawyers from both sides are permitted to interview witnesses in advance, ask them questions, and have a court reporter make a record of what is said. It is done under oath, and tends to keep witnesses from changing their stories when they reach court.

Another tactical consideration in auto-negligence cases centers on the client's recovery from injuries. Professor Freedman points out that when the suit is filed, "you may not be sure of the physical injuries. A latent injury may be discovered months later. And you may not be able to amend the complaint."

Most lawyers and judges I have asked about this agree that it is a valid reason for exaggeration in such a complaint. In such cases the lawyer may assert that the plaintiff "did suffer, on and about the body, cuts, bruises, lacerations, contusions," and every other injury imaginable.

Professor Hazard excuses this in part on the grounds the lawyer doesn't have time to draft a really specific, yet all-inclusive complaint in most cases. So he uses a form complaint, and tells "Miss Jones to pick up paragraphs 8, 9, 11, and 13 here."

Beyond this, the layman doesn't even "know what the language means because it is lawyers' language, and so may question it." Yet "a perfectly upright, thoroughly honest lawyer will write his pleading in the same way."

Press most lawyers about it and they will admit that what goes on before and in court includes "a strange exchange of distortions." But they defend the profession, often with a shrug, saying, "This is the way it works."

Professor Hazard blames much of the problem on our society itself and the American confusion over honesty and truth. The use of evidence stems from a fear of making decisions.

"The average person gets so upset when he is asked to judge on the skid marks that he sucks his thumb and asks for the psychological reassurance of a witness who was there and saw something happen."

How reliable are witnesses?

Take a criminal preliminary hearing I watched in Oklahoma.

A Negro youth was charged with stealing a credit card, and with trying to use it as his own.

A store manager in his late twenties was called to the stand. He testified that a young Negro came into his store to buy a jacket, and tried to pay for it with a credit card.

The store manager decided to check the bank because the

customer was young. The bank didn't know the card had been stolen. It approved the purchase. But the telephone call took so long the young man fled—leaving the card behind.

Some time later—the store manager couldn't remember whether it was three weeks or a month—the police dropped by with a "mug shot"—a picture of the young defendant.

When questioned, the young store manager admitted he didn't recognize the defendant from the picture. So later that day he went to the police station and picked the young man in the picture out in a police line-up.

"What was so special about the man you picked out? What made you remember him?" the young store manager was asked.

"Well," he said, "the boy who came into my store was a Negro, and he was slim, and this fellow is slim, and they both seemed to be about the same height, so I knew it was him."

I wondered how many other young men fit the description, and how the store manager picked him out of a line-up after three or four weeks' delay after waiting on him briefly in a store. It was not a crime of violence, where the youth's face might be burned into the memory.

Most judges, I found, would want more evidence. But in this case the young man went to jail to await trial in district court. Again, because of the long time lag, I was unable to learn his final fate. But for months I wondered if the wrong man was being held.

At the same time, I doubt that the young store owner was consciously lying. If he was puzzled at first, his testimony in the preliminary hearing will force him to stick to his story or admit he was wrong. It will be reinforced by the fact that he was able to stare at the young Negro for several minutes in court, and the next time he appears he will have even less trouble recognizing him.

Professor Freedman and several others I interviewed contend that while much false information gets into court every day, most witnesses think they are telling the truth. A witness is a gossip under oath, in a sense. As we observe, we tailor our views to fit the circumstances. We delude ourselves. Our imagination works in strange ways.

"Every lawyer knows that the lawyer who gets to a witness first has an advantage," Professor Freedman explains. "I am convinced red lights turn green while lawyers talk to witnesses."

This by the use of "suggestion," hard questions, a plea for sympathy for "the poor guy in the hospital who is wrongfully blamed for this," and other psychological devices.

Remember, the name of the game in the adversary process is "Fight to win for your client."

Perhaps more significant, our power to recall what we see is limited. Our eyes and our minds fool us.

Chief Justice Robert Finley of the State of Washington's Supreme Court tells of a Boy Scout test that involves looking at a collection of objects for a few minutes and then writing down a list of the objects.

"They only write down part of what they see, and sometimes they put down things they didn't see," he says. "Yet they remain positive that these objects were in the collection."

An Oregon lawyer, who asked to remain unnamed for obvious reasons, tells of representing a high-pressure, high-volume auto dealer.

"My firm's duties included forcing unpaid contracts," he says. "From time to time people complained that the contract was not the one they agreed to during the transaction. We really didn't think much about it until one of the purchasers was a lawyer, known by one of our people to be an honorable and trustworthy man. When he told us the contract on his car had been tampered with, we resigned the account.

"That takes a firm with a fairly strong sense of honor," the lawyer continued. "You think twice before you kick out a client that may be worth $20,000 or $25,000 a year. Now say, instead of a car dealer, it was Amalgamated National Steel Corporation [a name he made up to make his point]—well, that's another story.

"Business fraud is a bloody mess," he added. "You ask any lawyer, and if he is honest with you he'll admit it goes on all the time."

What this lawyer didn't say about the used-car firm case is

revealing in itself. While his firm was so convinced that fraud was involved that it resigned the account, the firm did not consider reporting it to the authorities. The car dealer presumably continues to operate in the same way.

Most lawyers consider it unethical to betray the sacred trust between client and attorney by turning a dishonest client over to the prosecutor.

The same firms that handle contracts and business deals and help with lagging collections have the second responsibility of defending their clients in court—even with the full knowledge that the client has done something wrong.

Lawyers may be so-called "officers of the court," but, as has been pointed out earlier, their first obligation in the adversary system is to fight with all their might to protect those who hire them.

Those are the rules of the game. And the good lawyers are caught up in it with the bad.

The President's commission report says: "Perjury has always been widespread; according to Pollock and Maitland's standard history of English law, 'our ancestors perjured themselves with impunity.'"

We hardly need to look to our ancestors. If perjury were prosecuted instead of being ignored, perhaps a third of all divorced couples would have criminal records. Perhaps more.

If the statistics are right, one out of four marriages ends up in divorce court. It is easier to get a marriage license than a library card in most states, for many libraries require at least two references. Yet to get a divorce we require one or the other spouse to be at "fault." In New York, where fault has been limited to adultery, it became common to lie, and even to get a friend or hire a firm to "discover" the husband cheating on his wife.

In many states divorce court has become a tragic joke.

Where mental and physical cruelty are accepted as grounds for divorce there is hardly a man or wife alive who cannot find an excuse to end the marriage. Even if it means lying.

A wife who flies to another state where laws are more lenient bends the truth by saying under oath that she is a resident of that state, only to leave it permanently the morning after the decree is handed down.

There are other examples of deliberate perjury. Traffic court is one of the best spots to hear examples. For the traffic officer insists a man was going 45 miles per hour in a 35-mph zone, while the poor "victim" swears he couldn't have been doing "more than 30 at most." The judge finds the man guilty, but he never asks the prosecutor to charge him with perjury.

Drunken driving is also a common charge that brings conflict and falsehood into the courtroom.

"The man was weaving all over the road, failed to stop at a sign, and nearly ran down two pedestrians," the officer may testify. "When I went up to his car I could smell alcohol on his breath, and his speech was slurred."

The defendant, now dressed in his best suit, his wife standing beside him, says: "Your Honor, I did have one beer with my supper. On my way home I began feeling ill, so I wasn't driving as carefully as I usually do. Those people in the street were half a block away, and I was driving slowly. I admit that I didn't come to a full stop at the stop sign, but I did slow down and make sure no cars were coming. As I said, I wasn't feeling well, and I was in a hurry to get home."

If the judge finds the man guilty, it is hard to believe that perjury has not been committed. The policeman can be excused for making an honest mistake.

But not in all cases. Professor Freedman tells of a Washington, D.C., case. Two Negroes were walking a white woman home from a club where all three worked as musicians. It was a tough neighborhood, and the men felt it unsafe to let the woman go home alone.

While they were walking, he says, a squad car rolled up. The policemen stopped the trio, used foul language, grabbed one of the men's instrument cases, and finally arrested both men for disorderly conduct, leaving the woman alone in the bad neighborhood.

When the policemen were asked in court why they had stopped the men, they testified they had a burglary report on the police radio and the two men matched the description.

When the police radio log was checked, no such report was found.

Later the officers appeared before the police trial board and were found guilty and fined. But no perjury charge was pressed.

After considerable pressure the case was reported to the grand jury, but the grand jury refused to indict, Professor Freedman says, adding he is convinced the presentation had much to do with the grand jury's decision.

Search-and-seizure laws, which make it difficult for police to make valid arrests in narcotics cases, also lead to false testimony.

In one Eastern city a public defender tells of a policeman who testified that he had been watching a man who looked like a narcotics suspect. The policeman said the man reached into his pocket and pulled out a handkerchief, and when he did a small packet fell on the sidewalk. The policeman recognized it as the kind of packet that often contains narcotics, so he picked it up before the suspect could bend down and get it. And the lab told him he was right about the contents.

Certainly a plausible story. Except the same story was told 16 different times by policemen in the city—each with a different suspect, and all in a period of a few days.

It seemed evident the officers had searched the defendants illegally, discovered the narcotics, and then testified in a way that would make the arrest lawful.

To enforce the law, policemen may break the law. There is evidence they sometimes lie in court because it is their job to get a conviction. Society demands it. And judges look the other way.

The coaching of witnesses can be a difficult area for many honest trial lawyers.

"Our witnesses get a tremendous hammering in court," says Professor Hazard. "The good lawyer dances with them, uses the rapid feedback, jumps around ignoring logical order, until the average witness gets all flustered and goes to pieces.

"Unless he is prepared for this he can really get slaughtered."

But there is a thin line between coaching a witness in how to stick to his story under these difficult conditions and showing him how to slant testimony or to withhold information by being "honest," and admitting that he "forgets," or he "doesn't know." Just as there is a subtle difference between making sure the witness "understands the consequences of saying certain things in court"—things that might open him up to criminal prosecution. Either way—by telling the truth or by lying—he may lose. But the greatest risk seems to be, in most cases, in telling the truth.

This will remain the case until perjury laws are enforced—if the fear of punishment is really the way to deter crime.

The President's commission asserts: "There is no apparent reason for distinction between perjury and other crimes. Sound prosecutive direction, proof beyond a reasonable doubt to a judge and jury, and the other traditional safeguards applicable to every criminal case provide adequate protection against the unwarranted charge and conviction of perjury."

It seems obvious that when any law is ignored by prosecutors and judges, some citizens will break the law. It is true of prostitution, gambling, and other vice. Towns stay wide-open until the crackdown comes.

But when our system of justice and the officers of our court *encourage* violation of the law—as is the case in divorce court, and too often in other kinds of cases too—the system tends to break down.

In Chapter V we noted that Dean Pound compared the adversary process with a football game. But even in football there is a strong sense of fair play. Gouging the opponent's eyes, blocking from behind, and standing off side is not acceptable.

In court both the coaches and referees—the lawyers and judges—should encourage sportsmanship. It could have an impact on our nation's attitude toward the game of law, and help bring order to our society.

CHAPTER XIV

The Jury: Safety in Numbers

While the professionals retain their rigid grip on our system of justice, one segment belongs to the people: the jury trial.

The reason for this is clear: Many Americans, including leading trial lawyers, lack confidence in our laws and our judges.

Because polite language has been scraped away, this sounds harsh. Like any generalization, it is subject to criticism and modification. But no matter how you slice the arguments used in support of the jury system, you find the distrust of judges and doubts about inflexible laws at the core.

Says Jacob D. Fuchsberg, former president of the American Trial Lawyers Association, a member of the President's Commission on Civil Rights and on the legal services advisory board of the Office of Economic Opportunity:

"Judges have no monopoly on intelligence, insight, or fairness. They are ordinary human beings like anyone else. I believe the opinions of 12 people are better than the opinions of one—and I don't care whether they are 12 lawyers, 12 judges, or 12 laymen.

"When 12 people must come to a decision, the prejudices that are inherent in most people get worked out in the discussion that is involved. I am sure most lawyers will agree that they find they get a more objective and fair judgment from 12 people.

"The conscience of a community is better reflected through a jury."

Donald K. Ross, spokesman for the 4,800-member Defense

Research Institute, a Milwaukee-based organization supported largely by insurance companies and their lawyers, says about the same thing.

"We feel a jury of 12 people can better decide an issue than anything else man has devised up to this point. A jury is better than a judge because with a jury there is always the give and take of 12 persons. Thus prejudice and bias can be reduced to a high degree in the jury room.

"While a judge has special legal knowledge, he is still just one person, filled with the prejudices and biases that are a part of each one of us.

"Another thing we like: the jury system is comparatively free of politics and pressures."

One of the nation's leading experts on the jury, Hans Zeisel, of the University of Chicago, and co-author, with Harry Kalven Jr., of the 12-year study (and book) *The American Jury,* points out that "in 20 to 25 percent of the cases where the jury comes to a different verdict than the judge would have come to, the jury is often in the position to 'do justice' in the individual case without breaking the law." This is because the lay jury "does not have to give reasons for its verdict."

Many judges, "confronted with the letter of the law, and without the freedom the jury has" to bend the law, are "glad to have had a jury" because it can render more humane justice.

The theory that judges can be as fair as a jury "assumes that judges are perfect human beings," he adds, "an assumption that is unfortunately far from the truth—especially in the United States where we have so many judges and therefore not always people who are beyond reproach. One need not point out the recurring instances of judges who have to be removed because of flagrant misbehavior."

And he sees another problem resolved by a jury.

"In big metropolitan areas as many as one out of every four court suits are directed against the city or against a transit authority, which is usually controlled by the city. In view of the fact that the judges in these cities are, in some measure, dependent on the good will of the mayors, who have a hand in their appointment or candidacy for election, this is probably a conflict of interest that should be avoided by the retention of the jury."

Even with these strong arguments in favor of the jury, a growing number of judges, lawyers, and legal scholars would scrap the 700-year-old system—unique to the English-speaking world.

Among other things, the critics contend:

- The jury system creates delays and causes court congestion.
- Jury trials are too costly.
- Because testimony is so often technical, many jurors do not comprehend what is going on. Or they may not understand the law. Or follow the thread of logic in a case.
- It is hard to round up a jury that really represents a fair cross section of the community. Many citizens are "too busy to serve." Or feel compensation is too low for the time spent. So they ask to be excused by the hundreds.
- Juries are unpredictable.

Yet those who support the jury system are quick to grumble, as does Jacob Fuchsberg: "Those who oppose it are largely academicians and judges and lawyers who have little practical experience with the system."

Congestion and Delay

The most valid criticism centers around the fact jury trials take more time than trials before a judge. Professor Zeisel says "the best estimate is that the bench trial would take 40 percent less time than the jury trial."

In Philadelphia and in a number of other cities I visited it can take days and even weeks to select a jury. This is especially true where a criminal case has made headlines for several days running. Or when the prosecutor intends to ask for the capital penalty and prospective jurors who oppose capital punishment are excused.

Because of the time it takes to conduct a criminal jury trial, judges in Chicago and in other cities are reported to give those who demand a trial by jury longer sentences if convicted.

Professor Zeisel waves a danger flag when he finds fellow professionals urging that state courts follow the lead of Great Britain, where the jury system originated. For there the civil jury has been abolished.

"If we abolish the jury in civil cases to cure court delay, we must look forward to the day when our courts will be up to date. Then we will be confronted with the question: what system of adjudication do we really prefer, trial with or without jury?

"There is one thing to be learned from court history—namely, that abolished institutions never come back. So we had better make up our minds now as to what we want. Because if we should like to preserve the right to jury trial in civil cases, then we must look for other remedies for court congestion."

Jury Trials Too Costly

One judge, Matthew J. Jasen of Buffalo, N.Y., points out that more than $5 million in taxpayers' money is spent on juries alone each year in the New York State courts.

"I'm in favor of the jury system," he says. "But there are many who don't believe it is necessary. To save the system, I am proposing a six-man jury. That would cut costs in half—a saving of over $2 million a year in our state."

Judge Jasen contends a six-man jury is "just as effective" as one with 12 members. In New York's lower courts, and in lower courts in several other states, six-man juries are used.

"Recently I looked at six-man juries used in the trial courts of Florida," he adds. "Every judge I talked to told me the plan is extremely satisfactory."

The logic of scrapping the jury system like an old car because it is too costly to keep it running is full of holes.

In a nation that can spend billions on alcohol, television, gambling, fashions, girlie magazines, deluxe autos, tobacco, professional sports, and even moon shots, the price we pay for something as essential as justice is ridiculously low.

Cost should not be a factor in the decision to retain or eliminate the jury.

A Pittsburgh judge, Henry Ellenbogen, calls the use of juries "a great system," noting that while "justice is not inexpensive, the precious rights and freedom of the individual are well worth it."

In a proposal for a foundation grant, designed to eliminate the waste of time and money involved in calling citizens for jury duty, the Institute of Judicial Administration in New York asserts:

> Each year many thousands of citizens are summoned to serve as jurors for two, three, or four weeks in courts located throughout the nation. Many of those called do not serve in a single case. And even those who do sit in one or two cases are likely to have most of their time wasted, with the consequence that they become apathetic and antagonistic toward jury service.
>
> The result is that many qualified citizens deliberately avoid such service, leaving the work to housewives, elderly persons, etc., so that a fair cross section of the community is not achieved.
>
> In addition large amounts of public and private funds are wasted in jury fees and expenses, in payments of salaries and wages to employees [many large firms now are paying wages while a man serves, and it is often part of a union contract], and in lost income to self-employed persons who sit cooling their heels while on jury "service."

One industrial firm alone paid out more than $250,000 to hourly rated workers for time not worked while on jury duty in 1965, the institute asserts.

"If a system could be devised to call only as many people as were genuinely needed for jury service, and to cut down on the waiting time of those called, the jury system would be strengthened and enormous savings would be made," the institute asserts.

Such a system, it suggests, could save taxpayers $1 million a year in New York City alone. It would be multiplied many times over for all the other communities which would benefit and then multiplied many times again for private savings in the form of salaries, wages, and income.

The Jury Doesn't Understand

Back in 1928 a Philadelphia attorney complained in a national magazine that

> most law suits present a plurality of complicated issues which single-track minds are utterly unable to grasp.
>
> To discriminate between conflicting items of evidence, to determine whether a skillful prevaricator is twisting facts to his own profit, to see when they are being grossly exaggerated or manufactured out of whole cloth, requires the highest degree of judgment, education, experience, and mental alertness. No greater demand can be made on the human intellect.

Said Granville Williams, an English scholar, in a series of lectures in 1955:

> . . . There seems to be a formidable weight of argument against the jury system. To begin with, the 12 men and women are chosen haphazard. Exemption is given to some professional people who would seem to be among the best qualified to serve—clergymen, ministers of religion, lawyers, doctors, dentists, chemists, justices of the peace, as well as all rank of the armed forces.
>
> The subtraction of relatively intelligent classes means that it is an understatement to describe a jury, with Herbert Spencer, as a "group of 12 people of average ignorance."
>
> There is no guarantee that members of a particular jury may not be quite unusually ignorant, credulous, slow-witted, narrow-minded, biased, or temperamental. The danger of this happening is not one that can be removed by some slight procedural change or adjustment.

In his 1962-63 report to the Harvard Law School, Dean Erwin Griswold, now U.S. Solicitor General, said: "Why should anyone think that 12 persons brought in from the street, selected in various ways, for their lack of general ability, should have any special capacity for deciding controversies between persons?"

Lawyer Walter J. Bilder, a frequent contributor to the *New Jersey Law Journal,* says: "The minds of jurors are notoriously susceptible to influences which are extraneous to the merits of the controversy and . . . the jury's verdict is likely to be determined by considerations which are irrelevant to a just determination of the case."

Part of the problem is that the language of the law includes familiar words with strange meanings. Latin, Old English, Middle English, and French words are common. And lawyers use words that are extremely precise in one sentence; words with broad meanings, like "adequate," in the next.

Take this paragraph from Tentative Draft 13 of the American Law Institute's "Restatement of the Law":

> Criminal proceedings are usually instituted by the issuance of some form of process, generally a warrant for arrest, the purpose of which is to bring the accused before a magistrate in order that he may determine whether the accused shall be bound over for further action by a grand jury or for trial by a court. The magistrate may, however, have a summary jurisdiction so that he may at the hearing dispose of the case by finding the accused either innocent or guilty. In either case, the issuance of the process constitutes the institution of the criminal proceedings. Not infrequently, however, an indictment is found by a grand jury or an information filed by a prosecuting officer without previous issuance of a warrant or other process. In such cases the return of the indictment or the filing of the information marks the institution of the proceedings. In all of these cases official action has been taken which constitutes a formal charge of criminal misconduct against the person accused.

While the paragraph is more clear than much legal writing, and perhaps laymen can make sense of it, it could (and should be) said more simply.

There are some in the legal profession working to bring this about. But other attorneys prefer to keep laymen in the dark. It gives the law an aura of mystery and helps a lawyer's ego. To wade through this stuff he has to be a "learned man." It may also help pad the lawyer's pocketbook as the man on the street throws up his hands and runs for help.

But others know you can't have it both ways. If the jury system is to be effective, then lawyers cannot play intellectual games, using words in ways that puzzle other intellectuals as well as the average citizen.

Lawyer Walter J. Bilder contends:

Aside from automobile-collision cases, a lawsuit is almost certain to involve a set of facts . . . which relates to . . . [an] experience which is wholly alien to . . . most, if not all, persons who become members of a jury.

Confronted with such a set of facts, the members of a jury will . . . [have] an attitude of incomprehension and inattentiveness and even boredom, aggravated undoubtedly by a feeling of resentment at having been compelled to leave their ordinary pursuits in order to settle a controversy which even fails to arouse [in] them [even] an academic interest.

Yet the study by Professor Zeisel and Harry Kalven Jr. shows that judges agree with juries 80 percent of the time. This should indicate juries are more competent than critics believe.

Prentice H. Marshall, who, in the fall of 1967, joined the law faculty at the University of Illinois after 13 years as a trial lawyer with a large Chicago firm, disagrees with those who say "juries can be bamboozled or misled by sharp lawyers." He contends the adversary process helps eliminate this. And weak or incompetent jurors are weeded out at the start as they are questioned by the lawyers or judge.

In answer to the charge "lawyers want dopes" on a jury, he says both sides want jurors who understand their arguments.

"I acknowledge that when trying a criminal case I am more inclined to accept a juror who has drifted around a bit, and perhaps expressed certain traits of irresponsibility," he says. "The prosecution looks for those jurors who lead a fairly rigid life.

"In a medical malpractice case, when defending the doctor, I want jurors who understand the problems of the patient, yet comprehend what the doctor and hospital face. I want jurors who are not inclined to decide for the plaintiff (the patient) solely because his medical condition did not improve or worsened. I would want to know if the juror has ever been hospitalized. When. Where. The nature of the hospitalization. I find out if he found the care he received satisfactory. Whether he left the hospital with any feelings against it. Or if anything that he experienced at the hospital would influence his decision in the case.

"I believe most jurors are very frank to admit it when they are prejudiced. I recall one case where a juror in the box stated he did not feel he could serve on a jury because his little girl died in a hospital."

And some judges see jury trials doing just the opposite of the things so often complained of.

"The jury should be retained, if for no other reason, to keep the lawyers on their toes," says Judge Ruggero J. Aldisert of Pittsburgh. "Nonjury cases tend to drag and the lawyers get sloppy."

Decisions are not as far off the track as some who oppose juries say they are, he adds.

"Juries usually come down with verdicts just about as I see it," he says.

Hard to Get Jurors

There is a great reluctance on the part of many citizens to serve as jurors. This is partly due to low compensation. Juror pay nationally runs from $4 or $5 a day to $15. In New York's supreme courts (trial courts of general jurisdiction) jurors get $8 a day, for example.

It is also partly because a large segment of better-educated citizens are excluded for one reason or another.

In many instances, lawyers, when selecting a jury, will refuse to accept business executives or others holding responsible positions. And they reject jurors for other reasons that are not always explained—in a way that makes citizens feel that the system must be wrong.

Says a Chicago office worker with four years of education beyond high school: "While my employer needed me badly, I didn't ask to be excused from jury duty because I felt I had an obligation, a responsibility to serve. For two weeks I reported in at the courthouse every morning at 9:30. Four times they called my number [for civil juries] in that two-week period."

But not once did she sit on a jury. Each time a lawyer on

one side or another excused her from the panel without giving a reason, but apparently, she says, on the basis of her religion.

"There were several others who did not sit on a jury," she adds. "They were excused by the lawyers because someone in their family was a doctor, nurse, policeman, or even if they had ever been in an accident.

"Some of them said it looked as if the less you know and the less education you have, the more qualified you are for jury duty.

"I'm certain of this: Next time they ask me to serve I'm going to say, 'Look here now, why should I come in for two weeks just to sit and read books and never serve on a jury? I have better things to do, and it caused problems for my employer because he was short of help at the time.'"

Unwillingness to serve is also caused by the poor administrative practices of the courts. I found, as I toured the nation, that would-be jurors wasted many hours sitting around waiting for cases to be called.

In many cities judges come in late (9:30 or 10 A.M.), take up to two hours for lunch, and leave early (sometimes before 3 P.M. and usually by 4 or 4:30). From time to time they may take an afternoon off to play golf or take care of personal business while jurors twiddle their thumbs.

While some juries are weighted with housewives and retired men, in other sections there is an overbalance of businessmen and others in the middle class. In the South a few Negroes are being called for jury duty. But most panels remain largely, if not all, white. Other sections of the country are equally slow to impanel minority groups.

Jurors—except in justice-of-the-peace courts—are not simply "hauled in off the street," as some critics imply. Often they are picked from tax rolls, voter registration lists, or rolls compiled by someone in local government.

In Maine the Chief Justice of the Supreme Court appoints two jury commissioners from each of the 16 counties—one Republican and one Democrat. These men make up a master list.

Judge James L. Reid of Portland explains how it works:

> The names on the master list, except in the smaller counties, are submitted from time to time by the municipal officers of towns and cities, at the jury commissioner's request. In a large county there may be as many as 2,500 names on the master list.
>
> Reasonably ahead of a term of court the commissioners call from the list a sufficient number of names to be summoned for jury duty, usually about 30. In the case of a murder trial, of course, the number will be substantially increased.

Since 1965 most counties have been sending out questionnaires to prospective jurors. Lawyers may read these before they begin selecting a jury, in an effort, he says, to permit counsel to "more easily get a cross-section jury of 12."

At a meeting of jury commissioners it was agreed that, among other things, "justices of the Superior Court should be firm in refusing to excuse from jury service except on the grounds of severe hardship or physical or mental infirmity," Judge Reid says.

(Under a bill signed by Governor Kenneth M. Curtis, May 26, 1967, Maine jurors are chosen at random from the voting lists instead of from a master list drawn up by commissioners as in the past.)

Los Angeles County Superior Court has a selection system that is undoubtedly better than most around the country, though it is far from perfect.

It uses 750 jurors a day in civil court in downtown Los Angeles alone, says William A. Goodwin, the jury commissioner. The names of roughly 3 million voters in the county are on IBM cards. Every sixth name in every sixth precinct is drawn.

"We're lucky to get one out of 10 we send letters to," he admits. The list of exemptions is long: Tollgate keepers, people who work on boats, jail and prison workers, railroad engineers and other workers, telephone and telegraph employees (the telephone company waives its exemption), policemen and firemen, members of the National Guard, those serving in the armed services, legislators, elected local officials and other governmental employees, teachers, ministers, druggists, hospital officials, physicians, Christian Science practitioners and readers, monks, and anyone who has already served on a jury within the year.

While the law doesn't exempt policemen's wives, judges usually do not accept them. And other excuses are accepted—like a housewife who says she lacks transportation (Los Angeles is short on public transit). Those who run "little one-man businesses" are let off.

After the cards are drawn by the computer, letters are sent out. Jurors have roughly a week to report. Mr. Goodwin prefers to give a prospective juror a time extension rather than scratch his name if he asks to be excused.

When the juror arrives he is screened for good health, ability to hear and see, and other qualities necessary to perform his duty. He then takes a written test to determine whether he has "sufficient knowledge of the English language and adequate comprehension and mental capacity to understand proceedings in a court of law." If that test is passed, then an interview is held, where, among other things, the jury commissioner determines whether the individual should be excused.

A prospective juror sits in the "jury pool," a large room with chairs, tables for chess and card playing, and other recreational activities. Each juror serves one month, and some never sit on a jury—despite the screening.

Yet I found less wasted time in Los Angeles than in other cities, including Chicago, which has a comparable court system.

Pay remains poor—often $5 a day plus mileage to and from the courthouse. A few states are pushing jury pay up, but it is doubtful it will begin to measure up to what a man can make back at the office or plant.

Juries Are Unpredictable

There seems to be little doubt that this is true, although again the Zeisel-Kalven figures tend to refute it, since judges agree with 80 percent of the jury verdicts.

The Texas jury in the fall of 1967 that reduced the amount awarded in an auto-accident case because the plaintiff was not wearing a seat belt might be considered unpredictable.

So might the jury that found a deputy sheriff and several white men guilty in the slaying of three civil rights workers near Philadelphia, Miss. Or so the reaction of many Southerners would indicate (I was in Louisiana at the time the verdict came down, and saw the reaction.)

Men accused of serious crimes have been convicted on little evidence, or set free in airtight cases after the 12 men and women finished their deliberations.

Warren Burnett, of Odessa, Tex., an experienced trial lawyer, contends that "one of the majesties of the jury system is the uncertainty of it. The only thing a trial lawyer is sure of is a darned good seat at the trial."

Judges told me it is especially hard to get a jury to convict in a drunken-driving case in many sections of the country. Someone on the jury can be counted on to vote for acquittal, remembering that only last Saturday night he had a little too much under his belt and just wasn't caught.

Yet in other areas juries are tough in drinking cases and similar violations.

One day when I visited the Chicago public defender's office a young lawyer and his friends were celebrating a victory in a narcotics-peddling case. The lawyer was jubilant because, he said, it is nearly impossible to win acquittal from a jury in this kind of case, even in Chicago where many people believe "anything goes."

Juries tend to be especially rough on cases involving sex and children, according to the University of Chicago study. Yet they tend to look the other way in rape cases involving girls near the age of consent if violence is not involved (called statutory rape).

Juries tend to represent the sentiment of the general public at any given time, handing down verdicts that agree with public opinion toward a type of offense.

When a jury does not like a law, it will shape its decision accordingly—either in leniency or severity.

And, according to the University of Chicago study, like each judge, each jury is different. From time to time a jury surprises everyone. Since jurors meet in secret, no one really knows how they hammer out a decision. When the Chicago researchers tried to find out through "jury tapping" they created a national uproar.

There is seldom a suggestion that jury trials be scrapped in criminal courts. But some judges and lawyers now suggest that auto-accident cases could better be handled by special boards.

They point out that not too many years ago when a worker was hurt he had to sue his employer in court. Now the problem is resolved through workmen's compensation. A similar system is being suggested for the auto crash—perhaps with no finding of fault and all parties involved in the accident being compensated for losses.

If there were no need to decide who was to blame for the accident—and thus who should pay—the dispute-settling role of the jury could be eliminated, proponents argue.

Similar boards or commissions are being proposed for other areas of court business—including traffic cases.

But trial lawyers oppose this, perhaps partly out of defense of their method of earning a living and perhaps partly for good reasons.

Says Warren Burnett of Odessa, Tex.:

"It is argued that boards and commissions are much more efficient than a jury. Efficiency isn't everything. It is . . . efficient to solve crimes by arm twisting or torture, too.

"Some people are always ready to rush in and sacrifice individual rights."

Illinois University's Professor Marshall can see value in what many would call a radical change—permitting jurors to ask questions. He urges the adoption of a system used in parts of California: note-taking by jurors.

He believes jurors can be asked to remember too much, and so transcripts of testimony should be more readily available to them. This is either discouraged or prohibited by some judges.

And he would improve the reading of instructions to juries. Too often judges mumble and drone and stumble, he says. Some have the clerks read the instructions.

"A good many of our judges have not had experience trying cases, and they are not familiar with the . . . law involved," he says. "They are reading words that are strange to them. They have no feeling for the concepts they are trying to communicate to the jury. They read without inflection or emphasis. Even otherwise good judges do this."

In criminal courts he believes "substantially less than 50 percent of the judges" were experienced criminal trial lawyers before taking the bench, and this has an impact on their handling of juries as well as on their ability to dispense justice.

Many argue that the jury is the last niche in our growing government where the citizen really takes part—beyond his trip to the voting booth every few years.

And Professor Marshall mentions an important factor that supports the use of the jury. The professionals, he says, get cynical and hardened to the system's imperfections.

"Those of us who work in the courts—the judges and lawyers—know that perfection cannot be obtained in our system of justice. That absolute truth cannot be obtained. And because of that, things go downhill.

"But this never happens to a jury. A juror is only in court a few times in his lifetime. He doesn't know what the professionals know. And so the juror strives for perfection."

Then, almost as an afterthought, he adds the point that is clearly the core of the question: "I believe the decision of 12 is better than the decision of one."

Until we upgrade the bench and the trial bar, and until outmoded laws can be scrapped, it seems certain that the jury is essential. It protects the public as a whole, and especially the little man.

CHAPTER XV

Who Owns the Courts?

When I started out, in late 1966, to study the nation's state courts for *The Christian Science Monitor,* a neighbor of mine—a normally bright and winning suburban housewife—said she couldn't understand why my newspaper would want to devote so much time, money, and space to such a dull topic.

After all, she said, she didn't expect to break any laws. So why should she care?

A few days later another friend, a responsible businessman with a major firm, reacted in about the same way.

Not only did they find the subject of justice dull, but they had been taught since childhood that our system of justice is the best of all systems of justice, and the third and equal arm of government in our democracy.

They didn't want me to find flaws in an old and reliable institution that served the nation so well in an era of gaslights and horses, even if there were things wrong with it in the age of space.

Nor did they want to be jarred out of the lethargy that grips so many Americans as they bask in affluence. It is easier to turn our problems over to that newly emerged omniscience called big government.

Without a doubt, both also have bought the theory (although they probably have not consciously thought about it) that our courts, and, in fact, our laws, are the private and exclusive property of lawyers and judges. This is a concept that has long been pushed by many members of the bench and bar.

These comments by my friends, and their attitudes, are common. They also are wrong. The very fact that so many Americans hold these views may help explain why there is so much turmoil in our nation today, and so many problems in our courts.

It seems axiomatic that problems arise when changes are needed, when old ideas and concepts and attitudes no longer fit the times.

Yet lawyers and judges, schooled in preserving the status quo, working with law built on precedent, in institutions that honor tradition, resist change.

Alexis de Tocqueville wrote:

> Some of the tastes and habits of the aristocracy may . . . be discovered in the character of lawyers. They participate in the same instinctive love of order and formalities; and they entertain the same repugnance to the actions of the multitude, and the same secret contempt of the government of the people. . . . I do not, then, assert that *all* the members of the legal profession are at *all* times the friends of order and the opponents of innovation, but merely that most of them are usually so.

Former United States Attorney General Herbert Brownell, president of the American Judicature Society, told me in an interview in his New York law office that "all of the great administrative improvements in New York in recent years came through the efforts of laymen. Citizens forced judges and lawyers to make changes."

As I toured the nation, I found too many lawyers and judges have vested interest in retaining the present system. Or they lack the courage to fight their professional brothers.

"It has to be laymen," Mr. Brownell explained. "They're the people who are hurt by the malfunctions of the courts."

Yet like my friends, millions of Americans, through apathy, fear, belief that the courts are sacrosanct, or conviction that mere citizens are unqualified to voice an opinion, are reluctant to demand change.

It is a curious fact that two once-silent groups—young people who were supposed to be "seen, but not heard," and American Negroes, who were to be neither seen nor heard—are suddenly forcing drastic changes in our basic concepts of law and justice, as well as in our very way of life.

There are other important factors, of course. One of them is Vietnam, a "different kind of war." Another is the rising crime rate. Population growth and the rush to urban areas must be taken into account. The muscle of our labor unions cannot be overlooked. Nor can we discount the education explosion, the two-car garage, and the amalgamation of white ethnic groups.

Even our jet airlines and superhighways play a part. The movement of industry into the rural South and Midwest is a factor. So are our growing affluence, our ever-increasing leisure time, and our expanding mobility. For all bring us in contact with people with different ways of life (and all make it easier for those so inclined to get into trouble).

And there is television, the friendly baby-sitter, perhaps the most potent educational tool yet devised by man, and too often the purveyor of violence and the bizarre into our living rooms.

Yet none compares in impact, at least at present, with the society-shaking wrath of nearly liberated Negroes, who are determined to convince America that the "white man's law" is flawed and unjust.

Nor do they compare with the growing rebellion we find in our homes as our highly educated and idealistic teen-agers challenge our society's half-truths and hypocrisies.

What are our young people trying to tell us about laws passed, at least in theory, to enforce morality?

They read of businessmen involved in price-fixing, who are arrested for dodging taxes, or are accused of being less than truthful about their products. Leading medical men contend cigarettes are a health hazard, yet selling cigarettes is so profitable, and the tobacco lobby so powerful, we do little except increase advertising budgets.

Our safety experts say speed kills while our auto makers spend millions selling speed. We preach brotherhood and individualism, and then rush to the clean white suburbs to buy look-alike houses with two cars parked in front.

We worry about our daughters and even our sons getting involved in sex, yet even toothpaste commercials emphasize sex appeal. We tell our youngsters not to fight, and then demand killing and violence in our television shows or write them off as dull. We tolerate a vicious crime syndicate. Divorce and even adultery grow as acceptable behavior as we glorify both in our movies and magazines. Parents lecture to children about obeying the law, then, with junior watching from the back seat, break the speed limit.

A prominent Chicagoan told me, not long ago, how he was stopped for speeding with his five-year-old sitting beside him. As was the custom, he handed the policeman a $5 bill with his license.

"My boy looked at me so seriously," the man said, "and then he said to me, 'Daddy, I didn't think you were supposed to do that.'" It was, he adds, the last time he bribed a policeman.

What are our young people saying to us when they turn their backs on high-paying jobs in industry, and ignore the house and two-car garage in the suburbs to enter the Peace Corps, to teach school, or to work with slum children? What are they saying when they openly flout sexual taboos, or wear strange clothing and haircuts?

The Negro revolution is, of course, another story. The Negro's impact on our law—and on our concept of justice—in the past 10 years is more evident than many Americans want to admit. We shake our fists at the Supreme Court for leading the way, not wanting to believe they are right.

So a nation that professes freedom and equality and justice as a basic concept is shaken when it is forcefully pointed out that we can be unjust, and that some Americans are more free and more equal than others.

Negro violence frightens us. But are there lessons to be learned?

I covered the Detroit riots for the *Monitor,* and the Chicago riots the summer before Detroit exploded. I was in Selma and spent days driving up and down the roads of Mississippi, and spent weeks in the Midtown slum of Gary, Ind.

I found American Negroes are both hated and harassed by other low-status groups in our society—and by American policemen. Psychologists tell us words can be more brutal than clubs.

Negroes pay more for bread, beans, and milk than I do in a white middle-class neighborhood. Easy credit is not very easy when, as I discovered, a television set that sells for $120 cash in my area can cost, with interest, more than $350 for a slum family.

Ghetto store owners are white. Admittedly, risks are higher, but not that much higher—at least until the riots broke out.

As I interviewed Detroit Negroes and watched them loot and burn, a pattern became clear. They were striking out at the white store owners and the injustice of high prices for inferior merchandise, and at legal usury.

They were striking out at slum landlords. And at the police and the institutions that represented the "white man's law" that seemed so unjust.

For those who are offended by this, I can only add that I am not condoning violence. I am reporting what I found as I probed Negro neighborhoods before and after the riots. (My first study of the Chicago and Detroit situation was in the spring of 1965.)

The courts have a major responsibility in all of this—as do our legislatures. As de Tocqueville pointed out well over a century ago, "The courts of justice are visible organs by which the legal profession is enabled to control the democracy."

But so do the rest of us—the citizens and taxpayers, the "little people."

Jeremiah Sullivan Black, Attorney General under President Buchanan and former Chief Justice of the Pennsylvania Supreme Court, restated a basic principle when he said, "Government is but an aggregation of individual rights and powers."

Roscoe Pound explained the conflict of our present era in his 1906 speech to the American Bar Association when he argued:

> Justice, which is the end of law, is the ideal compromise between the activities of each and the activities of all in a crowded world. The law seeks to harmonize these activities and to adjust the relations of every man with his fellows so as to accord with the moral sense of the community. When the community is at one in its ideas of justice, this is possible. When the community is divided and

diversified, and groups and classes and interests, understanding each other none too well, have conflicting ideas of justice, the task is extremely difficult. It is impossible that legal and ethical ideas should be in entire accord in such a society. The individual looks at cases one by one and measures them by his individual sense of right and wrong.

In 1966 and 1967 our leading thinkers debated our right to fight in Vietnam, and whether to bomb or not to bomb. We explain our actions, at least in part, by saying that we must show the Communists they will be punished if they continue to violate international law and try to take over Asia. This concept of punishment—or threat of punishment—as a deterrent is the same theory that we have so long used in enforcement of our criminal laws.

Until recently our highest concept of consumer law was "let the buyer beware." Now we are starting to recognize that the manufacturer has an obligation too. Most notable pressure has been on the auto makers, although there is growing interest in making the tobacco industry more responsible too.

In many states our laws make it easy for even incompetent tradesmen to put liens on our homes. It remains cheaper and wiser to pay than to fight the plumber or carpenter in court.

Our Internal Revenue Service has been accused of using high-handed and even illegal methods of gathering information and enforcing tax laws.

Hundreds of cities and towns depend upon traffic fines as an important source of revenue—giving little or no thought to enforcement as an important form of traffic-safety education.

There was a day when court-watching was an interesting sport, and a courtroom full of townspeople reminded lawyers and judges and the others who labor there that the courts belong to the people. Now we sit in our family rooms, watching television, while the bench and bar assume sole ownership of our courts by default. We elect judges we have never heard of, and seldom see, not caring whether they are brilliant or incompetent, or even buffoons.

As I looked at the nation's courts, it became increasingly

clear that reform will not take place without strong citizen action.

In the past few years a few women's clubs have taken on court-watching as community-service projects. Most are centered in the lower courts.

Pioneering work has been done in New England by the New England Conference of State Federation of Women's Clubs, headed by Mrs. Gerald E. Northrop, of Castleton, Vt.

But she says the work has only begun, and that some courts are throwing up barriers.

Mrs. Margaret Moore of the Indianapolis *News* blazed the trail for the rest of the nation when in 1962 a retired schoolteacher died after being knocked down by a purse snatcher. Letters poured in to the paper, and her editor suggested she do something.

From a group of 30 women called to a luncheon, the Indianapolis Anti-Crime Crusade was formed. Part of the program includes court-watching.

Now members of the organization sit in court every day and make reports—although they, too, had to battle resistance from some members of the bench and bar. Reports have been made on more than 70,000 cases, Mrs. Moore says. By confronting judges and others involved in the system of justice with their findings, reforms have been made.

But in most American cities the nuts-and-bolts machinery of the courts is largely ignored by public and press. Public interest too often focuses on the rich, the beautiful, or the prominent who are caught up in sordid crimes or divorce actions. Too little attention is paid to everyday procedures.

Court-watching can be a risky business, now that a whole generation of judges has come and gone with little or no public scrutiny. Earlier I mentioned the man in Louisville who was dressed down by a judge who dislikes people standing up before the jury goes to lunch, but thinks nothing of reading the comics on the bench.

But that was mild, compared to what happened to Frank Look, a 70-year-old Chicago salesman.

After conducting some business with his lawyer, Louis M.

March, Mr. Look decided to visit court with him—the first visit in 25 years.

When he sat down in court he had a cigar stub in his hand, and the bailiffs didn't like it. An argument developed, and Mr. Look finally beat a retreat to the hall, explaining the cigar wasn't even lit. The bailiffs said it was.

The judge ordered Mr. Look before the bench. Meanwhile, Mr. March became aware of the trouble and advised Mr. Look to apologize to the judge. Mr. Look did, but it mattered little, and the old man was sentenced to 30 days in jail for contempt of court.

It was de Tocqueville who said, "Some of the tastes and habits of the aristocracy may . . . be discovered in the characters of lawyers. They participate in the same instinctive love of order and formalities; and they entertain the same repugnance to the actions of the multitude."

It was Harry W. Jones, Cardozo professor of jurisprudence at Columbia University, who said, "There is much talk . . . about improving the 'image' of justice. Justice is not a commodity to be marketed by such means. The way to improve justice is to improve the reality of justice in the trial courts of the United States."

It was Herbert Brownell who said, when I asked him about who must bring about court reform, "It has to be laymen. They're the people who are hurt by the malfunctions of the court."

CHAPTER XVI

The Press Conflict

The people who live in the suburbs west of Chicago were stunned when 10-year-old Debbie Fijan was found murdered Feb. 11, 1966, after school.

In the public reaction that followed, newspapers, radio, and television stations and the national wire services sent reporters out to ask the Du Page County sheriff's office what was being done to capture the killer.

Sheriff Stanley A. Lynch was under pressure from all sides. And it wasn't long before his men nabbed a suspect—one of Debbie's teachers, Loren Schofield.

Debbie had been timekeeper at an elementary school basketball game on the afternoon she was slain. Loren Schofield coached that game.

On Feb. 15 one paper reported: "Schofield Questioned for More Than Nine Hours."

A Chicago newspaper story on Feb. 15 began:

> A young gym teacher who flunked a series of lie tests was charged with murder Tuesday in the stabbing death of 10-year-old Debbie Fijan.
>
> "I think I could have done it," the accused teacher, Loren Schofield, told Du Page County sheriff's police. "I am sick and I need help."

The following day Page 1 headlines in another paper announced: "Lab Tests Charred Clothes of Teacher. . . . Punish Killer, Girl's Father Pleads. . . . 'We've Got Our Man,' Sheriff Says."

On that same day a Chicago reporter wrote:

> Loren Franklin Schofield's inner torture was a secret he apparently betrayed to no one.
>
> His friends, neighbors, and acquaintances had his own word for it Wednesday, relayed by Sheriff's police, that he was "sick—I shouldn't be allowed to walk the streets."
>
> And yet no one among them had ever detected any sign that Schofield was the kind of man capable of the ghastly crime he is accused of, the mutilation-stabbing of 10-year-old Debbie Fijan.

Stories ran daily and usually were accompanied by pictures of the young teacher, the little girl, her parents, the sheriff, and others involved in the story.

Sheriff Lynch went on television so often that one paper reported Feb. 19: "His frequent appearances before the cameras prompted one law officer to refer to 'Lynch's Spectacular' and spurred newspaper reporters to ask him Thursday for 'equal time.' "

Then on Feb. 18 another paper headlined: "Coach Says He Did Not Slay Debbie. . . . He Changes His Statement." The story quoted Deputy Milton L. Rowe as saying he had found, on the teacher's clothing, "stains that might have been blood." Further down in the same story was another line: "The crime lab, in a partial report to Sheriff Lynch, has said that the stains found on the clothing which Schofield said he wore last Friday were not blood. . . ."

One Chicago reporter wrote:

> Several law-enforcement officials said privately that Lynch and Hopf [the state's attorney] already have a puny case against Schofield, which they have further weakened by frequent statements before television cameras and newsmen.
>
> Among the weak points, all admitted by Lynch, are that no motive has been established, no weapon has been found, and it is not known where death occurred.
>
> However, Lynch has repeatedly asserted he is sure he has the "right man" but has said that his men were "working on the theory" that there could have been an accomplice.

Loren Schofield sat in jail 15 days. His school suspended him from his job. Finally, bail of $50,000 was set, and his parents were able to scrape up enough to get him released.

On April 26, some 70 days after the arrest, a county grand jury listened to four hours of testimony. He was freed after only 35 minutes of deliberation.

But for Mr. Schofield, the nightmare isn't over. He and his wife and their child, and other close relatives, must live with the stigma of the accusations. No other suspect has been found. The sheriff—considered by most to be a responsible man—made flat, positive statements of Mr. Schofield's guilt.

In talking with residents of Du Page County I found some, and perhaps there are many, who still believe the ex-schoolteacher is the killer, and that he wriggled out of the charge by hiring smart lawyers, or on a technicality.

What does the Loren Schofield case mean to what is popularly known as the "fair trial–free press" dispute?

Curiously enough, both sides can argue it shows they are at least partly right—indicating the complexity of the problem.

To understand why, one must first understand the conflict.

The fair trial–free press controversy is tied to two amendments to the Constitution of the United States. The First Amendment is clear:

"Congress shall make no law . . . abridging freedom of the press. . . ."

The Sixth Amendment states:

"In all criminal prosecutions, the accused shall enjoy the right to a speedy trial, by an impartial jury of the state and district wherein the crime shall have been committed. . . ."

The assassination of President Kennedy, the slaying of Lee Harvey Oswald, and the retrial of Dr. Sam Sheppard in Cleveland have prompted lawyers and judges to take a new look at the amendments. Some have concluded—perhaps partly on the basis of emotion as well as logic—that there is a serious conflict.

Dozens of lawyers and judges told me that it may be impossible to pick an impartial jury and to keep it insulated from prejudice when the press is free to write what it wants before the trial begins.

In the case of Loren Schofield, the press can point out that he was released by a grand jury despite aggressive—and perhaps sometimes less than factual—reporting.

It can also be argued that Mr. Schofield can seek further justice through the courts by filing civil suits against those who wronged him. In fact this has happened. Mr. Schofield's lawyer has filed a $2 million suit against Sheriff Lynch and Deputy Rowe. It now is pending in neighboring Kane County. The attorney, Robert A. Chapski of Elgin, says he does not expect the trial to begin for several months.

Whether Mr. Schofield can win the suit, of course, is another matter.

While no suit has been filed against the newspapers or radio and television stations, Mr. Chapski contends the press played a key role in injuring his client. A scrapbook filled with clippings will be a major piece of evidence against the sheriff, he says.

Actually, it is being contended that the courts and the jury system are on trial in the free press–fair trial dispute.

Supreme Court decisions have not commented on what the press does as much as on what the courts do not do to guarantee a free trial.

The High Court did not, however, negate press responsibility for self-restraint and honest reporting.

A national survey of the fair trial–free press dispute by this writer reveals:

• A few of the nation's busiest trial lawyers and some judges assert that except in rare cases press coverage has little effect on whether or not a jury that can hand down a fair verdict can be selected.

"Given a good judge, pretrial publicity has no effect on the trial," says Warren Burnett, of Odessa, Tex., considered by many to be one of the best lawyers in the Southwest. "No system can be devised to meet the problems that arise in the exceptional case like Oswald or Ruby.

"I have seen judges set up a few simple ground rules and

inspire the respect of the press and everyone else involved. A good judge will change venue [shift the trial to another city].

"Some judges are reluctant to do this [because they like the publicity of a major case, or feel it will be a reflection on their ability to be fair], and so they clutch a case to their breast."

This is especially true in states where judges run for office. Like other politicians, judges may feel they need the publicity.

• Newspapers are often guilty of excesses in "big" cases. This is more often true in communities where papers are competing for business with other papers, or with radio and television stations.

Screaming headlines and titillating stories are examples of crass commercialism that "sells papers," regardless of who is hurt.

• Yet more often than not the problem of fair trial vs. free press stems from the actions of judges, prosecutors, or police officials.

• At least one other factor should be mentioned. Many judges and lawyers have a deep-rooted dislike and distrust of the press, which colors their views. This partly stems from pride and concern over criticism of their profession. Others see the press prying into affairs they would rather keep secret. But too often this dislike stems from newspapers that assign a green reporter to cover the police and court beat. Thus flaws in coverage of court and legal news are common.

But most attention is being paid in this controversy, at least by bench and bar, to their own ranks. This is partly because the press can do little about the suppression of news by the bench.

When the Supreme Court of the United States, in an 8-to-1 decision, overturned the 1954 murder conviction of Dr. Sam Sheppard because "virulent publicity" deprived him of his right to a fair trial, Tom C. Clark, then Associate Justice, placed the responsibility on the public officials involved—not the press.

Writing on a long list of errors made by the judge and other officials, Mr. Justice Clark said:

> The court's fundamental error is compounded by the holding that it lacked power to control the publicity about the trial. . . . The carnival atmosphere at trial could easily have been avoided since the courtroom and courthouse premises are subject to the control of the court. . . .
>
> The court should have made some effort to control the release of leads, information, and gossip to the press by police officers, witnesses, and the counsel for both sides. Much of the information thus disclosed was inaccurate, leading to groundless rumors and confusion. That the judge was aware of his responsibility in this respect may be seen from his warning to Steve Sheppard, the accused's brother, who had apparently made public statements in an attempt to discredit testimony for the prosecution.

Commenting on the case, George Edwards, Judge of the Sixth United States Circuit Court of Appeals, said recently: "That was the worst murder trial ever recorded. The trial judge's son was a member of the Cleveland police detective unit that investigated the case and laid the groundwork for the indictment. The trial judge and the prosecutor were both candidates for election to the common pleas bench during the trial. The trial was recessed on election day for campaigning. The trial judge and prosecutor posed together in mutual congratulations after they had been elected. The jury was not sequestered."

Martin S. Hayden, editor of the Detroit *News*, recently said at a seminar in that city: "The charges the bar wants to make [against the press] fall into the Cleopatra syndrome. You'll recall that when she learned that Mark Antony had been unfaithful she had the slave [who brought the message] killed. Ever since there has been a tendency to take it out on the bearer of bad news."

Defense lawyers contend that once the prosecutor or police give information—too often material that is not admissible as evidence in court—to the press, they have little choice but to issue counterstatements to protect the client.

"The press seems to fail to realize what they do by reporting everything that the prosecutor or police feed them," says John Flynn of Phoenix, a trial lawyer whose name became nationally prominent after he won the landmark Miranda case before the Supreme Court of the United States. [On July 15, 1966, the court threw out the conviction of Ernesto Miranda on charges of kidnaping and rape because it said he had not been advised by interrogating police of his constitutional right to remain silent.] Pretty soon the defense attorney is participating, and the case is being tried in the newspapers."

Reporting fiction, gossip, inadmissible evidence, and police and prosecutor conjecture continues.

Yet many papers are starting to weigh information made available to them in a criminal case carefully. They evaluate it for truth and motive as carefully as they do in other areas of reporting.

The Toledo *Blade,* and its sister paper, the *Morning Toledo Times,* have been among the pioneers, announcing in August, 1966, a set of guidelines they would follow in reporting criminal news before a trial.

They now print: (1) the name, age, and address of the accused person; (2) how the arrest was made and when and where; (3) the charge against the accused and the identity of the complainants; (4) the fact that a grand jury has returned an indictment and that a trial date has been set.

They are not printing, at the time of arrest: (1) any prior criminal record of the accused (which is not admissible in court unless the defendant takes the stand); (2) any reference to a confession other than the fact that an accused has made a statement to police—even then not indicating its nature; (3) any statements by officials or others, construed as detrimental or beneficial to the accused; (4) any statements by attorneys either detrimental or beneficial to the accused or concerning any defense that is to be made during trial; (5) any names of jurors selected for a particular trial; and (6) any arguments made in court in the absence of the jury or any evidence excluded in court.

This came about when the publisher of the two papers, Paul Block Jr., told his editors:

A maturing press must give some recognition to the realization that keeping a sharp eye on government and the effectiveness of law enforcement does not require us to jeopardize a life. Nor can we argue that thoroughly reporting any single case can keep the courts or police in line. This is a matter of over-all impact resulting from persistent watchfulness and a resulting awareness that we may blow the whistle at any time.

While honoring the Sixth Amendment to the Constitution, the two Toledo papers assert they have not backed off from their responsibilities under the First Amendment. In announcing the guidelines, the paper said:

> It should be understood, however, that we also have other responsibilities under the Constitution and that these cannot be waived. The First Amendment guarantee to a free press, for example, imposes an obligation to guard the public interest in all phases of governmental activity. Thus [we] will always investigate thoroughly—with or without the cooperation of official agencies—any evidence of malfeasance, misfeasance, or nonfeasance of anyone in public office.

While rejecting sensationalism, the Toledo papers also noted that guidelines will not apply when they see:

• The threat of a breakdown in law enforcement.

• A crime wave requiring more than normal information to reassure the public.

• Sensational reports spread by out-of-town publications or newscasts requiring the local newspapers to take account of the information or misinformation spread by others.

• Attempts to thwart investigations of misbehavior by public officials.

In an interview, *Blade* editor James C. MacDonald said reporters will continue to gather information about criminal cases and turn it into memo form for possible use after trial. And the paper will be more conscientious in covering trials, he adds.

The guidelines came about after the Toledo papers realized they were often getting only one side of a story in criminal reporting—the police side.

A man might be "convicted" in print shortly after a crime was committed "based on statements by public officials," and later an investigative reporter might discover that there was another side to the story, including negligence on the part of the accusing public officials, he explained.

While the *Blade* has pioneered in responsible crime news coverage, it has taken its lumps from other newspapers. They see its stand as close to surrender to the bar and bench, which, they assert, need to put their own house in order.

Some more militant editors interviewed call the exceptions to guidelines "loopholes" that make the guidelines a fraud.

There is little doubt that the press has a duty flowing from the First Amendment to serve as a watchdog for the too-often apathetic public. Wrote Mr. Justice Clark in the Sheppard decision:

> The principle that justice cannot be served behind walls of silence has long been reflected in the "Anglo-American distrust for secret trials." A responsible press has always been regarded as the handmaiden of effective judicial administration, especially in the criminal field. Its function in this regard is documented by an impressive record of service over several centuries.
>
> The press does not simply publish information about trials but guards against the miscarriage of justice by subjecting the police, prosecutors, and judicial process to extensive public scrutiny and criticism. The court has, therefore, been unwilling to place any direct limitations on the freedom traditionally exercised by the news media.

Adding "We sometimes deplore its sensationalism," he notes that the court has also held that "legal trials are not like elections, to be won through the use of the meeting hall, the radio, and the newspaper."

The fair trial–free press question has long been a smudge-pot controversy. High-octane fuel was thrown on it after President Kennedy's assassination and the televised slaying of Lee Harvey Oswald—and more recently in the Sheppard decision.

The Warren Commission said in its report:

> The experience in Dallas during Nov. 22-24 is a dramatic affirmation of the need for steps to bring about a proper balance between the right of the public to be kept informed and the right of the individual to a fair and impartial trial.

While the commission called for balance, many law-enforcement officials overreacted, clanged the door of information shut, and turned the key.

For example, in Fairbanks *Kassen's Weekly,* which bills itself as the "all-Alaska weekly," recently told its readers:

> Because of extreme difficulties in the coverage of court news, including at times being locked out of the courthouse while proceedings are in progress, we have decided to suspend until further notice coverage of our court beat and individual court cases.
>
> We shall, instead, concentrate on the operation of the court system in general.
>
> It is with great reluctance that we decide to suspend this coverage, but we feel the present inadequate hit-or-miss coverage is an injustice to both the public and the individual concerned.

While researching the *Monitor* articles, I ran into stiff resistance in Anderson, S.C., from Sheriff James H. Williams.

As in other cities, I asked for information about who was in jail and why they were there. A deputy told me he was not authorized to give out the information, although under South Carolina law it is public record. Sheriff Williams was the only one who could give it out, he said. And the sheriff would not be available until the following day.

Puzzled over this, I began checking around the courthouse. Soon I discovered that a seven-year-old and ten-year-old had been jailed on the sheriff's orders. And that an Indiana man had been jailed for months for failing to return a rental trailer, and was awaiting extradition to Indiana. And that others were being or had been held under questionable conditions.

The following morning I met the sheriff, identified myself, explained what I was doing, and asked to look at the records—as I had in cities across the nation.

He said the records were "none of your business."

I then went to the local newspapers—the Anderson *Independ-*

ent and *Mail*—to see if they could get the material I needed. I discovered that they found it as difficult to get information as I did.

After discussing the problem with *Monitor* editors, local newsmen, and with several courthouse officials, I engaged G. Ross Anderson Jr., a leading local lawyer.

The following morning Mr. Anderson asked for a court order opening the jail records to the public, as provided by the state statute.

Circuit Judge Harry Agnew first sided with the sheriff, saying that in his opinion the information requested was "none of your business." Later he denied our request because the word "sheriff" does not appear in the law. Instead the phrase "peace officer" is used, and the judge said he didn't know what that meant.

We asked if he would consider another writ—including the names of deputy sheriffs, since they were specifically mentioned in the law.

Judge Agnew said he couldn't possibly do that for a week or longer. Later a new motion was filed before a visiting judge in the name of the *Monitor*. G. Carey Hayes Jr., city editor of the afternoon *Mail*, joined in the action.

The visiting judge worked out a "compromise"—asserting we had the right to look at a book containing part of the information normally available to the press and public. But we were not allowed to look at record cards similar to those shown to me in other cities.

Sheriff Williams later was challenged in federal district court in Anderson by one of the men he had jailed, Joseph P. Furguile, who was represented by attorney Fox B. Cahaly.

On May 24 a jury in that court found Sheriff Williams guilty of violating the man's legal rights, and awarded Mr. Furguile $18,500 in damages.

Mr. Furguile was jailed for "investigation" on Sept. 2, 1965, when some rings disappeared from a woman's home, and was held until Sept. 27—25 days. The day after his release the woman notified the sheriff she had found the rings in a drawer in her home.

Mr. Furguile testified he was "never served with a warrant, never taken before a magistrate, never advised of his constitutional right to have a lawyer, and was never told he was being held for anything other than suspicion of larceny."

The freedom-of-information center at the University of Missouri's School of Journalism keeps a running tab on judges and others who block reporters from gathering news. The list is long. Examples:

Oct. 18, 1966—Officials in Luray, Va., clamped a lid of secrecy on the death of a man shot two days before. Police say they were ordered by Commonwealth Attorney A. E. Hackley to make no comment on the shooting, and Hackley also refuses to comment, saying ABA rules prevent him from giving out any information.

October 27, 1966—Starke County, Ind., Circuit Court Judge Marvin D. McLaughlin orders photographers not to take pictures of a defendant in the courthouse, in the jail across the street, or on the street between the two buildings. The judge also tells reporters to confine their stories to testimony presented in court, and announces that in future cases he will hold pretrial news conferences to outline to reporters what they will be permitted to report. In so doing the judge declares, he is following the Sheppard guidelines.

November, 1966—prosecuting and defense attorneys in the murder trial of Richard Speck issued proposed guidelines for coverage of the trial. Among points listed are: names of prospective or selected jurors will not be released; only what occurs in the courtroom and is a matter of public record should be reported; and witnesses should not be sought out and questioned before the trial for purposes of seeking information for pretrial publication.

Superior Court Judge Robert H. Beaudreau talks to Springfield, Mass., *Union* reporter Peg Shaw after a three-hour pretrial hearing held in open court and orders her not to write anything about it. Understanding the judge to mean she could not write anything until after the jury was selected, after it had been empaneled she writes:
"Before the trial started Judge Beaudreau denied a motion to suppress evidence on the grounds the evidence was secured by illegal search and seizure."
The following court day Judge Beaudreau declares a mistrial (be-

cause of what she has written). Several days later he finds Miss Shaw in contempt of court and fines her $100.

Thus the conflict grows.

It is the American Bar Association report, approved by the ABA House of Delegates on February 19, 1968, that is causing the greatest press concern. A number of editors already report some police officials and judges have used it as an excuse to shut off the news spigot. And in some instances it is reported the news blackout is used to cover wrong-doing.

This happened, in fact, before the ABA vote. A report issued by a committee of the American Society of Newspaper Editors tells the story:

> The mere possibility that the bar's tentative proposals for news restrictions may be . . . formalized is causing almost daily attempts to muzzle the press so law enforcement can operate behind closed doors.
>
> Quite naturally, more and more editors and publishers are beginning to fight back, and at all levels, at the police station, at the city hall where policemen get their orders, at the ballot box where judges and prosecutors are elected, and in the highest courts.
>
> . . . Bitterness is growing. Hard-liners have become more vociferous on both sides. A kind of open warfare threatens in the year ahead.

The ABA committee was headed by Paul C. Reardon, a justice of the Supreme Judicial Court of Massachusetts. He says his committee, during the three years they worked on the question, concluded that there is "a substantial number of cases, greater than is generally believed," where publishing news about a case "poses a significant threat to the fairness of the trial itself."

He also points out that the "principal source of this information was not the media," but rather "the attorneys in the case, and even more often, law-enforcement officials."

By their release of "ill-timed public statements of personal opinion or of matters that may turn out to be inaccurate, incomplete, or inadmissible in evidence" the entire community may "prejudge the case in a manner totally incompatible with the right possessed even by the guilty, to a fair and impartial trial," says Judge Reardon.

Most controversial is the committee's suggestion that police be restrained from talking with the press, and suggestions that judges use their power of contempt to limit publication of news that might affect the fairness of a trial.

Much of what is proposed in the Reardon report is included in the code issued by the Toledo newspapers. Yet it goes further —calling for penalties against lawyers, newspapers, and others,

In January, 1967, the Reardon report was answered by the American Newspaper Publishers Association, which contends that "there is no real conflict between the First Amendment guaranteeing a free press and the Sixth Amendment which guarantees a speedy and public trial by an impartial jury."

The ANPA report warned of the dangers "to the public in the restriction or censorship at the source of news, among them secret arrest and ultimately secret trial."

It quoted Federal Judge Frank W. Wilson of Chattanooga, Tenn.:

> History has taught us that if the public is to know, the press must be free to report. If it is to be free, it must be free to fail as well as to succeed, to err as well as to be correct.

He adds that when the press errs, it does not err so badly that it prevents a fair trial.

Discussing codes of conduct for newspapers, Judge Wilson says:

> In the preparation and negotiations on such codes, the participants should always bear in mind that freedom of the press is not their exclusive right to bargain with. Freedom of the press is the right of the public to know, not merely the right of any particular publisher to report as he chooses. No publisher or group of publishers and no member of the bar or bar associations has the prerogative to bargain away the public's right to know.

The ANPA report also states: "In a study covering a 10-year period from 1955 it was shown that American newspapers devoted only 3 percent of their space to crime news." In the same period the crime rate in America increased by 73 percent.

Just as only a small minority of criminal cases—less than 10 percent—ever reach the jury state, an even smaller minority of crime reports reaches public print [the report adds]. A survey in New York City in January, 1965, showed that of 11,724 felonies committed, only 41 of those were even mentioned in one newspaper that pays more attention than others to crime news.

Thus, rather than the curtailing of crime-news reporting, it would indeed seem that much more such reporting is needed in a day when crime is increasing by alarming proportions.

The ABA, editors, and publishers were joined in the free-for-all on Feb. 23, 1967, when the Bar of the City of New York's special committee on radio, television, and the administration of justice issued its own report, differing on several points with the ABA's Reardon committee. The New York report was headed by Judge Harold R. Medina, a retired member of the United States Court of Appeals in New York.

The Medina report argues that

guarantees of the First Amendment will prevent the use of the contempt power to control the news media even where the impartiality of a petit jury is endangered.

. . . Furthermore, more recent decisions of the Supreme Court suggest that the court has found in judicial housecleaning an alternative approach to controlling prejudicial publicity that is more consistent with the traditional American preference for an uncensored press.

The Medina committee in answering its own question—"During the pretrial period should the courts and the judges impose controls on the police, the lawyers, and the press?"—took a far different stand than that of the published draft of the Reardon report:

The prospect, in this pretrial period, of judges of various criminal courts of high and low degree sitting as petit tyrants handing down sentences of fine and imprisonment for contempt of court against lawyers, policemen, and reporters and editors is not attractive. Such an innovation might well cut prejudicial publicity to a minimum. But at what a price.

The committee also said it is "firmly of the opinion" that the courts do not have "any power whatsoever" over the police or the press during the early stages of the pretrial period except to control "activities in and around the courthouse."

"In the opinion of the committee, during the pretrial period the news media are restrained only by their own voluntary act from publishing information independently discovered by private persons, and protected by the First Amendment," it adds.

While the Medina report is highly respected, and undoubtedly has had an impact on the thinking of the Reardon committee, as has a report issued by the American Civil Liberties Union, it is the Reardon study that has the most impact on the press across the nation.

"Judge Reardon's set of amendments," says Mr. Murray, "moved toward the press viewpoint." And yet passage of the report was considered a defeat by free press forces.

Newspapers had not really opposed the first section of the report, for it deals with disciplining lawyers for giving out information prior to trial—something certainly within the ABA's scope of interest. But they strongly object to the bar's attempt to dry up news at the police station, and to suggestions that courts find those who fail to follow the guidelines in contempt.

Representatives of the press had asked for a year's delay in a final decision, so that a new $150,000 study could be completed. But the Bar would not wait, arguing that the press had three years in which to act. The press also urged voluntary guidelines be established in each state.

Already press-bench-bar guidelines have been hammered out in roughly a dozen states. Meetings are being held across the nation.

In the State of Washington, where much progress has been made in ironing out differences, the Bench-Bar-Press Committee, formed in 1964 and headed by Chief Justice Robert C. Finley, asked the Reardon committee to call a "moratorium on American Bar Association final action and recommendations" until state and local groups can meet.

The Washington State committee asserted that it believes

"this is a problem which can be resolved only at the state or local level," and that "any restrictive action taken by the American Bar Association would negate the progress and understanding achieved in this state and in other states."

The Washington committee was formed in 1965 and is made up of two members of the State Supreme Court, four Superior Court judges, two from the Magistrates' Association, five members of the state bar association, six newspaper representatives, two from the weekly papers, two from radio, two from television, two from the wire services, one representative from the University of Washington School of Communications, one from the state Prosecuting Attorneys' Association, one from the Association of Sheriffs and Police Chiefs, and a representative of the State Board of Prison Terms and Paroles.

The guidelines are impressive and, according to Justice Finley, "the State of Washington has both free press and fair trial."

There is little question that guidelines are needed, and that the press should carefully and objectively consider its responsibility to the public.

There is some evidence that the bench and bar are beginning to put their house in order. The comments by Mr. Justice Clark on the responsibility of the courts indicates the need, as have the findings of this writer.

CHAPTER XVII

Judges Go to School

It was in San Francisco that I watched a municipal-court judge try to hold a preliminary hearing in an auto-theft case without a defendant present. The defense attorney had to remind the judge that this was illegal.

Earlier, the same judge had been stumped by a legal question in another preliminary hearing on the same charge involving a different man. The defense attorney contended police engaged in illegal search and seizure, a common argument raised today in the nation's criminal courts. This is a point most judges can rule on quickly.

This man called both the prosecutor and the defense lawyer to the bench for a whispered conference—although a jury was not involved. The three talked for several minutes, riffled through a lawbook, then took their places again.

The judge told both to file written arguments within three weeks. He said he would decide after studying the briefs whether to bind the defendant over to a higher court for trial or let him go.

In an interview he explained that criminal law has been changing rapidly and it is difficult to keep up.

Further probing disclosed that he was a recent lame-duck appointee of defeated Governor Edmund G. Brown. This man's experience in court—especially criminal court—was nearly nil. Like a majority of the nation's judges, his background was political—eight years in the California Legislature.

Most court reformers like Glenn R. Winters, executive director of the American Judicature Society, see the need for a better system of selecting judges.

Until this comes about, however, most call for a pragmatic and relatively new answer: reeducation and retraining.

"As recently as 15 years ago the thought of judges' going back to school would have seemed ludicrous to most members of the legal profession," says Professor Delmar Karlen, director of the Institute of Judicial Administration at New York University.

"Ten years ago the only training available to American judges was on-the-job training. A man was a lawyer one day and a full-fledged judge the next. Everyone seemed content that donning of judicial robes made a man competent to perform all duties of office."

Mr. Karlen asserts this is not so, and a tour of the nation's courts clearly confirms it: Most lawyers are poorly prepared to take the bench.

Why?

The reasons are many, and Mr. Karlen touches on several of them.

We have no career judiciary, as in continental Europe, where a man enters the judiciary at an early age and then, under the supervision of experienced judges, works his way up in the judicial hierarchy from one court to another.

Under our system, a man becomes a judge at a fairly advanced age—usually in his 50's—and then, without any supervision from senior judges and without any systematic progression from one court to another, assumes full responsibility in a court in which he may have had no previous experience.

Our system also lacks the safeguards that exist in England, where the judges are chosen on a non-political basis from a small select group of experienced trial lawyers—the barristers. American judges are not chosen from any such small group; they come from office practice and academic circles [or legislative bodies] as well as from the litigating bar.

Laurence M. Hyde, who gave up a lifetime job on the circuit-court bench in St. Louis to become dean of the four-year-old

National College of State Trial Judges based in Reno, Nev., recalls his own experience: "When I went on the bench in 1962 in St. Louis, I went to an experienced judge, and he showed me where to park my car and how to get into the courthouse on Sundays. I had no more orientation than that."

Judge Hyde's early experience on the bench helps explain his enthusiasm for programs to educate judges. It also indicates why judges should come from the ranks of the nation's best trial lawyers.

"I was pretty well qualified for civil jury trials," Judge Hyde continues, "because that was my practice as a lawyer." (At the time of his elevation to the bench, he was considered one of the most brilliant young lawyers in the Midwest.) In probate, equity, and appeals, his experience and training as a law student and practicing lawyer were also of value.

"Yet," he points out, "as a judge I was faced with problems of child custody and other family problems—things that are tremendously important to both the individuals and to the community. Wrong decisions can create great problems.

"I had no guidelines given to me and no information on agencies available to help with family problems."

Judge Hyde was next assigned to the juvenile court and had exactly the same problem—although his predecessor did give him a little more background information.

"Then I was assigned to the criminal courts for a year, and handled all kinds of cases, including murder and robbery. My preparation for this was one freshman course at law school and handling a few criminal cases for indigent defendants in my 10 years as a lawyer.

"I had no information on the correctional system or facilities for rehabilitation of these defendants that were appearing before me.

"I brought my own prejudices and theories to court and made judicial decisions without anyone to question them or point my prejudices out to me."

He adds: "Except for those who have been prosecutors, my experience is fairly typical of state trial judges."

Contact with courtrooms across the country bears this out.

The transition from lawyer to judge is more difficult than most lawyers realize, judges interviewed disclosed. Sometimes even the little things can trip a man up.

Judge Hyde recalls the appointment to the bench of a competent, experienced trial lawyer: "He knew his job well but had paid little attention to courtroom procedure. On his first day, he took the bench and waited for the lawyers—and the lawyers waited for him. Much to his embarrassment, he simply did not know how to get a trial under way."

As the law changes and grows more complex, it is clear that legal education must move out of the days of the family farm and of the horse-drawn plow. Judges are not alone in their need of help. In more than 100 interviews with lawyers across the nation, I was told that lawyers, too, are sadly prepared for court work by the law schools.

"Law schools do not teach you to be a trial lawyer," says Samuel Langerman, a Phoenix, Ariz., attorney and national vice-president of the American Trial Lawyers Association.

The law has become so complex, he says, that it is impossible for all lawyers to know all areas of it. Courts across the nation keep changing the rules. There is new legislation, and the attitudes of the courts change as society changes.

"Take products liability," says Mr. Langerman. "The whole concept has changed from 'buyer beware' to 'seller, stand behind your product.' This affects the clothing you wear, the airplane you fly in, food, and nearly everything else you come in contact with. How does the older lawyer find out about this? If a New Jersey court hands down a significant decision, how do lawyers in Minnesota and California find out about it?"

Seminars for lawyers and judges are the answer, he said. His organization has conducted more than 41 in the past year. "The legal profession is undergoing, belatedly, a great increase in self-education."

Yet this is only part of the solution, and, in fact, only part of the problem.

Perhaps the greatest shortcoming of American judges is that

too often they were mediocre or even poor lawyers. Too few of the nation's state trial judges in courts of general jurisdiction may be classed as having been really "successful" in the practice of law.

And the really brilliant lawyers—with a few exceptions—refuse to sit on the minor courts, where, in fact, many judges have had no law-school training, or even a college education. Yet it is in the minor courts that 90 percent of all Americans appear.

"A judge need not be vicious, corrupt, or witless to be a menace in office," says Maurice Rosenberg, professor of law at Columbia University. "Mediocrity can be in the long run as bad a pollutant as venality, for it dampens opposition and is more likely to be tolerated."

Others go further and ask why mediocre men are even permitted to become lawyers—a profession that is ranked high by most Americans.

The state bar examinations—the tests that must be passed before a lawyer can hang up his shingle—have also been criticized as relatively easy and hardly evidence that a man is capable of arguing a case in court.

The nation's lawyers and judges are beginning to see the need for education and training beyond law school.

It is not a rapid awakening, to be sure. Thousands of lawyers refuse to attend the seminars and special courses now being held around the United States. Lower-court judges—those who need help the most—often are overlooked. This is especially true for the 10,000 or more nonlawyer judges in the United States, although some states have made inroads in this area as well as in the higher-level state trial courts.

And the North American Judges Association—formed to help minor-court judges—may, as it grows, solve some long-standing problems, including widespread ignorance of the law.

Most seminars for lawyers or judges (and there are some notable exceptions) are too short to make an impact—three or four days at most. But for many lawyers, who contend time is money, this is too long to be away from the office. And judges complain that with a backlog of cases they really don't have time either.

At several seminars I attended, lawyers and judges complained that speeches are too often shallow. Many of the experts who addressed the seminars spent much of their allotted time bragging about their own brilliance, past victories, and the amount of money they make.

"When is he going to say something?" asked one attorney impatiently at a seminar in Chicago after a nationally known lawyer rambled on for half an hour about his exploits. Several others in the paying audience walked out and didn't return until the speaker had finished.

Even when speakers have something to say, they aren't always listened to. At a traffic-court seminar I attended in Concord, N.H., many of the "student" judges and lawyers grumbled and in low tones disputed statements by the speakers. Several men around me contended that they weren't going to change their ways simply because the American Bar Association (which was sponsoring the seminar) said they should. Clearly they were not there to learn.

In spite of these and other shortcomings, the very fact that the number of seminars has grown from nearly none 10 years ago to two or three a year in many sections of the country is heartening for those trying to upgrade the system of justice.

Little more than a century ago most lawyers were trained in law offices as clerks or apprentices. While the aspiring lawyer might gain plenty of practical knowledge, he was short on more formal education. This was acceptable in a society where for most citizens an eighth-grade education was considered sufficient.

Now most attorneys are law-school graduates.

"But law schools are still teaching students where to look for the law instead of how to practice it," says Mr. Langerman. "Fortunately, they are trying to remedy this. In addition, our organization [the American Trial Lawyers Association] started a program of student-advocacy programs. Last year we appeared at 11 law schools. This is a meager beginning. This year we will expand and use films showing students how to handle a case from initial interview with a client to the jury verdict."

But this isn't enough, he adds. Practicing lawyers and judges need help through continuing education.

In the past six or seven years steps have been taken in this direction. Reformers standing on the drought-stricken land tend to see this as a cloudburst. Actually, it is more like a light, welcome shower that hopefully foreshadows a steady downpour.

Some reformers appear to be using a kind of sales psychology by saying "Everybody's doing it." The theory is that if the idea —court reform—is reasonable, if you say it long enough and loud enough, enough people will eventually decide they are out of step with "everybody else" and will make the claim "Everybody's doing it" valid.

Seminars for judges started way back in 1947. They were pioneered through the American Bar Association's traffic-court program, headed by James P. Economos. In June, 1947, Mr. Economos put on the first five-day traffic-court school for judges and prosecutors at the New York University Law School.

Sessions begin at 9 A.M. and run until 5 P.M., with both classroom lectures and an interchange of ideas included. Jointly sponsored with the Northwestern University Traffic Institute and the host law school, emphasis is on helping the participants better understand the traffic problem and their role in solving it.

In addition to this, more than 200 three-day regional seminars have been held. Twenty-one, from Alaska and Hawaii to Montana, Illinois, Texas, and Florida, were held in 1967.

Despite the success of this program, thousands of minor-court judges—many of them laymen without legal background —still have not been reached.

And other groups have been slow to follow the lead of Mr. Economos.

It was eight years after the traffic seminars began that Frederick G. Hamley, then Chief Justice of the Supreme Court of the State of Washington, suggested in a speech to the section of judicial administration of the American Bar Association that a seminar for appellate judges would be of value.

Russell D. Niles, dean of the New York University Law

School, said that "with some trepidation" he was willing to join in this bold experiment.

Justice Finley, of the state of Washington, attended the first session in 1956. He recalls some of the reactions of judges sitting on the highest state courts.

"There were some strong misgivings and strong criticism of the whole affair," he says. "Justices wanted to know what the whole thing was about.

"Some members of that first group said, 'This is sort of an effort on the part of these law professors to brainwash us, and we're not going to be brainwashed by some big-dome professors from all over the country.'"

Since that first session, the "quizzical, wary attitude toward judicial re-education has gradually disappeared," he adds. All Washington State Supreme Court judges—except the newest appointee—have attended.

"Our Washington judges are most enthusiastic about the seminar," Judge Finley adds. "We think it has benefited individual members of our court, as well as the Washington Court system as a whole."

Rather than a classroom setting, "everyone sits around one large table and discussion is free and uninhibited," says Professor Karlen, of the Institute of Judicial Administration.

Two seminars for intermediate appellate court judges were held in the summer of 1967, one in New York and a second in Reno, Nev.—another major step forward.

While it was not until 1956 that state supreme court judges recognized the value of the seminars pioneered by Mr. Economos and his traffic-court judges, it took even longer to reach the state trial judges.

There are at least two reasons for this. Low-level performance and mediocrity at best have long been the accepted standard for most county officials, and trial judges are part of the county courthouse crowd. More significant, it is hard for a man given a robe, "elevated to the bench," as the saying goes, and given the authority to stand in judgment of fellow mortals, to stifle ego and brush aside pride and admit that he might *learn* something.

Had not the supreme court judges already launched their school, and had not subtle psychology been used (being *chosen* for the trial-judges school became an honor), the plan might never have succeeded.

Recently retired Associate Justice Tom C. Clark is credited with lending the program much-needed prestige by taking a major part in it and by securing funds from private foundations and breaking down other barriers.

It was a slow building process. First he helped form the national Conference of State Trial Judges. Then he headed the Joint Committee for the Effective Administration of Justice (made up of 15 professional legal groups). A series of seminars for state trial judges was held beginning in 1961. These were similar to seminars held earlier around the country for federal district judges.

By 1964 the National College of State Trial Judges was established. In 1964 and 1965 two sessions were held at the University of Colorado at Boulder, and were financed—like the earlier seminars—by the W. K. Kellogg Foundation.

One hundred students were accepted each year—new men on the bench. Hundreds were turned down.

In September, 1965, with a 10-year grant of $2,390,000 from the Nevada-based Max C. Fleischmann Foundation, the college was moved to the University of Nevada at Reno.

In 1966 two sessions were held—one for 109 judges at Reno; the second at Boulder, for 105 judges. Both were supported by the founding grant from the Kellogg Foundation.

By 1967 only 400 of the 3,700 state trial judges—roughly one-tenth—had been through the school.

Two sessions were held in 1967, each with 150 judges, the first from July 3 to July 28 at the University of Pennsylvania, the second from Aug. 7 to Sept. 1 at Reno.

Now roughly 700 of the nation's 3,700 state trial judges have had the broadening experience of the school—although, like all education, there is no guarantee it will "take."

Emphasis is on practical aspects of the judge's job as well as theory, and teaching methods center around discussion groups where all judges are urged to contribute and exchange ideas.

Dean Hyde points out: "There is no other professional group in the United States that does not hold seminars—that does not become involved in continuing education."

He believes the interchange of ideas between judges from across the nation resulting from seminars is especially valuable.

The primary goal, says Dean Hyde, "is to somehow reach the judge before he takes the bench." Many states have now developed their own seminars for judges, and a few have actually reached the judge before he gets to the bench.

Chicago, long beset with more than its share of political hacks on the bench, now has a regular training program, pioneered by Chief Judge John S. Boyle.

On the Thursday after each November election, new judges go through a five-day indoctrination session. Five days won't turn a lawyer-politician into a judge, but they will help a new man understand his assignment and give him confidence.

Other judges from downstate have voluntarily taken part, but attendance for Cook County judges has been mandatory.

The old system of judges holding semisocial annual conferences has been replaced in Illinois—as well as in a number of other states—with educational seminars.

In December of 1966, 218 magistrates (the lowest-level judge in the new Illinois circuit-court structure) from across the state discussed the civil procedures, motions, evidence, the handling of traffic cases, criminal procedures, and other basics. The first indoctrination session was held by Judge Boyle in the fall of 1964 when the magistrates attended 10 Monday-night classes two hours in length.

Many states are working hard at upgrading their courts. California municipal judges were holding a weekend session while I toured that state.

On June 15-17, 1967, minor court judges in the western part of the State of Washington met in Spokane. A second session was held later in the month, in Seattle.

Both were sponsored by the Washington School of Law in cooperation with the University of Washington State Magistrates Association—considered by legal experts to be one of the best associations in the nation.

Again subject matter was basic: pretrial, trial process, post-trial, public image of judges, canons of judicial ethics, law of evidence, law of property, commercial law, law of torts, current constitutional development in criminal law, and relationships of courts and law-enforcement agencies.

While the seminars help, they are no substitute for better selection of judges at the outset. A number of men who work in the Cook County criminal courts—prosecutors, defense lawyers, and public defenders—complain that the new judges are assigned there and that many, if not most, are incompetent.

"By the time they understand their job they have some seniority and ask to be transferred," one official complained.

Removing the judiciary from politics is one step that is often recommended, but seldom followed. It is difficult to do this in a political system that believes in rewarding legislators, precinct captains, ward leaders, and those who make sizable financial contributions to the party with judgeships.

As has been pointed out, judges often are simply mediocre lawyers in robes.

The quality of the bench is obviously tied to the quality of the bar. Even well-meaning politicians, determined to appoint or slate only the best possible men, find it difficult to get top lawyers to agree to accept the appointment or run for office.

And already there is a critical shortage of competent trial lawyers.

In the past few years a number of organizations have tried to resolve this dilemma through continuing education. It has been a struggle.

"Lawyers are so impressed with themselves—convinced that they are intellectuals—that some run around with closed minds refusing to learn or even listen," says one of the Midwest's outstanding trial lawyers.

A number of groups are trying to resolve the "lawyer problem."

The American Bar Association was once considered, by many lawyers, to be only a fraternal organization. Now emphasis has been on education and improving the profession and the law as well.

Local and state bar associations are also changing in character.

The American Trial Lawyers Association—only a dozen years old—is quickly overcoming its ragtag, second-rate reputation. Those who had opposed it have seen it change and grow. Emphasis is on education of lawyers—initially those who were involved in auto-accident litigation, and since 1966 criminal defense lawyers.

Its members like to say they represent the "people," for the organization has crusaded to improve auto safety, worked to protect consumer rights, and has been, among other things, challenging the drug industry.

Seminars have been held across the nation, with some of the biggest names in the profession lecturing.

Most lawyers found these sessions well worth the time—especially with so many rapid changes in criminal law taking place as the federal Supreme Court and other appellate courts hand down new rulings.

A few schools have been offering educational programs for practicing attorneys for years. The University of Michigan's Advocacy Institute, which helps lawyers polish trial techniques, is 18 years old.

In 1960 the Institute of Continuing Legal Education (ICLE) took that over as the University of Michigan and Wayne State University Law Schools joined hands with the Michigan Bar Association.

The shock waves of interest that followed recent High Court rulings in criminal law helped the ICLE go national in 1966.

It has also entered the book business—publishing more than 20 a year on the law. And for four years it has conducted conferences for Michigan trial judges under the sponsorship of the Michigan State Supreme Court.

Now some law-school professors and practicing lawyers are suggesting internships for green law-school graduates. The idea is that backstopping these new lawyers with continuing education programs will greatly improve both the profession and the bench in the next decade.

While all this is important, more judges—especially those in the minor courts—should have specialized training. And better men should replace the hundreds of poor judges on the bench.

"More than the teacher, the engineer, or lawyer, the judge acts directly upon property, liberty, even the life of his fellows," says Columbia Professor Rosenberg. "His human frailties are perilously magnified by the nature of his day-to-day work.

"Judicial office today demands the best possible men—not those of merely average ability who were gray and undistinguished as lawyers and who will be just as drab as judges."

It seems clear that if we demand more of the bench now, these standards will be met and even raised in the future. Some courts have had a tradition of excellence, and a second-rate lawyer finds it hard to become a judge.

But in too many courts mediocrity is acceptable and incompetence tolerated and even encouraged by lawyers who like to manipulate judges.

While it remains difficult to change our selection process, there can be little doubt that even this will be resolved in time.

At present education is the answer.

CHAPTER XVIII

Recipe for Reform

What can be done to improve justice in the United States?

The list of problems covered in this book is long. Yet it is not exhaustive.

For each court in each county in each state is different. Each has its own set of challenges. These are closely tied to the experience and temperament of the judge, the size and quality of the bar, the people who live in the area, and the kind of justice they demand.

Court reform is not an easy task because courts are complex institutions. Too many citizens see them as the private property of the professionals—the judges, lawyers, policemen, prosecutors, and the others who work there.

One organization, the American Judicature Society, has been hammering for court reform ever since it was founded in 1913. Its executive director, Glenn Winters, has been on the job 27 years, and only in the past six or seven years has he seen much progress.

It was Arthur T. Vanderbilt, former Chief Justice of the New Jersey Supreme Court, who said, "Judicial reform is not a sport for the short-winded."

Money has long been a problem in court reform. State legislatures, hounded for funds by educators and highway builders and a dozen other groups, too often have neglected the courts.

Foundations have been slow to enter the field. It was only 10 years ago that the Ford Foundation entered it, and officials admit court problems are so gargantuan that private money can only brush away a little accumulated dust.

In Washington, the Senate subcommittee on improvements in judicial machinery, headed by Senator Joseph D. Tydings of Maryland, is pressing for legislation that would provide $5 million a year for three years "to encourage improved judicial administration in state and local courts." It would set up an office of judicial assistance to help local courts uncover their problems and to improve the caliber of judges and court personnel through educational programs.

It was Robert Finley, Chief Justice of the Supreme Court in the State of Washington, who had the courage to suggest that we need more than the surface reform proposed by many members of the bench and bar. In a rambling discussion that lasted nearly until dawn we talked of how, in many ways, our states have outgrown the present court system.

"We need to take a good look at our courts . . . at what we call the administration of justice," he told me. "We should look at the court structure, the state constitutions, the statutes, and the rule-making powers of state supreme courts.

"We should keep what's good and throw the rest out."

Yet, as is so often the case, whether the problem is polluted water or big-city slums, states wait until the federal government moves in.

Already federal district courts have been forced to hear civil-rights cases because some state courts have been less than just—at least in the eyes of many Americans.

While the trend in our courts is not too different from trends in other areas of government, there is a difference. Our founding fathers made it clear there was much merit in separate state and federal court systems. Improving the administration of justice remains a local responsibility.

This book centers on the problems of the state courts because the people can do something about these courts. And state courts handle the bulk of court business in our nation.

The following proposals for reform are really not radical, although they will seem so to some. They were culled and collected from this writer's tour of the nation's state courts. They come from interviews with judges, lawyers, private citizens, police officials, sociologists and social workers, and corrections officials. They come from the reports of the President's Commission on Law Enforcement and Administration of Justice. They come from reports and studies by professional groups like the American Judicature Society, the American Bar Association, the American Trial Lawyers Association, the Institute of Judicial Administration, the National Council of Juvenile Court Judges, and the National College of Trial Judges.

Because each state, county, and court is different, suggestions cannot be applicable to all. Yet the suggestions are universal enough to be valid in most areas, and hopefully are already being practiced in many.

What Citizens Can Do

1. Invite judges, lawyers, prosecutors, policemen, juvenile officers, probation officers, corrections officials, and others working in the state system of justice to speak before clubs and other groups. Do your homework and ask them searching questions. Discover what the local problems are.

2. Form a special citizens group to study the local system of justice, perhaps patterned after the Indianapolis plan, under which citizens become volunteer court watchers, keep statistics, present findings to local officials regularly, and demand reform.

3. Find out if qualified professionals are being hired for important jobs like probation officer and whether pay is adequate to attract good men as judges, policemen, etc.

4. If public officials insist on using the spoils system of politics, form a group to study the problem, and work to get it changed over to the merit system.

5. As an individual sit in court. Is the judge: Attentive? Concerned? Informed? Fair? Strong? Businesslike? Polite? Does he work a full day? How many days a week is he in court? How long are his vacations? Do witnesses, policemen, and lawyers show up on time? In criminal cases do the professionals—the judge, policemen, prosecutor, appointed defense attorney—have poise and skill?

6. Find out if your schools are teaching law and justice.

Do young people know what is lawful and right—and why it is lawful and right? Are special programs being held on the law, or system of justice, and its role in a free society?

7. Be willing to sit on juries. Consider it an obligation in a free society, like military service.

8. Demand decent local facilities for youthful offenders. Abandoned and battered children should not be jailed or housed with delinquents.

Help provide good foster homes for neglected children and those who have been in trouble because of horrible home conditions. Juvenile courts across the nation have complained of a shortage of first-class foster homes.

9. Since policemen are the first link in criminal justice, they should reflect a high degree of intelligence, be well educated, understand social problems, be mentally balanced, and carefully trained in police procedures. Citizens should demand this and be willing to pay for it.

10. Ask the American Judicature Society to hold a citizens' conference in your state to help bring about court reform. Since 1959, when the first was held, 36 conferences have been held in more than 30 states. Usually 100 leading laymen participate.

What Legislatures Can Do

1. Streamline the creaking court system—a hodgepodge of independent courts with varying and overlapping jurisdictions. This may require constitutional change.

2. Put the new, unified system under the supervision and control of the state supreme court. Connecticut's unique solution could well serve as a model. There a state supreme court justice was added to the high court to oversee the operation of the lower courts. Thus an already busy supreme court was not saddled with more work.

3. Establish a state court administrator's office. Give this administrator the power to check on judges and keep records and statistics on court business, and to file periodic reports, including comparisons of judicial hours worked, business completed, and backlogs of cases.

4. Establish a strong judicial council composed of judges, lawyers, and citizens to study court problems. Listen to council recommendations. Act on them.

5. Establish or aid associations of judges and court administrators (usually known as a judicial conference). Support them financially. Make attendance of meetings mandatory.

6. Provide funds for judicial education, and require all judges to attend a seminar of one or two weeks minimum before taking the bench. Also require a new judge to sit with an experienced judge before presiding over trials, as is done in Delaware.

7. Take judges out of politics—even if it requires a referendum and/or constitutional amendment. Nomination of judges by a blue-ribbon commission and appointment by the governor is usually considered the best solution.

8. Tie this to a good removal system. California's program is being copied by several states.

9. Establish a retirement age for judges, but also provide for a "senior judge" system that allows the more able retired judges to work part time if they wish when court business is heavy.

10. Provide adequate pay and liberal retirement benefits for judges so that leading lawyers will not find it a financial hardship to take the bench. Also encourage judges to retire when they can no longer work at full capacity.

11. Eliminate justice-of-the-peace courts and other independent minor courts, as Illinois has done. Replace these magistrates with professionals and promote the most able from the lower courts to the higher courts. In sparsely populated states, copy the system being used by several states, where circuit judges actually ride a circuit.

12. For civil matters involving only a few hundred dollars, establish small-claims courts with specially skilled judges as in Los Angeles, or work out a system of arbitration as Pittsburgh has (discussed earlier).

13. Establish a family-court system that treats the entire family and its problems as a unit. This would include divorce court and juvenile court, since the problems found in these

courts are often interrelated. The family court should be given adequate professional staff, including marriage counselors, social workers, investigators, and clerical help.

14. Consider removing social problems—family and individual—from the court system. Should courts be mere collection agencies for child support, as is the case in many states? Is it a judicial function to deal with alcoholism and vagrancy, or should the social welfare or mental health departments take over this responsibility? What about compulsive speeders? A study of these and similar questions would be of value, and could result in reducing court congestion.

15. Require courts to operate in a more businesslike manner, following modern court procedures, so that the time of lawyers, witnesses, and those called for jury duty is not wasted.

16. Establish uniform guidelines for all courts in the state, so that a lawyer from a neighboring city knows how to proceed and what to expect from the judge when he enters an unfamiliar courtroom.

17. Prepare, or have the judicial council prepare, guidelines for judges so that they know what is expected of them. This could include an indication of how many hours they should work under normal circumstances, how many civil cases can be handled in an average month, courtroom decorum, treatment of jurors, handling of witnesses, rules of evidence, and other basics.

18. Establish an "information center" that would—even for rural judges—provide points of law, citations, and information about recent decisions that affect court procedures. This could, in some cases, include a Teletype system similar to that being used by law-enforcement agencies to get information. Experimental use of computers indicates modern technology could help such an information center by listing citations to be transmitted by Teletype.

19. Provide funds for adequate court facilities, including accommodations for witnesses who now spend hours standing in corridors waiting to be called.

As Philadelphia Judge Herbert S. Levin has pointed out, it is hard to dispense justice with the hiss of steampipes in musty, dusty, hot, dungeonlike rooms, and with witnesses waiting in drafty, dreary corridors.

20. In urban areas establish 24-hour arraignment courts with adequate staff to properly process defendants. In most cities weekend courts should be used to prevent the arrest process from functioning as a sentencing or punitive action by police.

21. Establish, by statute, the length of time a man can be held by law-enforcement officials before appearing before a magistrate, and the days, weeks, or months a man can be held without a trial.

22. All charges against a defendant should be dismissed if he is not tried within the legal time limit or steps have not been taken to begin the judicial process.

23. Require the prosecutor to file a public report every two weeks listing all cases that have been delayed and the reasons for the delays.

24. Tighten up on continuance of cases, so that both lawyer and prosecutor must show the court good reason for postponing cases.

25. In states where judges handle both criminal and civil cases, the cases should be called in order of importance: criminal cases where the defendant is in custody, first; where he is on bond, second; and civil cases, third.

26. Eliminate the old "term" of court except where judges ride circuit, and then require special terms for jailed defendants.

27. Require policemen to attend all hearings involving their cases and compensate them for their time.

28. Establish standards for sheriffs' offices and local police departments. Require each to have men with skills other than shooting and fast driving. Schedule educational seminars. Test policemen for intelligence. Add to local police budgets with state funds, if necessary.

29. The merger of many small police departments into larger units—perhaps countywide—could improve the quality of the men and the very basic "justice" they mete out as they are confronted with problems hourly.

30. It is widely suggested that traffic offenses, except the more serious cases like manslaughter and drunken driving, should be taken out of the courts and turned over to a traffic board or commission.

31. An alternative: upgrade traffic courts, so that cases are heard by highly qualified lawyer-judges who understand the impact the auto has on our society.

32. Police who handle criminal investigations and disputes and disturbances might be freed of traffic duty. Separate units, like the Ohio Highway Patrol, could specialize in traffic control—but be trained in police work so they could nab suspects on the road and backstop criminal agencies.

33. Local governmental agencies should be prevented from using traffic fines and tickets as a source of revenue, regardless of need. Traffic court should promote safe driving. It should not be a fund-raising agency.

34. Consider alternatives to trial by jury for auto-accident cases. Solutions may include a board or commission that operates in a manner similar to workmen's compensation. Consider revamping insurance practices and litigants paying court costs.

35. Raise jurors' pay and issue certificates of recognition for service.

36. Increase the amount paid witnesses, so that the time off from work they must spend in court does not impose such a financial hardship.

37. Consider revamping the state bar examination and licensing system so that lawyers are divided up into general practitioners and specialists. Set guidelines for both, and make sure trial lawyers are actually capable of trying a case.

38. Require prosecutors to be skilled attorneys. Set pay high enough to encourage the best men to make the job a career. Provide adequate staff, including skilled investigators and competent clerical help. In sparsely populated states, divide the state into districts and have the prosecutor ride circuit, or have a deputy assigned to each county in the district. Eliminate the part-time prosecutor.

39. Establish a meaningful public-defender system—either full time or appointive, perhaps patterned after the Houston plan (described earlier), under which every member of the bar is subject to public-defender service. With a full-time office, establish pay levels comparable to those of the prosecutor, so that the better lawyers will make the defender's office a career. Provide adequate clerical and investigative help.

40. Establish a program patterned after the Manhattan Bail project that will permit more people to get out of jail on their own recognizance—if they appear to be good risks.

41. Examine the purpose of a corrections system and see if—in the light of the growing crime problem—your state system is corrective or simply punitive.

42. New institutions are needed to replace or backstop traditional prisons, work farms, jails, and mental hospitals. Pay of those who work in corrections should be increased. Emphasis should be shifted from hiring guards to employing more people with educational and sociological skills.

43. Establish probation offices in all court districts or a statewide office that is adequately staffed. Require all probation officials to be professionally trained. Require each probation department to hire women probation officers to handle women probationers.

44. Consider giving prosecutors the right to appeal an adverse ruling, especially in the pretrial stage or when essential evidence is suppressed.

45. Form a study commission for continual review of state laws. This is to throw out horse-and-buggy statutes and to avoid conflicting legislation.

What Educators Can Do

1. Give law students more opportunity to learn about trial work—both civil and criminal.

2. Make courses in writing and public speaking mandatory so lawyers become more articulate as a group.

3. Round out curriculums so that they cover the whole spectrum of the law. Increase emphasis on trial work.

4. Encourage students with specific talents to enter fields of law that match their talents—rather than pushing them to sign up with a Wall Street law firm for prestige or money.

5. Launch basic law and sociological research projects, using the courtroom, lawyer's office, prosecutor's office, defender's office, police station, jail, prison, slum neighborhoods, and court records. These projects would help educators, lawmakers, and court administrators understand how the system of justice is really functioning; where problems exist; how improvements can be made; what to do about court backlogs; and perhaps even how to resolve the nation's growing crime problem.

6. Consider your obligation to teach students ethics. Point out to them that leaders in their field are now emphasizing that it is a profession, not a business, and that their key role is to serve, not turn a fast buck.

7. Launch a legal internship program, so that young lawyers are competent to go to court and to provide other legal services to clients.

8. Encourage the establishment of a curriculum in court administration, perhaps a joint effort of the schools of law, business, and sociology.

9. Work to improve the "language of the law." The use of common words with uncommon meanings (prayer, for example); of Latin, Old English, Middle English, and French words (*amicus curiae*, aforesaid, demurrer); of words designed to perplex laymen (pursuant to stipulation); weasel words (adequate, due care); and words of extreme precision (perpetuity, never, all) should be re-evaluated.

What Judges Can Do

1. Accept the office only if you are willing to work full time as a public servant.

2. Stay awake. Pay attention, no matter how routine or dull the matter seems.

3. Run your own courtroom. Prevent prosecutors, lawyers, court clerks, politicians, or others from grabbing control.

4. Study. Attend seminars, special courses, and judicial

conferences. Read current professional journals on recent decisions and mounting problems.

5. Try to see through whatever prejudices and quirks may affect the quality of the justice you are dispensing.

6. Recognize the judicial powers you have been given and use them carefully. Understand that fellow human beings are standing before you, and that what you do will affect their lives, their families' lives, the county welfare budget, and the stability of the community.

7. Work carefully with other judges in the district and the state. Meet with them to see that justice is uniformly and fairly administered. Exchange ideas with them. Discuss sentencing, rules of evidence, and other basics.

8. Sentence no one to a juvenile home, mental hospital, jail, or prison until you have carefully examined the facility and understand its ability to cope with inmates. Be aware of serious shortcomings.

9. Urge all law-enforcement agencies that operate in your district to file a weekly report showing how many men are in jail, how long they have been held, and what the charges are against them. Large cities should follow the Los Angeles system, where daily checks are made and a complete list, punched out by a computer, is available to the public around the clock.

10. In multijudge courts push for assignment according to experience and skill rather than by seniority or chance. Assignments should parallel your experience as lawyers whenever possible.

11. Teamwork in multijudge courts is essential. Urge that court rules, hours, and procedures be established as a group effort. As in Memphis, you should not consider going home or to the golf links until fellow judges have a clear calendar, with no cases waiting. Regular meetings to discuss law, trends, and difficulties have been found to be profitable.

12. Recognize the need for a competent court administrator —a man with business experience or training in public administration. Work with him. Evaluate what he says, even if suggestions seem new or radical.

13. Welcome the public into your courtroom. Make it possible for them to hear what is going on. Cut down on whispered conferences when a jury isn't present, so the public will be confident that you know what you are doing and that you are not hiding anything.

14. Conduct business whenever possible in open court so the layman feels confident you are more than a politician dispensing favors or giving reprimands.

15. Keep your courtroom quiet. Require your bailiff to act as a gentleman, and to treat those who come into the courtroom—criminal or civil—as he would want to be treated. Ask your clerk not to rattle papers, react to testimony in a way that might influence a jury (with disdain or disgust, for example), and to treat those who enter the courtroom courteously.

16. Call your docket in order. Do not let your aides be persuaded or bribed into shuffling the docket when lawyers, witnesses, and those involved in the cases at the top of the docket are present.

17. Recognize that your first obligation is to dispense justice to the public—not to please or appease lawyers.

18. Recognize that while settlements in civil cases are desirable, this is not necessarily the primary function of the judge. It can, in fact, reduce respect for the courts. As New York's Judge Bernard Botein has said: "Forced settlements convert the courthouse into a countinghouse." Also recognize your own skill or limitations in hammering out settlements. It takes a special talent, and without it you are wasting everyone's time.

19. Require lawyers to file certificates of readiness in civil cases to avoid delays.

20. Refuse to resort to assembly-line justice, regardless of congestion or other court problems. Instead, bring problems of crammed dockets to the attention of the public, to local units of government, and to state lawmakers.

21. Consider the use of key punch and computer operations to keep track of cases, making assignments, docketing, and researching courtroom problems. Cook County, Ill., is one area pioneering in this field. Equipment may be used on a

shared-time basis with the county auditor or treasurer or other governmental bodies.

What Lawyers Can Do

1. Be prepared when you enter the courtroom. The old concept of flying by the seat of your pants or the smoothness of your tongue leads to charges of ineptness. Look up the law.
2. Do not ask for excessive continuances. As one of the nation's most prosperous lawyers points out, continuances are not profitable to you, and in most cases simply jam up the courts and reduce public confidence in your ability.
3. Avoid trying to "butter up" the judge. If he is half competent, he can see through it, and this may prejudice him against your client.
4. Avoid chicanery. An educated public can see through it, and it only hurts the profession as a whole, you as an individual, and your client. The "image problem" of the law profession can only be improved by improving individual habits and performances.
5. If you engage in plea-bargaining in criminal court, and you handle few criminal cases in your practice, consult an experienced criminal trial lawyer. Otherwise your client may learn in prison that you have bargained away more years than he might have got without the "deal."
6. Be punctual. Showing up late bogs down the courts and raises tempers, and may affect the justice your client gets.
7. Recognize, that, as Robert B. McKay, dean-elect of the New York University Law School, asserts, lawyers have a "responsibility . . . not simply to their client with whom a private . . . arrangement is made . . . for a fee," but "for the betterment of the entire social structure."

What Prosecutors Can Do

1. Take pride in seeing justice done, rather than in building an impressive conviction record.
2. Investigate all cases carefully. Screen arrests. Assign men to cases early. Give them investigative and clerical help.

3. Recognize your responsibility to prosecute law violators, to society as a whole, and to the families of men and women you prosecute. Understand the impact of your actions on the local community, the welfare rolls, and the individuals and families involved.

4. Refuse to run for office simply to "learn the trade." Only a competent trial lawyer can represent and protect the people in criminal cases. If experienced lawyers refuse to take on the job, it is probably because the pay is too low or there is a need for a district or statewide prosecutor system.

5. When you must hire inexperienced men, institute an in-service training program where green lawyers work as a team, as in Chicago, or with experienced prosecutors.

What Bar Groups Can Do

1. Muster the courage to stand up to incompetent or corrupt judges, clerks, bailiffs, and other court employees.

2. Adopt national, state, or local codes of ethics and *enforce* them.

3. Push for improved court facilities, better pay for judges, more competent court employees, judicial education, improved police departments, improved correctional practices, uniform court rules, better law-school curriculums, and answers to the many other court and court-related problems.

4. Launch or support programs of continuing education for young lawyers as well as refresher courses for experienced attorneys. See that they are more useful than many now being held.

5. Begin conversations with groups where long-standing conflicts may exist, including social-welfare agencies, and the press. Groups such as real-estate brokers, whose work increasingly gets into areas affected by civil-rights laws, should also be included. Work to improve understanding of opposing points of view.

6. Expand member participation in legal aid and defense for the indigent, especially among more affluent members of the association.

What the Press Can Do

1. Report court news honestly and fairly—seeking accuracy and balance rather than sensationalism. Guidelines for fairness and self-restraint may be necessary.

2. Serve as a guardian of the people, respecting both the rights of society and the rights of individuals who appear in the civil and criminal courts.

3. Ferret out dishonesty and incompetence in the courts and court-related facilities.

4. Crusade for improvement of the adversary system; law schools; judicial training and education; judicial selection, tenure, discipline, and removal; legal ethics; and other problem areas.

5. Evaluate editorial policies that give special treatment to court news about certain individuals or special groups—either for reasons of prominence, friendship, or power, or because they are members of minority groups, or lack influence, money, or power.

This is not an exhaustive list of suggestions. Rather, it may better serve as a starting point for discussion in most communities, large and small.

What Is Being Done

Court reform, as has been pointed out earlier, has been slow in coming. But Mr. Winters, of the American Judicature Society, sees a trend that he calls "the court-reform bandwagon."

In the fall of 1967 New York was in the throes of a constitutional convention. Plans to radically improve the state court system did not succeed, however. Other states have completed constitutional revisions or are making plans for them. Among them are: Michigan, Florida, Maryland, Illinois, Rhode Island, Pennsylvania, and Massachusetts.

In 6 of the 50 states, judges are selected on a merit system of nomination and appointment, according to Mr. Winters's tally. Missouri pioneered in this field in 1940 but has not made the system statewide. Alaska was first to do this, beginning with statehood in 1959. Iowa and Nebraska followed in 1962. Colorado has the most far-reaching plan, adopting a system in 1966 that includes the lower courts. In 1966 the Vermont Legislature passed a statute putting a statewide merit plan into operation. Utah's Legislature took the step in 1967.

Kansas, Alabama, and Florida have some courts under the merit-selection plan. Illinois and California allow judges to run unopposed on their records after initial election. New York, Oklahoma, and Minnesota (as well as Puerto Rico) fill vacancies on the bench through a merit system of nomination and appointment, where governors or other officials have voluntarily decided to operate in this way.

In four states merit selection of all or some judges will eventually go before the voters. Oklahoma approved the plan in July of 1967. In North Dakota, where the plan was rejected in November, 1966, voters will get another chance in 1968. So will Idaho voters. Indiana is working at it.

What of discipline and removal?

California is credited with the best system of removing or reprimanding judges for misconduct or disability (adopted in 1960), as was pointed out earlier. Texas was first to follow, then Florida, Nebraska, Maryland, Ohio, Utah, and Vermont.

New York was the pioneer, establishing a "court on the judiciary" some 20 years ago. Illinois adopted a similar plan in 1962, and Oklahoma voters approved its version in 1966.

In Texas, Louisiana, Alabama, Michigan, and Puerto Rico "removal power is vested, on varying terms," in the state supreme courts, according to Mr. Winters. New Jersey has the law but lacks legislative implementation.

Alaska has a constitutional provision for a board of inquiry—made up of judges and doctors to investigate charges of physical or mental disability.

Several states are considering the California plan in drafts of constitutional revisions.

Other areas of reform?

Seven states—New Jersey, Alaska, Hawaii, Illinois, Colorado, Michigan, and North Carolina—have completed, at least to a large extent, statewide court unification, plus "an effective statewide court administrative office." Again add Puerto Rico to this list.

Illinois has done away with the justice-of-the-peace courts. So has Connecticut. Virginia, California, Missouri, Tennessee, Maine, Ohio, New Mexico, and North Dakota are among the states where minor courts have been improved in varying degrees.

Progress has been made, and is being made year by year.

For a man like Mr. Winters, who has devoted most of his working life to trying to bring this about, it can only be seen as a bandwagon.

But as this book has pointed out, there is still a long, tough trail ahead.

Index